ean

DELICATELY POISED ALLIES: GREECE AND TURKEY

Problems, Policy Choices
and Mediterranean Security

Also from Brassey's

BIRAND
The Generals' Coup in Turkey

CAHEN
The Western European Union

COKER
Shifting into Neutral?

DROWN
A Single European Arms Industry?

GROVE
Maritime Strategy and European Security

GROVE
NATO's Defence of the North

SLOAN
NATO in the 1990s

DELICATELY POISED ALLIES: GREECE AND TURKEY

Problems, Policy Choices and Mediterranean Security

JAMES BROWN

BRASSEY'S (UK)

Member of Maxwell Macmillan Pergamon Publishing Corporation

LONDON · OXFORD · WASHINGTON · NEW YORK · BEIJING
FRANKFURT · SÃO PAULO · SYDNEY · TOKYO · TORONTO

UK (Editorial)	Brassey's (UK) Ltd., 50 Fetter Lane, London EC1A 4AA, England
(Orders, all except North America)	Brassey's (UK) Ltd., Headington Hill Hall, Oxford OX3 0BW, England
USA (Editorial)	Brassey's (US) Inc., 8000 Westpark Drive, Fourth Floor, McLean, Virginia 22102, USA
(Orders, North America)	Brassey's (US) Inc., Front and Brown Streets, Riverside, New Jersey 08075, USA Tel (toll free): 800 257 5755
PEOPLE'S REPUBLIC OF CHINA	Pergamon Press, Room 4037, Qianmen Hotel, Beijing, People's Republic of China
FEDERAL REPUBLIC OF GERMANY	Pergamon Press GmbH, Hammerweg 6, D-6242 Kronberg, Federal Republic of Germany
BRAZIL	Pergamon Editora Ltda, Rua Eça de Queiros, 346, CEP 04011, Paraiso, São Paulo, Brazil
AUSTRALIA	Brassey's Australia Pty Ltd., PO Box 544, Potts Point, NSW 2011, Australia
JAPAN	Pergamon Press, 5th Floor, Matsuoka Central Building, 1-7-1 Nishishinjuku, Shinjuku-ku, Tokyo 160, Japan
CANADA	Pergamon Press Canada Ltd., Suite No. 271, 253 College Street, Toronto, Ontario, Canada M5T 1R5

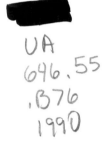

First edition 1991

Library of Congress Cataloging in Publication Data
Brown, James, 1934–
Delicately poised allies : problems, policy choices, and Mediterranean security / James Brown. — 1st ed.
p. cm.
1. Mediterranean Region—National security. 2. North Atlantic Treaty Organization—Mediterranean Region.
I. Title.
UA646.55.B76 1990 355'.03301822—dc20

British Library Cataloguing in Publication Data
Brown, James 1934–
Delicately poised allies : problems, policy choices, and Mediterranean security.
1. Mediterranean region. International security
I. Title
327.116
ISBN 0-08-037689-4

Printed in Great Britain by BPCC Hazell Books
Aylesbury, Bucks, England
Member of BPCC Ltd

Dedicated to

My Mother, Father and Uncle John
MAY THEIR MEMORY BE ETERNAL
and
Aunt Ann

Contents

List of Maps

List of Tables and Figures

Tables

Figures

Preface

This is a comprehensive study of the political and national security policies of Greece and Turkey and how their actions and interactions have influenced NATO's strategies in the South Eastern Flank. Historically, both nations have experienced significant internal turmoil and military interventions, which have affected their perceptions of external threats and the methods by which they formulate policy. Compounding this are historical animosities that exist between Athens and Ankara, colouring their views of each other and creating difficulties in establishing a cohesive defence posture for the Alliance as a whole, and in particular, the South Eastern Region. These problems are largely political, but they also have vital military and operational aspects which have made it difficult to integrate the two nations' separate and somewhat disparate national defence efforts into a common framework. It is important to understand these fissures because the defence of this region has remained primarily a national responsibility. From time to time, when a spirit of compromise has characterised their internal politics, the goodwill has transposed to the international arena. More often, however, the battles that dominate the search for domestic order find their complement in foreign and national security policies, which often appear narrow and intransigent.

Relations with the United States are, and will continue to be, more difficult to manage than relations with traditional or new enemies, since relations with Washington became important issues on the domestic scene as well. For both Greece and Turkey, dealing with the United States is a major foreign policy preoccupation and both have a very real fear of becoming partial satellites or pawns of Washington.

From the Alliance's perspective, the principal problem in the South Eastern Region derives from the fact that because the area is neither a geographic nor a political whole, it is not subject to a single military strategy. The strategy of this region is little more than a juxtaposition of at least three operational theatres. It is also true that the United States and Soviet Union use the Mediterranean, at least partially, to support and foster their policies elsewhere, while Greece and Turkey, at different times, in varying degrees, and for diverse motives, do so for their own ends. The coordination of policies between NATO and these two quarrelsome neighbours represents a challenge that is greater in this region than anywhere else in the Alliance. This continues to be true even though tensions are currently easing in other sectors.

Understanding the attitudes of both Ankara and Athens is an essential precondition for analysing the kinds of defence preparations each has undertaken, and any analysis of this area requires assessments beyond the sources of foreign threat and military balances. It must examine, for example, the roots of national security policies. In the case of both Greece and Turkey, this refers not only to security against internal tensions, but extends to external intimidation or direct attack. The political balance between left and right or between civilian and military is perceived as something that requires careful management, if not all-out manipulation. Foreign and defence policies are built to forge a national consensus that is aimed at strengthening community and statehood. The image that their political leaders present to the outside world is crafted to create an internal sense of purpose and must often be seen in this light. The nature of the foreign policy choices and the international relations environment that are managed by the political leaders also have domestic consequences. Although this is generally accepted for all states, it is particularly true for these two nations and it forms the object of this study, given their particularly turbulent recent histories.

With the rapid changes in the Soviet Union and Eastern Europe toward pluralism and democratic government, the world order as we have known it since the post Second World War period has been dramatically altered. The Cold War appears dead, and both alliances—NATO and the Warsaw Pact—must now come to grips with the re-evaluation and restructuring of their defence policies. The withdrawal of Soviet forces from Eastern Europe has begun; and the political environment today appears less threatening than we have known for quite some time. But the need for a cohesive NATO is still crucial. The Soviet Union remains the dominant military power on the European continent, and the possibility of economic and political instability in the Soviet Union or Eastern Europe may lead to different kinds of challenges for NATO, unlike those we have previously encountered. These implications will affect a whole range of issues associated with the security interests of Greece and Turkey and NATO. What follows, against the backdrop of recent history, is an examination of the issues outlined above. It suggests that NATO's South Eastern Flank members, Greece and Turkey, will continue to impose their national interests more aggressively on the Alliance, making the development of a coherent NATO policy in this region even more complex and less cohesive than have been heretofore the case.

On a very personal note, I have attempted to be fair in setting forth the arguments that affect the bilateral relations between Athens and Ankara. I realise that national pride will be a factor in how this book is evaluated. In my defence, I can only ask the reader to examine the volume as a whole and not dissect it issue-by-issue and thereby hurry into inaccurate judgements. If this is done, I am confident that the reader will conclude that there is more that binds these two nations together—culturally, historically and politically— than all the rancour that divides them.

I owe a debt of gratitude to many individuals and organisations.

A number of officials within the United States, plus the Greek and Turkish political and national security communities, provided critical perspectives and insights for many of my arguments, and I warmly thank them all.

I owe a special debt to William P. Snyder who reviewed and criticised this manuscript and made many constructive comments and suggestions that were invaluable.

My thanks also to the Department of Political Science and its chairman, Dennis S. Ippolito, for their assistance and moral support; it was indispensable. To the Ora Nixon Arnold Fund, whose financial assistance made it possible for me to take several trips to Greece and Turkey, I am most appreciative. Mrs. Mary McComas was of enormous help in preparing the manuscript, and I am deeply grateful to her. Finally, my gratitude to Jenny Shaw, Publishing Director, and the very competent staff at Brassey's for all their sincere interest and efficient assistance in seeing this volume come to closure.

All errors in fact of interpretation in this book are, of course, my sole responsibility.

CHAPTER 1

A Legacy of Fragmentation

Like the Maginot Line, the perimeter of NATO's defence, though it is formidable, is incomplete. It leaves unguarded the flanks and the rear of the Alliance. In other words, the threat to the allies is not global and no longer regional.

The Honourable Robert Strausz-Hupe

THE SOUTH EASTERN Flank of the North Atlantic Treaty Organisation (NATO), consisting of Greece and Turkey, constitutes one of the principal strategic points of the NATO Alliance. It offers a wide range of perspectives, more than any other NATO region. It is isolated from Central Europe, and is topographically fragmented. Both Greece and Turkey have long contact lines with Warsaw Pact members and the Soviet Union.[1] This region is closer than other sectors of NATO to the most volatile international tension area of our time—the Middle East, the Persian Gulf, and unstable and unpredictable Libya. The South Eastern Flank is also critically important to the West for its oil supply, commerce, and communications. Admiral William H. Rowden commented that 'one half of the oil consumed by France, Spain, and West Germany and all that of Italy, Switzerland and Austria arrives through Mediterranean ports'.[2] Western Europe's dependence on the Mediterranean trade route for other important commodities is comparably heavy. Thus, the principal focus of orientation for the NATO forces in this region is maintaining freedom of transit in the Mediterranean.

For the Soviet Union and the Warsaw Pact, the Mediterranean stakes are a bit lower, but by no means negligible. It has been estimated that approximately 60–70 per cent of the Soviet Union's supplies to Vladivostok are shipped through the Mediterranean, which is also the principal Soviet trade route to its Arab and African clients and customers. Naval power, therefore, plays a dominant role in defence planning and force projections for NATO, the Warsaw Pact, and both superpowers.

In order better to understand the importance of the Mediterranean, a broader perspective of this waterway is necessary. The most fundamental characteristics of the Mediterranean Sea are its

1

size and its shape. It would take an American aircraft carrier, making 25 knots, about three and a half days to cover the Mediterranean's length of 2,045 miles, measured from the Straits of Gibraltar to Beirut, Lebanon. Its area is 969,100 square miles, or if you include the Black Sea, about 1,158,300 square miles.

Another feature of the Mediterranean is that it is virtually enclosed, and though its coastline is irregular, the sea itself is rather neatly divided into two distinct basins. The only corridors to and from the larger oceans are the Straits of Gibraltar and the Suez Canal. (The Turkish Straits—the Bosporus, Sea of Marmara, and the Dardanelles—connect the Mediterranean with the more enclosed body of water, the Black Sea.) The Strait of Gibraltar, straddled by Spain and Morocco, is only eight miles wide and is one of the most congested waterways in the world. About 200 miles inside ths strait, the sea balloons out to the north along the coast of Spain, France and Italy.

In order to reach the eastern part of the Mediterranean ships must pass through the Straits of Sicily and Messina. Once on the other side, the sea bulges out again, this time to the south, forming a great bowl along eastern Tunisia, Libya and Egypt. Curving back up and around Israel, Lebanon and Syria, the Mediterranean envelopes Cyprus and runs alongside Turkey until it reaches the island-dotted Aegean Sea, another subsidiary. After passing western Greece, the Mediterranean becomes the easily definable Adriatic Sea, washing the shores of Albania, Yugoslavia and Italy.

For naval operations, the Turkish Straits, along with the Straits of Gibraltar and Sicily, are critical chokepoints, with the former controlling access to and from the Black Sea. If all of these Straits were closed to shipping, any vessel inside the Mediterranean would be trapped and ships outside could not get in. Some of the other chokepoints in the Eastern Mediterranean are the approaches to the Aegean Sea [a line drawn from the southern Greek mainland (Peloponnesos) to the island of Kithira to north western Crete] and east of Crete to the island of Karpathos to Rhodes and on to the coast of Turkey (Fethiye). In the region south of Kithira Island and east of Crete, and Cape Andreas off the eastern tip of Cyprus, the Soviet Union uses these areas as 'bases at sea'. It enables Soviet ships anchored at these spots, as well as others in the Mediterranean, to monitor Western naval activities and to take on food and fuel. The anchorages also compensate for the absence of Russian naval bases in the Northern and Western Mediterranean.

The region's strategic importance has been dramatically increased by events in the region. Turkey is the only Alliance member whose geographical position puts it predominantly in the Middle

East, and it sits on the flank of any Soviet thrust into Iran or the Persian Gulf. Straddling the Straits of Bosporus and the Dardanelles, it virtually controls the Soviet Union's only means of egress from the Black Sea into the Mediterranean. Similarly, Greece monitors Soviet use of the Aegean Sea and contributes to the naval readiness of the Adriatic Sea. For example, a Soviet guided missile cruiser of the Slava class coming from the Black Sea has a trip of some 820 miles from the point where it enters the Turkish Straits to Port Said in Egypt, the entrance to the Suez Canal. Geostrategically then, both Greece and Turkey lie athwart the direct avenues of Soviet expansionism into the Arabian Peninsula and Africa.

Since these two countries joined NATO in 1952, the bilateral relations between them have been vexing for the Alliance, and the situation has deteriorated markedly since the Cyprus crises of 1974. For all intents and purposes, military cooperation between the two allies has been non-existent since then, thereby sharply limiting NATO's ability to parry Warsaw Pact and Soviet moves in the region. Both countries tend to evaluate their national security concerns from a nationalistic perspective, thus detaching them from the 'Atlantic' perspective. Relations with the United States are more important to Greece and Turkey than their NATO commitment.

Both superpowers, however, have other important clients in the Eastern Mediterranean and so they too have interests that transcend their respective alliances. These complex relationships could lead to circumstances wherein the superpowers confront each other exclusively in defence of their interests or those of their client states.

There are three common denominators shared by all. First, the Mediterranean Sea washes their shores and is seen as a vital thoroughfare. Second, the presence of the United States' Sixth Fleet and the Soviet Union's Fifth *Escadra* condition events. Finally, the politico-economic conditions of Greece and Turkey, as well as of other nations in the region, in most cases reveal signs of more or less marked instability, leading to expectations that changes might occur and thereby alter the existing *status quo*.

Joining the Club

Until North Korean forces crossed the 38th Parallel to attack South Korea on 25 June 1950, there was very little enthusiasm among NATO's founding members for extending the Alliance beyond its original boundaries. The arguments against including Greece and Turkey in NATO, at a time when both countries were pressing for admission, were summarised as follows:

the conception of an alliance composed of socially and economically homogeneous countries did not 'readily lend itself to the thought of Greek-Turkish participation'; 'most parties to the North Atlantic Treaty would probably be reluctant to see a broadening of their security commitments, the immediate benefits of which they (could) not perceive'; and

there would be 'obvious complications resulting from enlarged membership.'[3]

By May 1951, these concerns had been overtaken by events in Korea and, at the next meeting of the North Atlantic Council in Ottawa in September of that year, the members unanimously invited Greece and Turkey to join NATO, with only Norway and the Netherlands still expressing reservations.

At the time, NATO strategists in Europe and the United States saw Korea as the Soviet Union's opening gambit, perhaps to be followed by military pressure on Kars and Ardahan in eastern Turkey, or a re-ignition of the Greek Civil War as a preparation for moves on Thrace and the Dardanelles. Thus the immediate advantage of admitting both countries to NATO far outweighed other considerations. In both instances Moscow hoped either to incorporate the countries into their sphere of influence or to attempt to establish friendly governments and therby eliminate American and British influence in this region.[4] Confronted by what appeared an imminent Soviet threat, no one, least of all the United States, was disposed to dwell on the long-term implications of admitting two states with historical bilateral differences and little inclination to resolve them.

A month before the Ottawa meeting, the British Embassy in Athens raised with United States Ambassador John Peurifoy the desirability of warning the Greeks 'to refrain from stirring up issues (i.e. Cyprus) that might cause difficulties with fellow members'. Peurifoy pointed out 'the Department's reluctance appears to attach conditions of any kind to Greco-Turkish adherence to NATO and presumed this would apply to any formal change of Greek policy re Cyprus'.[5]

Greek and Turkish willingness voluntarily 'to refrain from stirring up issues' lasted until the beginning of September 1955, when diplomatic developments in London affecting Cyprus resulted in anti-Greek riots in Istanbul. Since then there has been scarcely a year when both countries were not more preoccupied with their bilateral differences than with the Soviet threat. Since 1974 this preoccupation has been almost on a daily basis.

From the standpoint of the United States, sponsorship of Greek and Turkish membership of NATO was really a way of institutionalising, and at the same time sharing the responsibility to implement, the commitment to defend them undertaken by the United States under the Truman Doctrine of 1947. This marked the adoption of George Kennan's policy of 'long-term patient but firm and vigilant containment' of Moscow's expansionist tendencies. It was this doctrine that first established a defence relationship to Greece and Turkey which was eventually to lead to both countries' accession to NATO in February 1952. For their part, Athens and Ankara initially regarded their NATO membership as essentially a reinforcement of American guarantees.

Since 1952, the significance of the NATO link has changed perceptibly for both countries. Greece has come to regard its NATO membership as a buffer, not primarily against the Warsaw Pact but against Turkey, and as a reinforcement of its ties not to the United States but to Europe. Indeed, one of the significant benefits of NATO membership to Athens is that to some extent, it 'Europeanises' the small but conspicuous American military presence in Greece. While NATO has not been popular in Greece since 1974, its security policies are less suspect than those of the United States, which are believed by many Greeks to be unduly influenced by Turkey.

Ankara has also come to look at NATO, to some extent, as a buffer against over-reliance on the United States. Turkey is uncertain of doing business with the United States, whose security policies, in Turkish eyes, are unduly influenced by Greece, the American-Greek lobby, and by other internal American considerations. During the period of the United States-Turkish arms embargo between 1975–78, Ankara relied heavily on the continuing flow of military assistance from another NATO member, the Federal Republic of Germany, to compensate for the interruption of supplies from America.

While the problems that divide Athens and Ankara are mostly political, they affect the military and operational aspects of both Alliance members. These differences spill over and directly affect NATO planners in coordinating NATO and national plans for the cohesive defence of the area. For example, Greek and Turkish armed forces have not regularly participated in joint military exercises together for some fifteen years. The last NATO military exercise in which the two governments permitted their forces to cooperate directly was in the spring of 1982 (DISPLAY DETERMINATION). On a very limited basis Greece and Turkey participated recently in a medium-scale naval exercise in November 1989 (DETERRENT FORCE 2/89). In fact, most of the exercising that Greece and Turkey have undertaken in the Aegean Sea since 1974 has not been against a common foe, but against each other. Greece today views its Warsaw Pact neighbours as being a lesser threat than Turkey, its NATO neighbour. Unlike Greece, Ankara leaves no doubt that it believes the principal menace to Turkish security remains the Soviet Union and its surrogates.[6] Turkey, in fact, feels little threat from Greece and has been puzzled by Athens' actions since Prime Minister Andreas Papandreou's ascension to power in 1981. Turkey is convinced that Greece seeks to undercut Ankara's position in NATO and other international fora (EEC, WEU).

If the most obvious benefit NATO gained when Greece and Turkey joined the military organisation in 1952 was a defence presence in the South Eastern Mediterranean, the most obvious liability that NATO incurs from the present situation is a lack of coordination that loudly calls attention to itself in every European forum where the two allies are represented. It should be observed that the defence of this region within NATO was for many years relegated largely to second class status. It was not until the late 1970s and early 1980s that numerous high-ranking Alliance officials warned that insufficient attention was being paid to this sector. In 1985, the United States Ambassador to NATO, David Abshire, observed that 'critical deficiencies'[7] existed, that both Greece and Turkey were relatively weak, and that NATO had an obligation to repair these. Even today, most Alliance members focus their security concerns on the Central Front threat. Although Abshire heightened awareness of the problems that existed for over 25 years, Greece and Turkey appear geographically too distant and not germane to their defence interests, but at least now the issues are officially on NATO's agenda.

Issues that Divide

Henry Kissinger wrote some 20 years ago, 'Of course no alliance can perfectly reconcile the objectives of all of its members. But the minimum condition for effectiveness is that the requirements of the alliance [should] not clash with the deepest aspirations of one or more of the partners.'[8] For over a decade, this minimum condition has not been met on NATO's South Eastern Flank. Ever wary of involving itself in 'political' issues, the Alliance has tended to look the other way and not take any serious initiatives to resolve underlying Greco-Turkish issues.

Both protagonists presently believe that NATO is not impartial. Each is convinced that the Alliance tilts in favour of the other. The Greeks believe that strategic considerations—the notorious *realpolitik*—invariably give Turkey more weight in NATO councils because of its larger population, troop strength and border with the Soviet Union.[9] The Turks, on the other hand, believe that the weight of their membership is limited by its purely strategic character, and that NATO tends to side with Greece for historic, cultural, and religious reasons. In other words, both Ankara and Athens consider that NATO undervalues their membership, albeit for different reasons. Paradoxically, NATO's hands-off policy, while intended to project the Alliance's impartiality and encourage both nations to settle their own disputes, is more likely to be having the opposite effect. Ankara and Athens logically surmise that the South Eastern Flank is accorded low priority and this gives them little reason to place NATO priorities before their own. There are two major disputed issues: Cyprus and the Aegean Sea.

Cyprus

Since its emergence in the 1950s, Cyprus has been the focal point of Greek-Turkish relations. Occupied by Great Britain in 1878 and a British colony after 1925, this island was no exception to the rule of anti-colonial struggle that affected the British Empire following the end of the Second World War. Greek Cypriots, who represent about 80 per cent of the island's population, continually appealed to Athens for support and for *enosis* (union) with Greece. It was not until 1954 that the Athens' government of Alexander Papagos embraced the cause of the Greek Cypriots. When Archbishop Makarios, political and spiritual leader of the Greek Cypriot community, introduced the issue to the United Nations, London responded by including the previously neutral Turkish Cypriots and Ankara in the conflict.[10] The foundations of intercommunal conflict were thus laid and what began as a struggle for independence, gradually deteriorated into a confrontation between Greece and Turkey. With the establishment of Cyprus' independence in 1960, hopeful observers expected that the situation on the island would stabilise between the two groups.[11] This was not to be.

In late 1963 the Cypriot President, Archbishop Makarios, proposed several constitutional amendments to streamline some of the nation's unwieldy institutions and procedures. Among these were proposed changes to curb the power of veto of the Turkish minority in legislation and to whittle down the representation of the Turks in governmental services to a level more representative of the total Cypriot population. Fighting between the two communities erupted, and Ankara threatened to invade the island to protect the Turkish Cypriot minority. This led to the now famous letter that President Johnson sent to President Inonu warning Turkey of dire consequences if Turkey chose to invade Cyprus.[12] President Inonu backed off. The Johnson letter was a very bitter pill for Ankara to swallow. Turkey subsequently assumed a more critical position toward the United States and modified its pro-NATO stance. It remained for the 1974 Cyprus crisis to precipitate the most serious damage to the relations between Turkey, Greece, the United States and NATO, to the benefit of the Soviet Union.

On 15 July 1974 the Greek Cypriot military forces, on orders from Brigadier General Demetrios Ioannides, the military strongman in Athens, backed a right-wing *coup d'état* that would have forced *enosis*, and done away with any semblance of constitutional government on the island. Archbishop Makarios barely escaped with his life through the back door of the presidential palace. This time, Ankara invoked its right of intervention without waiting for reaction from Washington.[13] The result was the collapse of the Cypriot Greek coup, and a few days later, the military dictatorship in Athens which had instigated this scheme; so, after seven years, Greece returned again to democratic government. As on previous occasions when the Cyprus issue flared, the overriding United States' concern was not the rights or wrongs of either side or the fate of the two communities on the island, but rather a way to limit the potential damage to NATO and to the American strategic position in the Mediterranean. Thus the United States sought to defuse the situation and, above all, to prevent a war between Greece and Turkey that would be disastrous for all concerned. While the American intervention in 1963–64 had succeeded in averting a confrontation between the two NATO allies, it did nothing to further a permanent solution to the Cyprus problem. Furthermore, and most important, American involvement aroused the resentment of both Greece and Turkey, each of which felt that Washington had betrayed it in supporting the other.

United Nations Security Council Resolution 353 called for a cease-fire, the withdrawal of foreign troops, and the initiation of negotiations. Two Geneva conferences were unable to settle either the form that the internal constitutional and administrative structure should take or the territorial arrangements between Greek and Turkish-Cypriot communities. Following these failures, a second operation was launched by the Turkish armed forces from 14–17 August which consolidated the Turkish foothold, left Turkey occupying about 40 per cent of Cyprus, and thus further hardened the positions of the adversaries. The most immediate impact was felt by NATO with Greece's withdrawal from the military wing. Six years would elapse before Athens would return to the integrated military command structure.

The most serious cause of friction between Ankara and Washington (resulting from the Cyprus crisis) was the arms embargo imposed by the United States Congress in 1974 and ultimately rescinded by that Congress in 1978.[14] This action was regarded by most Turks as an insult to a loyal ally and aroused widespread Turkish indignation. Ankara questioned what sort of reliance could be placed on an allied nation whose vital decisions were made by the legislative body that enjoyed power without accepting responsibility for it, and which was so vulnerable to pressure from special interest groups. Turkish pride and national sensibilities had been offended. Predictably, Turkey responded by temporarily closing twenty-six United States military installations. Former Defence Minister Haluk Bayulken warned the United States that 'a[n] embargo against Turkey will be perilous for Turkish-US relations.' The . . . 'Turkish people will not tolerate another test of pressure like an arms embargo.'[15] This action, no doubt, will, in the future, manifest itself in an 'unanticipated way in how Ankara proceeds in its relations with NATO and the United States'.[16]

The Cyprus imbroglio has festered for some three decades. It culminated on 15 November 1983, when the Turkish minority declared the Turkish Republic of Northern Cyprus an independent state. This move is fraught with dangers. The emergence of this state affects the political and military map of the area. It not only increases tension between the East and West but also complicates life in NATO and exacerbates the tension between Greece and Turkey.

A number of diplomatic initiatives have been taken by the United States, Great Britain and the United Nations. Specifically, United Nations Secretary General Javier Perez de Cuellar has focused the discussions on creating a bizonal, bicommunical, federal solution, all to no avail. Bridging the gulf that divides the two communities looks insurmountable, and there seems little alternative to the current stalemate. Any major new diplomatic initiative by the United States and NATO or the United Nations would almost certainly fail; the political situation today is simply not ripe in Cyprus or in Greece and Turkey for meaningful dialogue.

The Agenda of Aegean Issues

Hostile relations between the two NATO neighbours over Cyprus, which had almost resulted in full-scale war, also furnished the occasion for challenge on another front: the Aegean Sea. Those issues have more serious ramifications than the Cyprus dispute. They directly affect the sovereignty and vital interests of both countries and the solidarity of NATO. Indeed, the interests which Greeks believe most threatened by Turkey are found here, while, for Turkey, the Aegean is the other area against which Ankara believes NATO discriminates. As a result, the Aegean and the morass of technical, yet highly charged, issues it encompasses constitute the second and potentially more dangerous cause of friction between Greece and Turkey.

The term 'Aegean' is really shorthand for a set of interests contested by both countries.[17] These differences stem partly from geographical peculiarities of the region and partly from the respective historical perceptions of the disputants. The Aegean Sea is a semi-closed sea scattered with more than 3,000 Greek islands and islets. The Greek islands in the Eastern Mediterranean are very close to the Turkish mainland (in some cases less than half a mile) and more than 100 miles from the Greek mainland. These facts of geography exacerbate for the Turks continual Greek reference to the 'historical rights' of Greece in the Aegean.

From a geostrategic perspective this archipelago canalises maritime traffic in lanes going through at least four main island complexes. Greek or NATO forces operating from these islands can obstruct the passage of any ship through the Aegean. Thus successive choke points form a narrow corridor for the Soviet fleet to pass through. These begin at the Bosporus, continue through the Dardanelles, and end at the Fethiye-Rhodes-Karpathos-Crete-Kithira-Peloponnese line, which can block not only the exit of Soviet vessels from the Black Sea but also their effort either to return from the Mediterranean to their bases or to blockade Turkish or Greek ports and thus interrupt communication within the Alliance. General Bernard Rogers, Supreme Commander Allied Forces Europe, was well aware of the strategic value of such a corridor when he stated to the Turkish journalist Ali Birand:

> It is important not only to keep the Aegean vis-à-vis the Soviet forces which pass through the Straits, but also impede the Soviet forces of the Mediterranean to enter the Aegean in order to regain the Black Sea going through the Straits. I am interested in all measures taken to deter those two possibilities.[18]

There are a number of disputed issues: questions of control and sovereignty of the islands and their seas, the continental shelf, the airspace over the sea and the resources in it. On these essential bilateral issues, the two parties have fundamentally disagreed about the way to resolve their differences. Greece, in general, has looked to international law and has advocated recourse to international bodies, and essentially considers the continental shelf issue negotiable. Turkey, viewing the Aegean as a unique situation for which durable solutions must be political rather than legal, has generally proposed settlement through bilateral negotiations, and seeks resolution of the full range of issues. Further complicating the Aegean agenda are the rights and obligations of Greece and Turkey through their participation in major international conventions of the 20th century and, since 1952, membership in NATO.

Control of Airspace

In 1931 Greece extended its airspace to ten miles without regard for the breadth of its territorial waters, which was then three miles and was extended in 1936 to six miles. This is a breach of international law, embodied in the 1945 Chicago Convention on International Civil Aviation, whereby the breadth of national airspace must correspond to the breadth of territorial waters. Subsequently in 1952, the International Civil Aviation Organisation (ICAO) decided that the Aegean controlled airspace (except the band of Turkish national airspace some six miles off the coast of Turkey) should form part of the Athens Flight Information Region (FIR) for air traffic control purposes. All planes, civil or military, flying west were required to file flight plans and to report positions as they crossed the FIR boundary after leaving the coast of Turkey. Planes coming from the opposite direction were required to report to the control centre in Istanbul as they entered Turkish FIR. Following the Cyprus conflict in 1974, Turkey issued, on 6 August, NOTAM 714 (notice to airmen) and declared a 'security zone' west of the FIR line agreed upon by both Ankara and Athens in 1952. Greece countered with NOTAM 1157. This effectively gave Greece control of all civilian and most military traffic over the Aegean.

In 1980, in the context of improving bilateral relations, Turkey withdrew NOTAM 714 and allowed the re-establishment of the pre-1974 FIRs. Direct civilian air links between the two resumed shortly thereafter. Nonetheless, Greece almost daily continues to protest what it considers to be Turkish violation of Greek airspace. Turkey, on the other hand, complains that Greece abuses its FIR rights and duties to restrict Turkish military aircraft and air force exercises over the high seas of the Aegean.[19]

In summary, Greece claims that it alone should control air defence operations over the Aegean and it cites its control of the Athens FIR to support its argument. Turkey claims that air defence responsibilities in the area should be shared.

The Continental Shelf

The continental shelf problem is one of the more acute Aegean issues, and, according to most knowledgeable persons, one of the more readily solved. It has been aggravated by the two states' desire to exploit the resources of the sea. Once again, the two sides' legal arguments are difficult to reconcile. Greece adheres to the 1958 Convention on the Continental Shelf, which provides islands with a continental shelf area, and has signed the 1982 United Nations Convention on the Law of the Sea that reaffirms Athens' position. If applied to the Aegean, this view denies Turkey almost all continental shelf rights and turns the Aegean into a *de facto* Greek lake, by virtue of the same 3,000 Greek islands. In all, Greece has claim to about 70 per cent of the Aegean.

Turkey supports neither convention and maintains that the Aegean has special characteristics which require a special solution. She proposes to seek political relief to the question of delimitation of the continental shelf, based on the principles of equity and equality.

Both parties have refrained from any initiatives or acts relating to the continental shelf which might prejudice negotiations.[20] Through the years, both Ankara and Athens have explored for oil in this region and tensions between the two have been vexing. In March 1987 a new history of the continental shelf was written. In a period of two weeks, the political situation so deteriorated that the military forces of both nations were placed on a high state of alert. War between the two seemed inevitable. It took the personal intervention of both Prime Ministers (Papendreou and Ozal) to diffuse the state of affairs. Each government pledged to refrain from further provocative activities in the Aegean.[21]

Territorial Limits

Another issue that affects the continental shelf and airspace controversies is the dispute over maritime limits claimed around the islands. Both Greece and Turkey currently claim six-mile territorial seas off their respective Aegean coasts, but Greece, following the concept of the United Nations Law of the Sea Treaty, reserves the right to increase its limit to 12 miles. This position is unacceptable to Ankara.[22] A Greek declaration of this kind would be considered by Turkey as *casus belli*. Under the present existing six-mile territorial sea limits, Greece possesses approximately 44 per cent of the Aegean Sea and Turkey 7.5 per cent. The remaining 48.5 per cent is part of the high seas. In the case of an extension of territorial waters to 12 miles, the Greek share of the sea would climb to about 71 per cent and that of Turkey to about 9 per cent. Moreover, the continental shelf problem would be solved very readily in Greece's favour. Obviously, under these latter circumstances, Turkey's communications to and from the Mediterranean would be intolerably restricted, with serious consequences for her defence and economic and commercial viability. There is little evidence to suggest that Greece intends to exercise its rights, but nevertheless, in the overall scheme of Aegean issues, this is the most troublesome one.

The Lemnos Issue

Another quarrelsome issue is the militarisation and fortification by Greece of her islands off the Turkish coast. Ankara views these actions as violations of the Lausanne Peace Treaty of 1923 and the Italian Peace Treaty of 1947 (see Fig. 1.1).[23] The Turks interpret Greek militarisation of the Aegean islands as provocative, but have opted to take a low-key approach except for Lemnos. This island is strategically important in an East-West context for the security of the Aegean and the entire Mediterranean. It dominates geographically the mouth of the Dardanelles.

Treaty Provisions	Lausanne Convention, 1923* Articles 4 and 6	Treaty of Lausanne, 1923 Article 13	Italian Peace Treaty (Paris Treaty 1947) Article 14 and Annex XIII
Islands affected	Samothrace, Lemnos, Imbros, Tenedos, Rabbit Islands	Mytilene, Chios, Samos, Nikaria	Dodecanese islands
Military installation	'No fortifications permanent artillery organisation, . . . no military aerial organisation, and no naval base.'	'No naval base and no fortification . . .'	'Naval, military and military air installations, fortifications and their armaments (prohibited);'
Armed forces	'No armed forces shall be stationed in the demilitarised zones and islands except the police and gendarmerie forces necessary for the maintenance of order . . .'	'Greek military forces . . . will be limited to the normal contingent called up for military service . . . as well as to a force of gendarmerie and police in proportion to the force of gendarmerie existing in the whole of the Greek territory.'	Restrictions on 'the basing or the permanent or temporary stationing of military, naval and military air units . . . does not prohibit internal security personnel restricted in number to meeting tasks of an internal character.'
Personnel arms	Armament 'will be composed only of revolvers, swords, rifles and four Lewis guns per hundred men, and will exclude any artillery.'		Internal security personnel may be 'equipped with weapons which can be carried and operated by one person . . .'

Treaty Provisions	Lausanne Convention, 1923* Articles 4 and 6	Treaty of Lausanne, 1923 Article 13	Italian Peace Treaty (Paris Treaty 1947) Article 14 and Annex XIII
Naval activity	'Turkey will retain the right to transport her armed forces through the demilitarised islands of Turkish Territory, as well as through their territorial waters . . . (and) Greece shall be entitled to send her fleet into the territorial waters of the demilitarised Greek Islands . . .'		'The basing or the permanent or temporary stationing of . . . naval units' in 'the territorial waters concerned' is prohibited.
Other provisions	'Turkey and Greece shall have the right to organise in the said . . . islands in their respective territories any system of observation and communication, both telegraphic, telephonic and visual.'	'Greek military aircraft will be forbidden to fly over the territory of the Anatolian coast. Reciprocally, the Turkish government will forbid their military aircraft to fly over said islands.'	Naval and air obstacles, military training in any form and production of war materials prohibited.

*The Montreaux Convention (1936) does not contain any provisions specifically referring to the islands demilitarised by the Lausanne Convention.

Source: *Compendium of International Agreements and Other Legal Documents* Headquarters, Allied Forces Southern Europe, Naples, Italy, January 1985.

Fig. 1.1 Comparison of Demilitarisation Treaty Provisions

Lemnos has gained visibility because the Greeks want NATO to recognise their forces on the island and to include Lemnos in NATO exercises. Since 1984, Athens has stationed an Army brigade on Lemnos and, in the annual NATO Defence Planning Questionnaire, Greece includes these forces as NATO-committed in an attempt to obtain Alliance recognition.[24] In Turkish eyes this is essentially a ploy to force the Alliance and Turkey to recognise the militarisation of the island as legal, thereby weakening Turkey's stance in relation to the entire range of contested Aegean issues. Greece points out the incongruity of NATO not being able to exercise in peacetime the defences of territory which they must protect in wartime. This issue is at the heart of the Greek refusal to participate in Alliance exercises. Athens will not take part without receiving a *de facto* NATO endorsement of its position.

Aegean Command and Control

Greece and Turkey also differ over NATO command and control responsibilities. Athens opposes the current arrangements that have been in effect since Greece withdrew from the NATO military command structure in 1974. Since then, NATO air defence of the Aegean has been the responsibility of the 6th Allied Tactical Air Force (SIXATAF) based in Izmir, Turkey, and commanded by a Turkish general under the direction of NATO commands in Naples, Italy. At present, Greece does not have responsibility for any Aegean command, and has only marginally participated in NATO military exercises since 1974.[25] Three attempts by Supreme Commander Allied Forces Europe (SACEUR) General Alexander Haig (1978–79) and a fourth by his successor General Bernard Rogers (1980) have come to naught. The latter's plan is perhaps the most viable. According to this proposed settlement package, a new allied air force command (SEVENATAF)—similar to 6th ATAF—would be established in Larisa. Athens maintains that decisions on the limitation of the operational control zones of the two headquarters should precede the establishment of 7th ATAF. Turkey, meanwhile, wants to maintain its share of operational responsibility for half of the Aegean, mainly because Ankara does not believe that Greece has the capability or willingness to provide adequate coverage for Turkey's Aegean coast.

The Aegean Sea disputes affect NATO matters in many important ways. Among them is the disruption of NATO military exercises because of Greek and Turkish objections to certain war game scenarios. Lemnos is not included because the Alliance does not want to interfere in this bilateral dispute. Alliance manoeuvres are also disrupted because Greece claims the right to prohibit NATO exercise participants from using facilities on Greek soil if Athens does not take part.[26] Likewise, Athens' effort to advance its position on Aegean airspace creates safety problems during NATO exercises and aggravates tensions between exercise participants and Athens. For example, Greece continually claims Flight Information Region violations during military exercises because American and Turkish aircraft do not comply with Greek demands that they should file flight plans. This leads to Athens repeatedly charging the United States and Turkey with airspace violations. And finally, Greek-Turkish problems have blocked the construction of NATO-funded projects for some Alliance countries. Greece, for example, opposes the construction of a low-frequency transmitter in Canakkale, Turkey, because it claims the station would provide coverage of the northern Aegean, including Greek islands.

If the element of national pride is set aside, and with it the heightened sensitivity to political risk that national pride entails, it becomes very clear that the present *status quo* works in no one's favour. Mineral exploration of the Aegean shelf remains unexploited by either party. Territorial sea and air space have become weak points to be defended rather than strong points in the common defence. The Athens FIR loses operational effectiveness as an air traffic control centre to the extent that Greece invests it with political authority which Turkey disputes. Aegean command and control lines, which assure interlocking defences when they are compatible, have produced military gridlock since 1974. Neither the two protagonists nor NATO benefits from a situation where military and economic interests are subordinated to inclusive tests of national sovereignty.

NATO's Mandate

There is no doubt that NATO's mandate, as conceived by the original signatories, did not include a responsibility for addressing internal disputes among the members. According to Sir Nicholas Henderson, a member of the 1949 NATO Working Group, when the French suggested that an 'article of conciliation' be introduced into the draft treaty, the other representatives rejected the idea as duplicating existing mechanisms, notably those provided within the framework of the United Nations. Henderson's comments are illuminating:

> Furthermore, the possibility of dispute between parties to the Pact of such serious nature as to defy solution by these existing agencies or under existing treaties seemed to some members of the (Drafting) Committee so remote as to make it unnecessary to establish a further agency conciliation as between the parties.[27]

This point was underscored later when plenipotentiary representatives agreed that, in public statements, all signatories would define the primary purpose of the NATO treaty as collective self-defence, under Article 51 of the United Nations Charter, but would not term it a 'regional arrangement' under Chapter Eight.[28] This presumed the avoidance of any implication that the Alliance charter aimed at regional conciliation and therefore encroached on United Nations prerogatives. The parties did, however, reaffirm 'their existing obligations for the maintenance of peace and the settlement of disputes between them'.[29]

Both Secretaries General, Lord Carrington and Manfred Woerner, have offered their good offices to both the Greeks and Turks to resolve the Aegean Sea issues, and the Deputy Permanent Representatives of NATO have established a working group on

Aegean affairs.[30] Substantive resolution of these multi-faceted issues is presently distant.

There will always be arguments for letting time take its course, for trying to keep NATO out of a family quarrel, for continuing to treat military consequences as though they had no political causes. In the meantime, NATO's South Eastern Region languishes, military planning and coordination are fleeting, and political consensus is an elusive commodity.

CHAPTER 2

Politics of Continuity and Change: the Greek Context

TODAY, SOME 35 years after Greece and Turkey joined NATO, the relations between these two countries, as we noted earlier, are anything but placid. Long-standing differences between them have been exacerbated by domestic changes and an ever-changing international environment. Foreign policy in both Ankara and Athens is but an extension and reflection of domestic bickering and alignments. The cohesion of NATO is of minimal concern.

It has not always been easy for Westerners to discern the real motivations of Greece and Turkey and to understand their problems and policies. This lack of comprehension is perhaps understandable. Geographically, both countries are set apart from Western Europe and in NATO circles the Central Front is the principal focus of defence policy. Also, the socio-political context of Greece and Turkey, their levels of economic development and special democratic traditions are exceptional. In design they may appear to be Western, but in reality the indigenous institutions and processes are quite different. Greeks speak of 'going to Europe', and, depending on their purpose, the classifications imposed by scholars make Greece a Middle Eastern, Balkan or Mediterranean state. Her institutions and political processes since her inception in 1821 have not operated in the fashion of their Western European counterpart. Greece hovers on the threshold between Europe and the non-Western world, between the 'developed' and 'developing' nations. In the case of Turkey, it is predominantly a Muslim state, albeit secular, unlike any other NATO member. This fact, along with both countries' close proximity to the Middle East, significantly colours their relations and mitigates NATO's policy in this region. For these reasons, a closer, more individual look at each nation's polity, (Chapter 2: Greece; Chapter 3: Turkey) an analysis of their contemporary political institutions, will help us understand the overall uniqueness of this troublesome sector of the NATO Alliance.

Greece

Post-Second World War Politics

The election of the charismatic Andreas Papandreou and PASOK (Panhellenic Socialist Movement) in 1981 reflected a shift toward the left and disillusionment with NATO and the United States. Papandreou's campaign centred on the slogan *allaghi* (change)— change across all sectors of society. According to PASOK's ideology, Greece is an economically underdeveloped state and is politically, economically, and militarily dependent on the West. The previous post-Second World War conservative governments pursued, according to Papandreou, a 'mono-dimensional' policy of dependence that led to a series of concessions, policy ambivalence and sacrifice of sovereign rights vital to Greek interests. Innovation in both domestic and foreign policy areas was called for. What appeared on the surface to be a watershed electoral event turned out in the end to be marginal in its political consequences. The rhetoric was excessive, but change came haltingly.

Historically, the single most important factor in the political development of Greece since its liberation from German occupation in 1944 was the Civil War (1947–49). This conflict, which claimed more than 80,000 lives, had the effect of polarising politics, institutions and ideology in a manner that has affected all sectors of Greek society. Specifically, the transition from coalition governments in the 1940s to single party right-wing governments in the 1950s was directly or indirectly affected by the Civil War. It set the tone for the politics that followed, such as the liberal centre after 11 years of conservative government monopoly (1952–63), and the brief interlude of liberal politics (1964–65), the clash of George Papandreou and the Centre Union party with the Crown which led to royal intervention in parliamentary politics and a series of caretaker governments (1965–67), the military régime of seven years (1967–74), the return of parliamentary government by Karamanlis (1974–81), and finally, Andreas Papandreou's PASOK party's accession to power in the 1981 elections. He was defeated in June 1989, and caretaker governments followed.

The dominant common characteristic emerging from the Civil War period was anti-communism and the resultant unconditional commitment to the Western Alliance. The Left was either muffled or fled the country. No attempt was made for any gradual reconciliation. Besides, the fear of communism reinforced the role of the King, concomitant with the allegiance of the military to him. This exaggerated a monolithic belief in a communist threat, which made all liberal and socialist ideas and principles suspect. The nation state 'presented itself both as a concrete agent of the professional and social integration of a large number of people and as the obvious highly valued symbolic entity of a collective identification'.[1] Its role expanded greatly in the post-war era: having undertaken the entire burden of reconstruction—the allocation of massive amounts of foreign aid and its promotion of national orthodoxy—its effect on society became much larger. High unemployment and a totally devastated economy turned the state into the principal public planning vehicle and chief employer, which continued until the 1970s. From 1940 to 1970 the population increased by some 19 per cent, while the number of civil servants increased by 140 per cent.[2]

The national ideology presented an image of Greece as a unified nation fighting leftist adversaries who threatened to undo democratic institutions. There emerged in this way a 'nationalist form of fundamentalism which . . . was defensive, exclusive, and parochial'.[3] Within the state apparatus, a cluster of agencies emerged, filled with functionaries (military officers, gendarmerie, and other guarantors of public order) who enjoyed relative freedom from parliamentary scrutiny.

It was the monarchy that perpetuated the heritage of the Civil War and its attendant anomalies. In this respect, the King and the Officer Corps often referred to the 'communist insurrection' and continued to invoke the threat from within years after it had ceased to have any real substance. There was little awareness of the contemporary Communist world and little understanding of the Left's changing character in Greece itself. During the elections of 1956, 1961 and 1963, the military, with the knowledge of the crown, intervened through intimidation in the political process. Veremis suggests, 'This was not an army of state-builders or modernisers, but rather the trump card of the state against the "internal enemy".'[4] As a symbol of national unity, the military—particularly the Army—felt that their main purpose was to protect the nation from communism, both from within and without.

The problems of political, economic and social reconstruction dominated the 1950s-60s. Relative stability characterised the unprecedented seven-year prime ministership of the conservative government of Konstantine Karamanlis and his National Radical Union (ERE) (1956–63). The monarchy appeared as secure as it had ever been, protected by the armed forces, the right wing political parties and, less directly, the United States.

This period of outward stability faced a new, stiff challenge by 1963 from the emergence of a strong liberal centre and a vocal left. Feeling his vested interests and those of his staunch supporters threatened, King Konstantine II thrust himself into the middle of these disputes. Reformist elements backed the eloquent George Papandreou and his left-leaning son, Andreas, against the conservative forces. Under the elder Papandreou, the Centre Union Party (EK) had as its objectives an end to political polarisation, reform the educational system, defend civil liberties and further the democratisation of the political process. The Party won an impressive electoral victory in 1964[5]. This reflected a merger of forces ranging from moderate right to socialist, and found support in the growing urban centres where the anonymity of populations tends to weaken traditional clientele politics. Collective grievances of a decade or more were freely and loudly voiced.

Determined to challenge the Monarchy's influence on the military, Papandreou came in direct conflict with King Konstantine soon after taking power. The clash with the elder Papandreou was over allegations that a leftist organisation known as *Aspida* (the Shield) had penetrated the military;[6] this ultimately led to Papandreou's dismissal. The dispute between the King and the Prime Minister caused a major political crisis and a power gap that climaxed in the military coup, 21 April 1967. *The Times of London* reported that Konstantine was 'strongly opposed to any changes in the army which might expose it to Communist penetration', whereas Papandreou was 'under pressure from his [Centre Union] party to rid the army of right-wing officers whose loyalty to his administration is questioned'.[7] The failure of Papandreou, despite his massive popular support, to consolidate his party's position and survive the confrontation with Konstantine betrayed the precariousness of post-war democracy in Greece.[8] It also underlined the opposition of extra-parliamentary forces such as the Monarchy and the armed forces to change and reform.[9] The personal linkage of the military to the Crown or to conservative members of parliament was essential for professional personal advancement. Paradoxically, this very dependence of the officer corps on the Monarchy or political patrons became a source of resentment among sectors of the officer corps who were most eager to profit from it.[10] Clandestine organisations permeated the armed forces in order to purge leftist elements from its ranks, while simultaneously promoting their own corporate interests and waiting to assert their autonomy.[11] From all outward appearances the armed forces appeared united and non-political. But, in reality, the officer corps retained the belief that it should act if it perceived a potential or actual threat to Greek national security. Thus the inability of the politicians and the monarchy to solve the political crises during the 1965–67 period encouraged certain officers who had come of age during the Civil War to institute the *coup d'état* of 21 April 1967.

There were at least five discernible reasons that appeared to predispose the officer corps toward intervention: the perceived communist threat, the political incompetence of parliamentarians, the decline in the growth rate of the economy, Greece's geostrategic role in NATO, and the professional grievances (promotion and salaries) of certain elements of the officer corps. Also, the military felt a sense of isolation due to their 'total institutional life'[12] and the widening gap between their own social importance and that of prominent businessmen, professionals and bureaucrats.

The 21 April coup prevented George Papandreou from winning the upcoming election. Except for his followers, most of the Greek population accepted the coup, recognising the politico-socio-economic factors that led to this action.[13] The longest period of military rule in Greece (1967–74) culminated when the Junta launched its ill-fated coup against Archbishop Makarios and the Cypriot Government in hopes of uniting Cyprus with Greece. This plot failed. The Greek armed forces were totally disgraced and forced to return to the barracks, and Turkey asserted its rights as guarantor under the 1959 London-Zurich agreement and landed forces on the island in the early hours of 20 July 1974 to protect the Turkish minority. The Junta had gambled that Turkey would not respond or that the United States would again intercede (as in 1964 and 1967) to prevent Turkish intervention, and it lost the gamble.

Discredited and diplomatically isolated, the Junta exited on 23 July bringing Konstantine Karamanlis (self-exiled in France since 1963) to power once again to assume leadership of a civilian government and hold elections. The electoral outcome in November 1974, four months after the fall of the military dictatorship, was an affirmation of Karamanlis' efforts to secure an orderly transfer of power without provoking the fallen military régime's followers.

The second historical issue to be addressed by Karamanlis was the status of the monarchy. Since independence, but particularly in the twentieth century, the debate between republicans and monarchists had soured the political scene, often resulting in violence and distorting the evolution of the parliamentary system. In December 1974, for the sixth time in this century (previously in 1920, 1924, 1935, 1946 and 1973), a referendum was held on the future of the Monarchy. In the fairest vote to date, 69 per cent of the electorate voted against restoration of the Crown. The constitutional issue that had historically plagued Greek politics was finally and definitely over.[14]

Karamanlis and the New Democracy Party's electoral victory in November 1974 was overwhelming. It captured 54.37 per cent of the votes (220 seats out of 300 in parliament), as compared to the opposition consisting of the Centre Union with 20.42 per cent (60 seats), Andreas Papandreou's PASOK 13.58 per cent (12 seats), the United Left 9.47 per cent (8 seats) and the Communist Party received less than 1 per cent of the total vote. Three years later, the outcome of the November 1977 elections (unthreatened by the possibility of a military coup) betrayed a growing shift of the electorate toward the left. In this election PASOK gained significantly, from 13.58 per cent of the votes in 1974 to 25.34 per cent. Simultaneously, New Democracy dropped to 41.84 per cent from an all-time high of 54.37 per cent.[15] This was a prelude to a PASOK victory in 1981.

After five years as Prime Minister, Karamanlis was elected President of the Republic by Parliament in 1980. During his term of office Karamanlis utilised the 'carrot and stick' to purge unrepenting officers while also attempting to establish a *cordon sanitaire* about the military, thereby neutralising them. During his term in office, he legalised the Greek Community Party (KKE), entered into negotiations that led in 1981 to Greece becoming a member of the European Economic Community (EEC) and removed Greece from NATO's integrated military command structure (a response to its passive stance during the Cyprus fiasco).

The victory of PASOK and Andreas Papandreou in October 1981 is attributable to a number of political factors. Its constituency focuses on Centre Union support and the generation which came of age during the seven years of Junta rule. Papandreou also capitalised on the left's desire for legitimacy and on the guilt feelings of some conservatives who had ideological affiliations with preceding right-wing governments. The reconciliation of conservatives with liberals and leftists, merging in a united front against the military dictatorship, was the most positive, albeit unintended, product of Junta rule, as it expanded the consensual base of post-1974 parliamentary politics.[16] Furthermore, PASOK was able to draw on a younger and more radical constituency to recreate the socialist promise that the elder Papandreou and the Centre Union had been unable to fulfil prior to 21 April 1967.

Papandreou's ascent to power created consternation in the officer corps. In an effort to allay any concerns on the part of the military, Papandreou kept for himself the defence portfolio and resurrected two foreign policy issues that strongly appeal to nationalism. First and foremost is the state of Greco-Turkish relations. Since 1974 all Greek governments have developed a consensus concerning the 'Turkish threat'. This preoccupation with Turkey is over the several key issues discussed in Chapter I. Papandreou dismissed any threat from the communist north and saw the east (Turkey) as Greece's major threat.

Greece's dealings with NATO and the United States is the second issue of concern. Papandreou followed a very calculated but contradictory policy. On the one hand, in 1983 he successfully negotiated a five-year Defence and Economic Cooperation Agreement (DECA) with the United States, while at the same time being very supportive of the Soviet Union in the foreign policy area (e.g. Poland, nuclear free zone in the Balkans). The DECA discussion between Greece and the United States over the several major installations and twenty smaller bases were stalled until after April 1990 when new elections were held. The United States announced the closing of two of these major installations in Greece (Ellinikon Air Base and Nea Makri Communications Station). This leaves the United States with two major bases (Irakleon Air Base and Souda Bay on the Island of Crete). These installations are a large part of the American presence in the Eastern Mediterranean. The Greek side demands that the Americans provide security guarantees to Greece against perceived threats from Turkey. If no agreement is forthcoming by November 1990, the United States will have to dismantle its activities and leave Greece.

Although Papandreou attempted to neutralise the armed forces during his tenure in office, in reality the Greek military, and in particular the officer corps, was politicised as in earlier periods of Greek history. Promotions and officer retirements, especially at the senior ranks (Lieutenant Colonel and above), were dependent upon an officer's support of Papandreou and PASOK or the appearance of being completely neutral. For one to hold power in the armed forces, a certain political coloration was required. Purges and massive dismissals at the generals' rank cowed the officer corps into submission.[17]

Indeed, in the post- Second World War era the Greek armed forces believe that they are the embodiment of national ideals and that they are a fixed and integral part of Greek history. The armed forces, modern Greece, and her history have become inseparable in the eyes of the military. It is commonplace for officers to boast that they more clearly represent the mainstream of Greek values and the views of a majority of Greeks than do the elected politicians and bureaucrats. This poses major difficulties for civilian governments in maintaining supremacy over the military establishment. An examination of the socio-economic background of the officer corps highlights the socio-economic differences between the military and civilian élites and suggests the bases for the suspicion and distrust between the two groups which frustrates rule by parliamentary government.

The Military: A Profile

The Service academies are the institutions that recruit and socialise the military élites. They view officership as a 'sacred mission' and the military cadets are called *evelpis*, meaning 'the best hope for the nation'. At times, governments have used the academies to indoctrinate cadets in the political values of an existing régime rather than in professional ethics; for example, during the late 1960s and early 1970s a very pro-Junta view and a denigration of all elected officials were proffered.

TABLE 2.1. *Geographic Origins of Greek Military Academy Cadets, 1985*

	Army %	Navy %	Air Force %	General population
Peloponnesos	15.26	11.47	17.01	10.25
Central Greece and Euboea	20.82	30.96	23.50	11.39
Macedonia	20.24	5.73	16.66	21.55
Thessaly	12.11	1.63	14.73	7.54
Thrace	6.80	2.45	4.83	3.77
Epirus	4.81	0.82	2.63	3.55
Crete	8.46	4.09	6.84	5.21
Ionian Islands	1.35	1.16	1.20	2.09
Aegean Islands	2.80	4.09	1.45	4.76
Athens Metropolitan Area	7.30	37.70	11.05	29.96

Source: *Meleti ths Sxoles ton Evelpidon (Study of the Army Academy)* a yearly study, Greek General Staff, Research Division, Athens, Greece, 1985.

The military recruits cadets primarily from agricultural and small towns, except for the Navy, which tends to recruit from urban areas. Close examination of the data in Table 2.1 shows that the Army and the Air Force tend to recruit from the same general areas in Greece, but the Navy draws from central Greece and Euboea, the Aegean Islands, and the Athens area. A partial explanation for the overrepresentation of Naval cadets from these areas may be that the recruitment patterns differ along socio-economic lines. Historically the Navy has been viewed as the more prestigious Service, with links to royalty, shipping magnates, and the more affluent sectors of Greek society.[18] This situation still prevails to a lesser degree.

The Army and the Air Force tend to draw from relatively poor economic regions whose inhabitants are attracted by the mobility, security, and prestige offered by the military. The regions of Macedonia, Thrace, Epirus and Crete contribute a high proportion of Army and Air Force cadets. In addition, these regions, except Crete, border on countries long hostile to Greece. Thus war, with its attendant chaos and devastation, has become a way of life for the people of these regions, all of which are known for their 'heroic' values.

Because the Army and Air Force cadets come mainly from rural areas, and one may infer that they tend to come from humble circumstances where the father's occupations may be those of farmers, tradesmen, or public employees, officers' careers serve as convenient vehicles for social mobility. There are two principal reasons why the military has become an avenue of social mobility for young men from rural areas. First, economic and technological developments and the expansion of civilian bureaucracies have broadened the opportunities in non-military careers for the best educated, who tend to reside in the urban areas. Second, public schools have given the rural lower classes the opportunity to receive the academic training needed to qualify for the academies, thereby enhancing their future career goals.

Another element indicating social background is the proportion of cadets and officers who enter through self-recruitment as sons of professional officers. The percentge is highest in the Navy (16.7 per cent) and considerably less in the Army (7.7 per cent) and the Air Force (5.7 per cent). The Air Force's relatively small percentage may reflect the fact that it is a fairly new service that has not had time to develop self-recruitment patterns.

The rural social backgrounds of the officer corps, especially the Army, coupled with its lower class occupation origins, support the contention of a 'fundamentalist orientation and lack of integration with other élites, especially political élites'.[19]

As indicated elsewhere, kinship ties and family connection characterise modern Greek politics and life. This also extends into the military. No matter what the political complexion of the régime may be, political leaders have cultivated support from individuals (clientage) within the military; while officers may have resented the system, they have not hesitated to use the exchange of favours (*rousfeti*) as a means of career advancement.[20]

For most Greeks, the basis of any régime and even obedience to authority depend on personalities and clientage networks that tie individuals to particular incumbents. In this kind of setting actual inheritance of political position is common.

The significant number of parliamentarians from families with histories of political involvement indicates the existence of a network of political influence at provisional and local levels.[21] In fact, during the 1946–65 period Legg found that political families have retained strong holds on political offices.[22] The advantages offered by particular regional backgrounds are related to clientage, and most Greek politicians retain strong ties with their place of birth, even if they live elsewhere. For example, Karamanlis' most recent government (1977) had seven cabinet members from Macedonia; only Athens with ten posts had more.

One major note of importance is that politicians and political families tend to represent the more affluent sectors in regions, while members of the officer corps are recruited from lower socio-economic strata.[23] These differences colour the officers' perceptions of each other and the various Greek institutions, resulting in political mischief on the part of the armed forces.

The Military: A Socialising Experience

All Greek citizens capable of bearing arms are required by the 1975 Constitution to contribute to the defence of the country. Conscripts comprise some 66 per cent of the armed forces, serving tours of duty which vary depending upon the service (Army, 21 months; Navy, 25 months; Air Force, 23 months). Universal conscription maintains the armed forces. However, in the next decade, meeting manpower demands will be quite difficult for Greece because of zero growth in her population. Greece is now experimenting by permitting women to join the armed forces. It is hoped that enough women will enter to meet future personnel needs.

The conscription system operates effectively and is an accepted part of Greek life, particularly in rural areas where military duty may provide conscripts with their first ventures away from home and with training opportunities not otherwise available. Men from the rugged mountain districts of northern Greece generally expect Army service, and those from coastal areas and islands that are familiar with the sea and ships are more likely to receive Navy duty.

By the 1960s, universal military training was credited with having virtually eliminated illiteracy among men under the age of forty. Recruits deficient in basic literacy skills receive instructions in reading and writing as part of their military training. The percentage of recruits that fall in this category is less than 3 per cent. Personnel also receive technical and administrative training which contributes skilled workers to the economy. In 1985 a law was introduced permitting conscripts who are attending educational institutions to complete their basic military obligation by attending two-month training sessions during the summer.

Since the early 1980s, military units are fully integrated without distinction made based on one's political leanings. This has not always been true in the Greek armed forces. During and immediately after the Civil War, left-wing officers and conscripts were separated from the others and sent to a small island off the tip of Attica for military training and indoctrination. Upon completion of this

training, the conscripts were put into special units that were widely
known for their severity, and they were usually assigned to the most
unpleasant duties in the northern mountainous areas of Greece.
Until the Papandreou Government came to power, it was a fundamental and firmly adhered to assumption of the officer corps that no
person with leftist political ties could possibly be loyal to Greece. In
1983, a general amnesty was granted to those Greeks who had
fought in the Civil War on the side of the Communists. The assumption that conscripts and officers had to have a clean police record
(meaning that they had no leftist leanings) in order to be eligible to
enter the military was cancelled. Further, the social science curriculum at the academies has been changed. The historical discussions
of the Civil War have been tempered and the strong anti-communist
rhetoric that was part of the curriculum in the post-Second World
War period has been greatly softened. These changes have created
some consternation with many senior officers (Lieutenant Colonel
and above), most especially those who either fought against the
EAM/ELAS elements or were in some way affected by the Civil War.

Papandreou's efforts to shape the military were concentrated primarily upon the general officers' ranks. His elimination of background investigations heightened the entry of leftist elements
throughout all ranks in the military, and particularly the Greek
military academies, ensuring that a younger generation of officers
would be less conservative than the current corps. These steps taken
by Papandreou to shape the Greek military into his own political
image pose problems for Western security. The fact that many senior
military leaders shared Papandreou's anti-West attitudes weakened
Greek military ties to NATO. Those who did not share his views
tended to get in line rather than jeopardise their careers, a policy
that eroded the professional competence and morale of the Greek
military. PASOK's defeat after eight years in power affected the
promotion policies at all levels of the military and has serious implications for the United States and NATO, bringing the Greeks' ability
to fulfil their NATO mission increasingly into question.

Today the nation has a very positive view of its armed forces,
which are always an integral part of all celebrations on patriotic
days. The embodiment of the national ideals of the Greek military
and their link to Greece's heritage and War of Independence in the
nineteenth century are the *Evzones* (Honour Guard), who wear the
traditional costumes of the mountain warriors and are prominently
seen guarding the Tomb of the Unknown Soldier in Athens.

The preoccupation of the Papandreou Government with the
perceived 'Turkish threat' and the varied social and economic func-
tions of the Greek armed forces, as described above, has furthered

Greek national self-esteem and in turn has linked the Greek nation more closely to its armed forces. A military that was totally traumatised in 1975 has once again become the embodiment of Greek nationalism and the 'barracks' appear to be a far safer haven for them than excursions into the political arena.

Defence and Economic Considerations

Although the strategic commitment was the essential element in Greece's original relationship with NATO, economic considerations quickly followed. It was necessary, in the eyes of the United States and Western planners, to establish a viable economic base as a prerequisite for social stability. Toward this end, American economic and military aid poured in. In the period of 1944–65 total United States economic aid and loans were in excess of $1.9 billion while during the same period military aid totalled $1.6 billion.[24] This resulted in the reshaping and integration of the Greek economy to the West. Between 1965–74, the average yearly growth rate of the economy was an exceptional 6.7 per cent and *per capita* income rose to about $2,750. The fall of the military junta in 1974 and the eventual rise to power of PASOK did very little to lessen Greece's economic dependence on the West. For example, 74 per cent of imports and 78 per cent of exports in 1986 involved trade with OECD members.

Historically, the nation has been plagued over the years, regardless of the government in power, with the lack of any structural changes in key sectors of the economy. The State has never attempted to assume a leading role in establishing consistent policies toward the growth of industry, the balance of payments deficit and unemployment. Market forces, when permitted to operate freely, took the economy down a path that aggravated existing problems or created new ones.

The post-dictatorship period saw Greece's total external debt steadily climb to a massive $19 billion by 1986. Inflation during this same period hovered at about the 20 per cent level with unemployment rates of about 8 per cent annually, and budget deficits climbed steadily, reaching $3.3 billion in 1985.

Owing to the stablisation programme that Papandreou introduced in 1986, the Greek economy is now just beginning to realign itself. There have been some improvements in the budget deficit, domestic investments and trade. Inflation, one of the major targets of this austerity programme, has yet to be arrested, hovering at about 14 per cent for 1990. But, '(T)his is not enough', according to one analyst. 'Even 8 per cent would be high when other European countries have 3–4 per cent.'[25]

Perhaps the most characteristic aspect of this lack of a sense of direction and the expectation that solutions would appear from abroad[26] was the signing by Karamanlis in 1961 of the pact that led to Greece's full membership of the EEC 20 years later, in January 1981. PASOK was at first vehemently opposed to membership. In opposition, it had threatened to take the country out of the Community should it win at the polls. Then Papandreou promised a referendum to allow the Greek people to decide this question. This referendum was never held.

While most of the EEC is hurrying toward 1992, Greece still lags far behind the economic development of most of its partners. 'Closing the gap between now and 1992 appears to be a real long shot. We weren't prepared in 1981 and we won't be prepared for 1992.'[27] The most pressing need facing Athens in the near future is the continued financing of its deficit by foreign resources. The inflow of revenue from the West has increased considerably with Greece's entry into the EEC. Papandreou had worked hard to win improved terms, for Greece (especially the agricultural sector),[28] while American military aid remains a necessity for a country whose defence budget between 1980 and 1986 averaged about 19 per cent of the total budget (see Table 2.2). Real growth in defence spending has been negligible. Continued economic stagnation severely restricts Greece's ability to modernise her armed forces, even with United States assistance. Thus, Greece will continue to remain heavily dependent on foreign assistance, especially aid from Washington, for most of its major procurement programme as well as maintenance of its current force levels.

In terms of the share of the gross domestic product (GDP) going to defence, Greece, at about an average of 6.5 per cent, bears one of the heaviest defence burdens of NATO members. However, because its GDP is much smaller than that of other members, defence spending *per capita* is about average for NATO—roughly $242 per year. In 1986 United States defence assistance was equivalent to some 20 per cent of the Greek defence budget and about 150 per cent of the procurement budget. Overall, with the worsening economic situation in Greece, defence spending has declined by about 2 per cent in real terms since Papandreou's PASOK came to power. Defence spending as a percentage of the national budget has also declined from 23 per cent in 1981 to 12.2 per cent in 1989 (see Table 2.2).

As we noted elsewhere, Papandreou consistently stressed the independence of Athens' defence and security policies from those of NATO and the United States, and he fully understood that to criti-

TABLE 2.2. *Greek Defence Expenditure 1980–89*

	1980	1981	1982	1983	1984	1985	1986	1987	1988	1989
Total Defence Expenditure (billions $US)	2.27	2.58	2.6	2.2	2.1	2.1	2.4	2.97	3.1	3.0
Defence Expenditure as a Percentage of GDP	5.7	7.0	7.0	6.4	6.8	6.6	6.5	5.6	5.8	5.3
Defence Expenditure as a Percentage of Budget	23.0	23.2	21.8	17.5	18.2	17.5	16.1	21.9	13.1	12.2
Real Growth in Defence Spending	-8.2	23.5	-1.0	-8.2	4.4	0	0	1.0	-2.0	-2.5
US Military Assistance										
Totals (millions $US)	147.6	178.0	281.3	281.3	501.4	501.4	431.95	344.25	344.1	350.7
Percent of Greek Expenditure	6.5	6.9	10.7	12.8	23.7	23.8	17.9	11.6	13.2	14.9

Source: *Greece* (Greenwich, Conn.: Defence Marketing Services, 1989); *Greece and Turkey: US Foreign Assistance Facts* (Washington, DC: Congressional Research Service, 1989).

cise reduction in American aid to Greece was inconsistent with his declared independent policy. More importantly, however, Papandreou realised that as long as the 7 to 10 ratio was maintained, security assistance reductions adversely affected Turkey much more than Greece because of Ankara's far greater dependence on external aid.[29] Thus, Athens will calculate that its security interests vis-à-vis Turkey's are, ironically, protected by these reductions. The United States can expect strong pressure from Athens for increases in its military assistance programme, far in excess of the 1990 total of $348 million. At minimum, any government that comes to power will press for the maintenance of the 7 to 10 ratio and Athens may try to gain more in the DECA discussions and those related to United States base arrangements.

Greece allocates national funds largely to operations and maintenance, and reserves United States aid monies for equipment procurement. Any resulting cuts in American aid will make it more difficult for Athens to reach its NATO force goals, as it is unlikely to allocate funds for defence to offset aid cuts. Some procurement programme will require cancellation or be stretched out or delayed. Nonetheless, those military needs which the government deems absolutely necessary will be met. Athens will continue to give priority to maintaining its defensive capabilities against Turkey and in support of its NATO mission. The gap between Greece's military capabilities and those of the Warsaw Pact is not likely to diminish. Finally, Greece will continue to be dependent on aid from other countries to implement its modernisation programmes, especially those that require large expenditures (e.g. the Air Force's F-16/Mirage 2000 programme and naval modernisation).

The International Dimensions

Greek foreign policy since Papandreou's ascendency has dismayed the European community and its NATO allies. Greece has become a maverick among them. Athens took an international posture which seemed, on the surface, to favour the Soviet Union and the Warsaw Pact, and which contrasted with the oft-repeated statement of Karamanlis that 'Greece belongs to the West'. Recall that Greece was the only European nation that was a battleground for democracy when it staged a civil war at the beginning of the Cold War era.

The Papandreou electoral victory did not augur well for the interests of NATO and the United States. Throughout the previous period, Papandreou had campaigned on their negative roles and influences in Greece, specifically on the United States' support of the seven years of military rule and their non-opposition to the Turkish incursion in Cyprus. Stridently nationalistic, Papandreou, as the principal opposition spokesman, ceaselessly taunted Karamanlis and his New Democracy Party.

While in power, Papandreou made no sharp fundamental shifts in Greece's broader relations with either NATO or the United States. Indeed, by cutting through the political rhetoric and posturing, one could observe Papandreou extending, albeit with sharper language and different tactics, policies launched by his immediate predecessor, Prime Minister Karamanlis.

It was Karamanlis, in 1974, who sought to modify Greece's foreign policy path and to shore up the nation's shattered diplomatic status in the aftermath of military rule. Part of the objective of developing Greece's freedom to manoeuvre is mirrored in the decision to withdraw from the military command of NATO. Subsequent policy decisions clearly indicate Karamanlis' attempts to steer Greece away from the dominating influence of the United States. His crowning achievement was Greece's accession to the EEC in 1981.[30] Domestic opposition to membership came from the Communist Party (KKE) and PASOK, with Papandreou claiming that Greece would suffer economically and politically. While regularly emphasising that 'Greece belongs to the West', Karamanlis embarked on a concerted effort to expand and cultivate Athens' regional ties. Through these efforts he sought to take advantage of Greece's geographic position as a crossroad for three continents. He cogently summed up his views by referring to Greece as 'the Mediterranean balcony of Europe'. While improving Athens' already favourable relations with the Middle East, he concurrently concentrated on bettering her relations with its northern neighbours and the Warsaw Pact. Naturally, the spirit of *détente* facilitated these initiatives, and the Soviet bloc welcomed the overtures. This was an exceptional twist in Greek policy since Athens' main security concern in the post-war period was the threat posed by its Balkan communist neighbours, particularly Bulgaria. Beyond the benefits of increased trade, improved cordial relations permitted Greece to counterbalance the perceived threat posed by Turkey. The rewards of this *rapproachement* were reflected in the remarks of Defence Minister E. Averoff in a parliamentary debate in 1979 that Greece was in no way threatened by her northern neighbours.[31]

The perception of Turkey as the primary threat to Greek national security influenced and affected Athens' relations with Washington and NATO. It was in late March 1976 that the United States initiated a defence cooperation agreement with Turkey which provided $1 billion in American military aid for four years as payment for the use of American military installations in Turkey. The Greek

Government quickly initiated a similar agreement with Washington for $700 million. Although neither agreement was ever implemented, the precedent was established, at Greece's insistence, that henceforth the 7 to 10 ratio would be used to calculate military aid for the two feuding allies. To allay any Greek apprehensions, then Secretary of State Henry Kissinger sent a letter to Greek Foreign Minister Demetrios Bitsios stating that Greek-Turkish disputes 'must be settled through peaceful procedures and that each side should avoid provocative actions'. Moreover, Washington 'would actively and unequivocally oppose either side's seeking a military solution and will make a major effort to prevent such a course of action.'[32] While never deviating from the general commitment to the West, the post-junta rightist governments had succeeded in forging a more flexible foreign policy for Greece.

Rhetoric and symbolic gestures have abounded from Papandreou in his attempt to mold a more independent foreign policy within the framework of NATO,[33] a policy of less slavish identification with Western security concerns, in the manner of the French, in order to create a multi-dimensional foreign policy. Papandreou insisted that he did not believe in the Yalta division of Europe into two blocs and that he preferred to see eventual disintegration of both NATO and the Warsaw Pact, a Mediterranean with neither the US Sixth Fleet nor the Soviet Fifth Escadra, and a denuclearised Europe as a beginning to a denuclearised world. To this end, and despite Greek membership in NATO, he participated in the so-called Five Continents initiative, joining non-aligned and Third World countries to campaign for a moratorium on the development and deployment of nuclear weapons. He has repeatedly reiterated his intention to remove American nuclear weapons from Greece and refused entry to Greek ports of American nuclear warships.[34] He also stressed the notion of multilateral disarmament and the creation of a nuclear-free zone in the Balkans.

The 'Davos Spirit'

A constraint on PASOK's realisation of its more radical policy has been the tension in Greek–Turkish relations and Papandreou's sense of realism, which was partly motivated by the country's economic problems that necessitate friendlier relations with the West. The former tensions between the two NATO allies for 15 or so years can be described as a state of defensive confrontation (over the Aegean and Cyprus). By 1985 the rhetoric and strained relations had reached such intensity that Athens declared a new defence doctrine, an orientation of her forces toward the East (Turkey). An incident in the Aegean Sea over exploration rights in March 1987 brought the impasse to flashpoint and prompted NATO to appeal to both nations 'to avoid recourse to force at all costs'. The crises so disturbed the two countries' leaders that it set in motion a gradual process of reconciliation. It was initiated by Papandreou through an exchange of letters with Turkish Prime Minister Ozal and culminated in the Davos, Switzerland summit in January of 1988 when both sides agreed to work to improve bilateral ties. This meeting was particularly significant for Greece because Papandreou's policy since his election in 1981 had been not to meet with Turkish leaders until Turkish troops were removed from Cyprus.[35] Some tangible results occurred. Prime Minister Ozal visited Athens in June 1988, a monumental event in the relations of both countries,[36] and this was to be reciprocated by Prime Minister Papandreou. The latter did not take place, because of Papandreou's electoral loss. Also, Ankara agreed to revoke a decree, passed during the 1964 Cyprus confrontation, which froze the property assets of the Greek minority. Funds will now be allowed to be 'freely invested' in Turkey. In exchange, Greece has agreed to sign two protocols related to Turkish EEC association. However, Turkey's application for full membership is another matter. Greece has made it clear that Athens will veto it as long as Turkish troops remain on Cyprus.

The electoral defeat of Andreas Papandreou in June 1989 has brought the entire Greek political process to a halt, most especially in the area of foreign and defence policy. His demise was caused by an affair of the heart, plus scandals of embezzlement (Bank of Crete) and arms deals implicating Papandreou ministers. Unfortunately, no political party has been able to garner a majority in parliament, after two elections.

A Halt to the Political Process

In the June election, Konstantine Mitsotakis and the New Democracy Party received 44.2 per cent of the vote (144 seats out of 300 in parliament), Papandreou and PASOK, 39.1 per cent (125 seats) and the Alliance, a coalition of communist and leftist parties, 13.1 per cent (28 seats). Without a mandate from the electorate, an unorthodox partnership was formed beween New Democracy and the Alliance to give the hung parliament enough time to prosecute PASOK ministers for their alleged financial misdeeds.[37] With criminal charges brought against Papandreou and several of his ministers, new elections were set for 5 November 1989.

The second round of elections in less than five months again failed to give any party a clear majority. Once more New Democracy led with 46.2 per cent (148 seats), more than the party won in June, but still three seats short of a majority. PASOK received 40.6 per cent of the vote (128 seats), gaining in total percentage votes from the earlier election and increasing its seats by three. The remaining seats went to the Left Wing Coalition with 10.9 per cent of the vote and 21 seats, and independents received three seats. An all-party government was formed headed by Xenophon Zolotas, former governor of the Bank of Greece. The primary mandate of this government was to address social and economic issues and to set the stage for another election. Foreign policy and national security issues were held in abeyance.

New elections were held on 8 April 1990. The leader of the New Democracy, Konstantine Mitsotakis, emerged victorious with the assistance of Kostas Stephanopoulos, an independent rightist, who won one seat in parliament. Stephanopoulos pledged his seat to Mitsotakis, giving New Democracy a fragile majority of 151 seats. This is the first conservative government for Greece in nine years, Mitsotakis' principal rival, former prime minister Andreas Papandreou and PASOK, lost five seats, giving it a total of 123. Of the rest, 19 went to an alliance of leftist and Communists, and two seats went to Moslem candidates from the small ethnic Turkish minority that resides in the Western Thrace area. One went to an ecological movement and four seats to candidates running on a joint Socialist–Communist ticket.

The most immediate issue is the economy with a 14 per cent inflation rate, current-account deficit widening, and an overall slowdown in growth from 4 per cent in 1988 to the present 2.3 per cent. One additional issue that Mitsotakis must address immediately is the resumption of DECA negotiations with the United States. Athens will request additional monies and most likely restrict further American activities at these installations. Cyprus and the Aegean sea issues will not be placed on the immediate agenda for consideration.

The political challenges that Greece finds herself facing today and troublesome domestic political issues in Turkey (detailed in Chapter 3) have dampened significantly the 'Spirit of Davos'. Once again inflammatory statements and actions are permeating Greek–Turkish relations.

First there came Turkey's unilateral enlargement of the areas of the Aegean, Mediterranean, and Black Sea over which she claims jurisdiction for search and rescue puposes. Ankara backed off on this issue and was prepared to discuss it with Athens, but it remained a sore point. (Athens responded in kind in March 1989).

At about the same time, Greece voiced her insistence that the port of Mersin should not be included as part of the exclusionary area that borders Syria, Iraq and Iran and which Ankara wants barred from the Conventional Forces Europe (CFE) discussions in Vienna.[38] By virtue of its geographical location, Mersin is essentially a Middle Eastern rather than a European port, but it is particularly sensitive as far as Athens is concerned because of its proximity to Cyprus. This port is used by Turkey to support her forces on the island, and was the location from which Turkey launched her military operation in 1974. The 'Mersin question' has been shelved by Greece in the face of determined Alliance opposition not wanting to see this issue hinder the pace of the conventional arms reduction process. Athens has made it clear, however, that she still reserves her position and that this is still an open issue.

As we have seen, the existing temporary governments in Greece and the removal of Andreas Papandreou from the political scene have dampened the 'Davos Spirit'. In addition, further shadows were cast on chances of Greek–Turkish *rapprochement* first by Greece objecting to NATO denouncing the Bulgarian policy toward ethnic Turks and later, at the year's end, when Turkish public opinion became increasingly concerned about the situation of ethnic Turks residing in Greece's Western Thrace. The greatest storm was over the refusal, on technical grounds, of the candidacy of two ethnic Turks who planned to seek parliamentary seats in the electoral district of Komotini (Gumulcume) in the 6 November elections. This controversy escalated and finally climaxed in the sentencing and jailing of the two former parliamentary candidates to eighteen months imprisonment on charges of 'unacceptable and anti-national' behaviour. Magnified tensions between the Greek and minority Turkish communities go unabated and have led to several clashes with sustained injuries for both sides. Furthermore, both Greece and Turkey expelled their consuls from Komotini and Istanbul respectively. In addition, Greek and Turkish armed forces were placed on heightened alert. Unlike the March 1987 confrontation that was described earlier, today both parties are lacking in political leadership and governmental stability. It is doubtful, in the foreseeable future, that the 'Spirit of Davos' will be resurrected.

Papandreou also remained true to his statement of May 1985 when he predicted that Greece's relations with the United States and NATO would enter 'calmer seas'. By pointing out the diminished interest of the public in foreign affairs and the focus of his campaign on domestic problems, he was, in fact, suggesting that his public would grant him a free hand in conducting his foreign policy. Prime Minister Papandreou's new attitude was no doubt motivated by economic requirements which necessitate friendlier relations with the West, but it was also motivated by Greek concern over Turkey. For example, between 1982–86, out of a total of $1,580 billion spent toward purchasing arms, $775 million came from the United States, and $150 million from the Federal Republic of Germany, with only a negligible amount—$95 million—from the Soviet Union and Warsaw Pact, and the remaining $560 million from other countries. Greece's dependence on NATO for sophisticated arms and equipment remains very strong.[39] Present aid to Greece from the United States, some $348 million annually, is totally commercial credit and will go primarily toward the purchase of forty F-16s ordered in 1985 at a projected cost of $2 billion to match Turkey's order of 160 F-16s.[40] In addition, the Southern Regional Amendment (SRA) has benefitted Greece (and Italy, Portugal, Spain and Turkey) by providing her with the transfer of excess American defence equipment such as M48-A5 tanks, F-4E Phantoms, two patrol boats, eight T-33 jet engines, small arms, equipment and ammunition. In 1988 the United States Congress also applied the 7 to 10 ratio to the SRA. This has had a very negative affect. The application of the ratio negates the funding of large stores of equipment to both nations.[41] Comparable aid programmes exist with other individual NATO members, i.e. surplus and obsolescent F-104 and F-5A fighters have been transferred to Greece by the FRG and Netherlands.

Papandreou's government yielded to certain harsh realities. A falling-out with the United States and consequently with NATO only improved Turkey's diplomatic and military position and accentuated Greek weaknesses. Clearly, there seemed to have been a fundamental shift in Greece's perception of the balance of power between Athens, Ankara and Washington. Speaking to officers in Ioannina in February of 1988, Papandreou stated:

> . . . for quite a long time we used to speak, both Cyprus and Greece, of a triangle. Greece presses America to put pressure on Turkey, for solutions to be found to our problems, above all, the Cyprus problem. I think that this scheme is now historically outdated. . . . It has to do with the strategic role chosen for Turkey by the Pentagon and the commitments are such that, as we see it . . . there is really no way forward . . . to effective solutions. For this we are obliged to base ourselves on our own powers and it is possible for us to lay the foundation of peace with Turkey but through a dialogue on equal terms.[42]

As a counterweight to Greek problems with Turkey, and as a general element in its desire for regional co-operation, Papandreou had pursued actively good relations with Greece's Balkan neighbours. This was an extension of a process begun by the military dictatorship and continued by the New Democracy governments. On 28 August 1987 the declaration of war against Albania, which had remained in force since 1940, was repealed in exchange for guarantees of greater human rights for the Greek minority living in the area once claimed by Greece as Northern Epirus. Shortly thereafter, a substantial delegation headed by five ministers, including Foreign Minister Karolos Papoulias visited Tirana to pursue industrial, tourist and energy links. This visit was reciprocated by a high level Albanian delegation headed by its foreign minister, Reis Malile. Athens has also been instrumental in seeking Albanian integration and participation in Balkan affairs.

Foreign Policy Outside NATO

Overall, Athens' relations with the Warsaw Pact countries are quite cordial. This *rapprochement* was initiated by Karamanlis, who exchanged official visits with Romania, Bulgaria and the Soviet Union, and furthered by Papandreou. Such effects have failed to proceed further than commercial agreements and declarations of intent. The relations with Bulgaria can be characterised as 'warm'. Repeated contacts between Papandreou and Bulgarian President Todor Zhivkov culminated in the signing of a Declaration of Friendship, Good Neighbourliness and Co-operation and included promises of mutual consultation in the event of a local or international crisis.[43] It is no more than a mere statement of friendly intentions. This document is typical of a long line of intra-Balkan efforts at improved relations between the states of the two blocs, and thereby contributes to the easing of tensions beween the Warsaw Pact and NATO countries.

In 1981 Papendreou abandoned the 'we belong to the West' policy and instead sought to play the 'Soviet card' with an eye to gaining greater leverage with the West and satisfying PASOK's own leftist elements. Papandreou took a number of positions in the name of Greek independence (e.g. labelling the United States as the 'metropolis of imperialism,' supporting Moscow's position on Poland and Libya, the downing of the South Korean airliner and calling for a nuclear-free zone in the Balkans) that strained United States/NATO–Greek relations and strengthened ties with Moscow. Although Athens has very little to show for Papandreou's pursuit of a more independent foreign policy, Moscow has undoubtedly benefited. At the very least, Papandreou's initial hostile attitude toward Washington probably encouraged a domestic environment more conducive to Soviet diplomatic propaganda and intelligence activities, and fostered a strong anti-American feeling toward American diplomatic and military personnel. No doubt Moscow welcomed the constant bickering among NATO members. Papandreou's efforts to expand Greece's economic ties with Moscow did not result in any significant increase in overall trade, nor did the Soviet Union tilt decisively toward Greece in its disputes with Turkey in the Aegean. Although Moscow subscribes to the Greek view of the need for a 'unified' Cyprus and has called for an international conference on Cyprus, doubtless the Soviets' long-term goals are to encourage Greece (as well as Turkey) to adopt more neutralist foreign policies so as to drive wedges in the south-eastern flank and increase its own presence in the region.

Relations with Yugoslavia, traditionally closer than with other neighbours, have been a bit strained by occasional disputes over the Macedonian issue. Greece's primary concern over this area is to maintain the territorial status quo and to avoid entanglement in the chronic conflict among the minorities in Yugoslavia and Bulgaria to create a Macedonian nation.

Both countries maintain close military contacts, but their nature and frequency have mainly been kept secret. It is to Yugoslavia's advantage that Athens does not move away from NATO because it may discourage the Soviet Union from taking risks in the Balkans. Greece, likewise, has maintained good relations in the Middle East in order to protect the Greeks of the *diaspora*, to promote trade and more recently to counter Turkish influence regarding Cyprus. This overall policy diverges from the views of the United States and some NATO members. The oil crisis, the Persian Gulf confrontation, religious fundamentalism and Arab nationalism have set the United States apart from Greece and some NATO members in its Middle East policies.[44] Since 1981 Athens has pursued a policy based on the principle that it should side with the underdog, but this has not been easy. It finds itself caught in the crossfire of inter-Arab and inter-Muslim disputes.[45] PASOK's relations with the Palestine Liberation Organisation (PLO) have been particularly good. It was Greece that provided the ships for the PLO's retreat from Beirut, and its leader, Yasser Arafat, has been to Athens on several occasions, most recently in January 1988. Papandreou has stated that the acts of violence by Palestinians are a part of a liberation struggle and do not constitute terrorism. In fact, this PLO linkage with Athens was instrumental in effecting the visit of Syrian President Hafiz Al-Assad in May 1986. Papandreou received Syrian support for Cyprus while supporting Palestinian rights to their own country.[46] Syria is the key to events in the Middle East and could facilitate Athens' role as a bridge between the Arabs and the West. During this three-day visit President Assad enlisted Athens' help to convey Syria's view on terrorism and the Middle East problem to the West.[47] In the case of the American action against Libya in April of 1986, PASOK faced a dilemma. How would it appease its own Third World supporters without provoking Washington? In the end it came down on the side of Washington in restricting the Libyan embassy in Athens from making provocative statements, and a large section of the Libyan mission was removed from Greece.[48] Athens was careful to differentiate its policy from that of its NATO partners by voting for a package of sanctions against Libya; it said that it did not feel bound to implement the decision until 'concrete proof' of Libyan involvement in 'specific terrorist incidents' was produced.[49]

The at times contradictory perceptions of the Papandreou Government were evidence of its attempt to walk the diplomatic tightrope toward the goals enunciated when it came to power, namely a 'natural, independent and multidenominational foreign policy'. Without question, PASOK created uncomfortable moments for the NATO Alliance. Given Papandreou's complete control over PASOK's party apparatus, his malleability in questions of political doctrine was incontestable from within the government. The opposition, the New Democracy Party led by Mitsotakis, has been unable to attack effectively PASOK's contradictory policies. In fact, PASOK's leanings toward closer relations with the Alliance took New Democracy aback. All that Mitsotakis was able to do was to attack PASOK in the foreign policy area by suggesting that it was following earlier New Democracy's positions. The distinctions in foreign policy beween the two parties was basically a difference in degree. New Democracy today is more open in its support of the West and more willing to criticise openly the Soviet Union and the Warsaw Pact, and makes Greece appear less of a renegade in Western political and military circles. New Democracy would doubtless continue to seek solutions to the issues that divide Athens and Ankara if it came to power, and could conceivably adopt similar tactics as PASOK, such as refusing to participate in NATO exercises, in order to register its protest.

Regardless of which major party is in power in Greece today, the basic rivalry is a very simple one. It is an indication of the smattering of political forces that can have an effect on the decision-making process. Under these circumstances various statements made by the leading political figures, as well as parliamentary discussions, fuel political debate and provide an atmosphere that seems to depict to the outside world that Greek politics take extreme and emotional forms. Inevitably, the stability of relations between Greece, the United States and NATO directly affects Turkey as well.

CHAPTER 3

Turkey: A Delicately Poised Ally

NO NATION that has maintained close relations with both the United States and Europe for the last three decades is so little understood as Turkey. In spite of this lack of understanding, Turkey, over this period of time, has been of major strategic importance to the West. In the wake of the Revolution in Iran and Russia's invasion of Afghanistan, Turkey (the only Moslem member of NATO) serves as a vital link to the Moslem world. It has special and obvious ties with the Islamic countries, and a sense of affinity with the developing and predominantly neutralist Third World.

The Setting

Sitting astride the strategic crossroads where Europe meets Asia, Turkey began her process of Westernisation some 100 years ago. The real turning point in this process, however, was the establishment of the Turkish Republic in 1923 by Kemal Ataturk.[1] That year marked the beginning of a systematic attempt to transform Turkey into a Western state. Under Ataturk's 'benevolent dictatorship', Turkey's diverse peoples were treated as one homogeneous 'Turkish' people. This 'tutelary' régime diligently pursued the dual goals of national security and modernisation (Westernisation); it utilised its power to impose systematically a radical set of six unifying concepts on the nascent republic. Formally embodied in the Constitution of 1937, the six tenets are republicanism, populism, nationalism, reformism, étatism, and secularism.

Ataturk unified his country, but only after first overcoming resistance from within the ranks of the military and Kurdish insurrectionists.[2] During the last years of his reign, Ataturk's 'legitimacy' was undisputed, supported as it was by a strong military. The Turkish Republic's tutelary incubation had yielded a centralised political and economic infrastructure on which to build the modern nation/

state envisaged by its founder. Ataturk's dream, that Turkey's destiny lay with the West, continues to this day to affect both her domestic and foreign/military policy.

The wisdom of Turkey's post-Second World War alignment with the West, and in particular with the United States, was scarcely questioned until the 1960s. Before 1939 there was a strong residue of Turkish goodwill toward the United States, based in part on the long record of American philanthropic and educational activity in the country.[3] American championship of national self-determination after the First World War was in welcome contrast to the imperialist ambitions of the European powers. Indeed, as Turkey faced the prospects of foreign occupation and partition in 1919, there was even some sentiment favouring the establishment of an American mandate over the country.[4] In the late 1940s, there was an almost perfect coincidence of American and Turkish interests regarding Communist activity and Soviet expansionism. As seen above, the civil war in Greece was raging during this time. In Iran, the Soviets were delaying their military evacuation, and instead were encouraging the formation of 'People's Republics' on the Turkish border. This pincerlike movement from Greece and Iran was combined with direct pressure from the Soviet Union for retrocession of the eastern Turkish region of Kars (a Russian territory from 1879–1920) and for 'joint defence' of the Bosporus and Dardanelles. Turkey rejected all such Soviet demands, while hoping for Western backing in any ensuing confrontation.[5] With the inability of Great Britain in 1947 to support Greece and Turkey, the United States stepped in to fill that gap—with the first clear statement of the policy of containment of Soviet expansionism, the Truman Doctrine. Yet this early coincidence of American and Turkish interests soon blurred out of focus.

The close bilateral relationship, which had been accepted by both sides in the face of the Soviet threat of the late 1940s, came gradually to be viewed in the 1950s as a convenient means to other ends. For the financially hard-pressed government in Ankara, American foreign and military aid programmes became a cornucopia of subsidies. For Washington, the Turkish Government became a ready source of diplomatic assistance with complex problems—as when pacts of friendship and mutual military assistance among Turkey, Greece, and Yugoslavia (1953, 1955) created an indirect diplomatic connection with Yugoslavia's President Tito, into which the United States did not care to enter directly.[6] Instrumental, manipulative relations, as outlined, work very well if the interests of both sides remain compatible. On the other hand, they are subject to sudden strains and recriminations when interests unexpectedly diverge—

as in 1962 when Washington considered trading missiles in Cuba for American missiles in Turkey without consulting Ankara; or when Turkish intervention in Cyprus (threatened in 1964 and carried out in 1974) upset United State's assumptions about Greece and Turkey as the solid South Eastern Flank of NATO.

In the mid-1940s, as Turkey and the United States were establishing their close strategic ties, Turkey was also embarked on a fundamental transformation of its domestic politics—from authoritarianism to democracy.[7] The first test of real democracy came in the general elections of 1950 when nearly 90 per cent of Turkey's electorate turned out to vote Ataturk's Republican People's Party (RPP) out of power. The Democratic Party (DP), which replaced the RPP, was founded in 1946 by four civilians who had been expelled from the RPP and exhibited no great devotion toward the ideals of Ataturk or its military/bureaucratic adherents. Once in power in 1950, President Celal Bayar and Prime Minister Adnan Menderes commemorated Ataturk's era by applying his monolithic authoritarian tactics to the exigencies of electoral politics. As the DP and RPP freely trampled the political rights of minor parties in the Parliament, the 'rules of the game' evolved by precedent. Intolerance of opposition and public criticism, aversion to compromise, and an inability to accommodate or adjust to change (to this day the pathological trademark of Turkish party politics) proved to be the downfall of the First Republic. In May 1960 a *coup d'état* by 38 Army and Air Force officers took power in the name of a National Unity Committee (NUC). This coup was due entirely to domestic causes. Menderes' Democrats had been elected and re-elected by enthusiastic rural majorities but had increasingly antagonised their urban following of workers, intellectuals and the press. A temporary economic recession in the late 1950s caused acute hardships and much dissatisfaction, to which Menderes responded by progressively curtailing the opposition's freedom of expression.[8] Press freedoms vanished in the tense and destructive atmosphere of 1958 and 1959. The armed forces came under pressure from all sides to take action. Notwithstanding its jealously guarded reputation for neutrality, the military could not ignore the crisis or even observe it with unanimous disinterest. Violent protests became rampant during the first part of 1960. Martial law was declared, thereby forcing the armed forces to stand in reluctant opposition to the DP's detractors. When on 21 May the War College cadets staged a protest march, the tide of sympathy was seen to have moved irreversibly against the government.

The Fateful Sixties

Beginning in May 1960, the National Unity Committee (NUC), led by General Cemal Gursel, ruled Turkey for almost 18 months. Declaring that Ataturk's principles had been violated by the previous civilian régimes, the NUC banned the Democratic Party and arrested its members; Bayar was jailed and Menderes was hanged for forcing a series of repressive and anti-democratic measures while in power. One faction in the military junta, under Colonel Alpaslan Turkes, favoured installing a permanent authoritarian régime. Turkes and thirteen fellow extremists were expelled from the National Unity Committee. But the majority under General Gursel saw its task as initiating the drafting of a new constitution with better democratic safeguards and returning power to civilian hands. Part of the solution was to dispossess the Parliament of some power; beginning in 1961, the State courts held ultimate judicial authority in constitutional disputes.

Translating Ataturk's six cardinal principles into a new constitution involved fundamental choices affecting Turkey's future. Within the NUC, two positions emerged. One view equated 'populism' with the inalienable right to freedom of expression, and hence of ideology. The other advocated a restricted pluralism, warning of the contrary effects of communism, fascism, and theocracy on 'nationalism' and 'secularism'. The former's wishes prevailed; the latter's fears materialised. Two decades later the debate is far from settled.

With the new constitution in force, the shadow of Kemal Ataturk loomed far mightier than the men in Parliament. Individuals and organisations now enjoyed unprecedented rights and freedoms, but with their government thus constrained, they also enjoyed lessened protection against one another's transgressions. It was in this permissive milieu that extremist groups took root in the early 1960s.[9]

The Justice Party (JP), meanwhile, plagued by its own intra-party factional competition, expelled its most extreme members. In what turned out to be a very politically astute manoeuvre, the JP abandoned Inonu's coalition and swept the 1963 provincial elections as the nation's chief opposition party. For better or worse, an irreversible drift away from centrist politics was gaining momentum in Turkey.

By the early 1960s, the traditional basis of American relations with Turkey was being increasingly questioned, especially by the far left. Yet any friction remained largely latent and subordinate to common security aims. The origin of open deterioration of United States–Turkish relations can be traced to the 1963–64 Cyprus crisis in which American intervention was highly resented. Turkey has never forgotten President Johnson's warning to Prime Minister Inonu that, if Turkey did not desist, it could not expect United States support in the event of a Soviet attack.[10] Moreover, in terms of security in the Eastern Mediterranean, the situation produced three important results: it led to a sharp deterioration in relations between Greece and Turkey; it intensified differences between both countries and the United States and gave them a strong emotional and at times irrational edge; and it contributed to a polarisation of domestic politics and an increase in domestic instability. One of the most important consequences of the Turks' ensuing foreign policy re-evaluation was a re-examination of bilateral defence arrangements. This resulted in the signing of a new Defence Co-operation Agreement in July of 1969, giving the Turkish Government more control over indigenous United States bases.[11] Another consequence was the initiation of efforts to improve relations with the Soviet Union. A third was an attempt to expand relations with the Arab world.

Government legitimacy was flagging by 1965. The imposition of martial law at various times during 1961–63 had inflamed the Left. Corruption was rampant, stigmatising the government as it had done in the 1950s. An attempted *coup d'état* by extremist officers in May 1963 did little to reassure the public of the armed forces' commitment to Inonu's administration.

The elections of 1965 brought the dynamic new leader of the JP party to power as Prime Minister, Suleyman Demirel.[12] Only three decades before, in the 1930s, Ataturk had enjoyed a strong grip on the nation while drawing blueprints for a self-governing republic. As recently as a decade earlier in the 1950s, Menderes too had demonstrated a taste of tight control while perverting Ataturk's democratic process. Now, under the Second Republic, more power resided in the ballot box than in the Prime Minister's office. Demirel needed support and votes, and for four years he refrained from repressing his opponents and tampering with debate in the press and and in the National Assembly. Through these tactics the JP earned some support, but the nation's problems were deeply entrenched, requiring more from the government than good behaviour alone.

Under the political circumstances of the mid and late 1960s, Turkish politics could be characterised as a 'silent partnership' in which the military maintained its full autonomy from the government while keeping a watchful eye over the parameters of civilian political life. In the midst of improving economic conditions and the progressive strength shown at the polls by the JP party, the incentive for military intervention decreased. In terms of civil-military relations, the régime increasingly moved to the centre of the continuum in the context of an uneasy partnership. Demirel was careful not to repeat Menderes' errors. He maintained good relations with the military and routinely consulted with the Supreme Military Council. He also worked to improve the economic position of the officer corps.

Intervention by Ultimatum

It was not until the internal weakening of the Justice Party and the manifestations of growing domestic turmoil that the military once again intervened in March 1971. The internally split Demirel government was unable to cope with the growing student unrest, campus warfare, labour union strikes, ethnic clashes and violent manifestations of anti-Americanism. Under the threat of a military take-over, Prime Minister Demirel resigned. Significantly, however, the armed forces refrained from an outright assumption of power, but permitted the establishment of a non-partisan cabinet to impose martial law, suppress newspapers, outlaw strikes and arrest hundreds of extremists from both the Left and Right.

The March 1971 intervention by the military became known as the *coup by communiqué*. The three cabinets of civil servants and backbenchers that ruled Turkey from 1971 to 1973 were approved unofficially by the Supreme Military Council, and only 'after much dickering, by rather sullen parliamentary majorities. Despite—or just because of—multiple approvals, none of them proved either "strong" or "credible".'[13] In 1972, moreover, Bulent Ecevit deposed Ismet Inonu in a bitter contest for the leadership of the Republican People's Party. It was Ecevit's programme of democratic socialism and his uncompromising stand against military intervention that turned out to be crucial elements in his victory. In April 1973 the military and parliament agreed on a bipartisan caretaker government to guarantee the freedom and fairness of the elections scheduled for the Autumn of 1973. In addition, Turkey's constitution was amended to close 'the loopholes' which had allowed extremists to operate so effectively for ten years.[14]

On 14 October 1973 civilian rule returned to Turkey, ending 30 months of indirect rule by the armed forces. The election revealed a shaken polity, as the six parties, none of which won a majority, failed to agree on a ruling coalition. Ecevit's rejuvenated RPP emerged as the strongest single party.[15] After much manoeuvring among the several parties, Ecevit put forth an unlikely coalition with the ultra conservative National Salvation Party (NSP) of Necmettin Erbakan. With martial law and the political vendetta (both Left and Right) over, Turkey's leaders turned to other matters amidst a sense of relative political normalcy. The two most pressing concerns were interrelated, namely the OPEC oil price/supply crises (Turkey imports 70–80 per cent of its oil) and growing tensions with Greece over oil exploration rights in the Aegean Sea. In addition, the Cyprus issue was shortly to loom (July 1974) once again, affecting relations with her NATO partner, the United States.[16]

In the Grand National Assembly extraordinary amounts of time were spent patching together coalitions that might secure majority support.[17] The 1973 bipartisan caretaker cabinet stayed in office for three months after the election it had been charged to administer. In 1974–75 a non-partisan government of civil servants remained in office for three and a half months after losing its bid for parliamentary confidence 17 to 372. After the 1977 election Ecevit's RPP, having secured 41 per cent of the popular vote, tried for one month to form a government, but fell short of a majority by 12 votes.[18]

Of the seven governments in office since 1973, only four met the requirements of majority endorsement in the Assembly. Two of these were coalitions of Demirel's Justice Party with the Salvationists and Nationalist Action Parties on the right. The remaining two were formed by Bulent Ecevit and his RPP. One was a coalition with Erbakan's Salvationists (January–September 1974) which Ecevit dissolved after the Cyprus intervention in the summer of 1974 in the vain hope of forcing an election that might give a majority to his party alone. The second was Ecevit's government that took office in January 1978, with the crucial support of a dozen defectors from the Justice Party. It fell to this government to conduct the delicate negotiations about re-financing Turkey's towering foreign exchange debt and to re-establish military co-operation with the United States. The elections of October 1979 brought about the ouster of Ecevit. His replacement, by a parliamentary minority, was led by Demirel and his Justice Party. To gain a parliamentary majority Demirel invited the 'unconditional support' of the National Salvation Party, the National Action Party and the National Order Party. This government's life was short-lived.

By August 1980 Turkey's domestic situation had reached a critical stage. Against the backdrop of a turbulent decade—coalition governments, political polarisation, personal animus between Demirel and Ecevit, urban terrorism, and fundamental socio-economic problems—the spectre of two unpalatable outcomes loomed: anarchy or military rule.

The September 1980 Intervention

The armed forces led by General Kenan Evren intervened on 12 September 1980. Warnings by the military that intervention was probable had gone unheeded.[19] These warnings were addressed not to one single party or to several politicians but to all constitutional institutions. General Evren stated, 'We have not eliminated democracy. I would particularly like to point out that we were forced to launch this operation in order to restore democracy with all its principles, *to replace a malfunctioning democracy.*'[20]

The sense of relief with which Turks greeted the restoration of order was virtually unanimous. Within a year the military government, through the National Security Council, had taken steps to reinstitute democracy. A new constitution, drafted to replace the 'liberal' constitution of 1961, was submitted to the voters, who overwhelmingly approved it. The new constitution sought to strengthen the office of President and the two-party system. The latter effort was designed to break parliamentary impasse which gave minority parties disproportionate strength in forming coalition governments. These and other constitutional changes, supported by implementing legislation, were quite significant. One constitutional provision banned the leading opposition figures (and some hundred or so lesser ones) from active involvement in politics until 1992. It was the intent of the military for new political actors to take the stage.[21]

The transition from military to civilian rule was initiated in November 1982 with the election of General Evren as President of the Republic[22] and culminated in November 1987 with parliamentary elections. In these elections former Prime Ministers Suleyman Demirel and Bulent Ecevit took part, and Prime Minister Turgut Ozal's Motherland Party was victorious.[23] This election was a milestone in Turkey's political evolution. Civilian rule was again restored, the process of democratisation became firmly entrenched, new parties and leaders emerged, and political respectability in the international community, especially in Western Europe, came to Turkey.

Since 1986 Turkey has witnessed a rapid multiplication of political parties as it did in the pre-1980 period.[24] Despite such misgivings, there exists a growing consensus among the élite and the population that Turkey cannot evolve into a workable and sustainable pluralistic democracy without representation of all political views.[25] This was evidenced in the most recent elections when Prime Minister Ozal suffered his first major setback in March 1989 when the Turkish people defeated Ozal's Motherland Party in the nationwide by-elections, receiving only 22 per cent of the total vote.[26] These by-elections were vigorously contested by the Social Democrats led by Erdal Inonu and the True Path Party headed by Suleyman Demirel. Both parties questioned Ozal's leadership abilities and his economic policies, most especially the inflationary spiral the nation now faces which has affected all strata of Turkish society.

Prime Minister Ozal and the Motherland Party's popularity reached an all-time low by September 1989. Concurrently, by summer's end, President Kenan Evren had decided not to seek re-election for another term to the office of President of the Republic. With no viable candidates in the offing and the political opposition highly fragmented, Ozal announced for the office in early October. With the Motherland Party in the majority and the two major opposition parties boycotting the presidential election in parliament, the Grand National Assembly elected Turgut Ozal with 263 votes out of 450. The legitimacy of Ozal's succession to the presidency is questioned by the opposition and to some extent the public. In constitutional terms, his election to the post is quite legal.

From the very beginning of his term as president, Ozal has let it be known that he would continue his influence in the government, especially on economic issues and foreign policy, as well as his continued involvement in the Motherland Party's politics. Predecessors holding the office of President of the Republic in the past and most especially President Evren stood above the political fray. Ozal will most likely use the extended powers accorded to the president in the 1982 Constitution to have his views on the choices Turkey will take enshrined in legislation, overseas commitments, and the personnel of the State. It appears that President Ozal may have plans to affect the political system by making it more dependent on the full authority of a president instead of a prime minister.

No sooner did Ozal become president than he artfully managed to pull various factions within the Motherland Party together and had them elect his faithful supporter, Yildirim Akbulut as prime minister and party boss. A frustrated opposition now watches Ozal continue to rule Turkey from the presidential palace. It is highly unlikely that any change will take place before 1992, when the next parliamentary elections are scheduled to take place.

The Kurdish Problem

The interplay of economic and security issues is most evident in South-Eastern Turkey. This is the home of Turkey's largest minority, the Kurds, who number between eight to ten million and are the resident minority in eight provinces bordering Iran, Iraq and Syria.[27] Kurdish unrest in South-Eastern Turkey is by no means a recent development. Since the early 19th century, this region has experienced periodic uprisings and other forms of Kurdish resistance. The present phase of violence that began in August 1984 has combined several features of modern guerrilla warfare not previously employed in Turkey. Today's insurgents are waging a tactically astute hit-and-run campaign exclusively in the rural, sparsely populated countryside. These elements are apparently benefiting from substantial foreign training and material support abetted by cross-border safe havens in Iraq, western Iran and Syria, and training camps in Lebanon's Bekka Valley. No doubt with the end of East-West tensions, Turkey's defence priorities will be shifting southward.

Although most Kurdish peasants are loyal to Ankara, they have resisted assimilation because of their traditional orientation and tribal communal structure. A small minority belonging to the Kurdish Workers' Party (PKK) emerged in the late 1960s. Its ideology is a combination of Marxism–Leninism and ultra-nationalism; its ultimate goal is to establish an independent Kurdish state under Communist rule in South-Eastern Turkey. Thus far, however, the question of outside support, tacit or otherwise, for the PKK has been more of a problem with Syria, where the PKK leader Abdullah Ocalan resides for most of the year. With the continued escalation in terrorism in this region, there is growing pressure on Turkey to take stronger action against Syria and Iraq. In January 1990, Ankara diverted the waters of the Euphrates River to fill a reservoir behind the Ataturk Dam, the centrepiece of the South East Anatolian Project (GAP), for revitalising this regiòn by cutting the flow of water to both Syria and Iraq. Turkey promised to unblock the river in one month (and did so!), but both Damascus and Baghdad were furious. This action by Ankara also sends a direct message to both capitals, that Turkey could, if necessary, cut off the flow of the Euphrates upon which both Syria and Iraq rely for the majority of their water supply, if the PKK continues its attempts to destabilise South Eastern Turkey.[28]

In response to the recent escalation in terrorism and loss of life, the government has developed a series of short- and long-term measures for curtailing violence. For the short term, the post of regional governor was created in July 1987 for the purpose of coordinating the efforts of security forces in the South East by making them more responsive to the insurgency there.

Ankara's economic development programmes for the long term are twofold. The first programme is Ankara's effort to bring a basic infrastructure—roads, electricity and schools—to all parts of this region by the end of the decade. This target will most likely be met. The second programme is the enormous South East Anatolian Project, that was mentioned above, for harnessing the Tigris and Euphrates rivers to produce billions of kilowatt-hours of electricity and to irrigate millions of acres of land across the south-eastern provinces. The focus of this effort is the Ataturk Dam, the fifth largest dam in the world, which is scheduled to be completed in the 1990s. Beyond this project, the GAP envisions an additional 10 dams and 13 separate development schemes over the next 30 years. Upon completion, the GAP, more than other organisations, has the potential to change the face of South Eastern Turkey over the coming decades, and this will go far toward assisting integration of the Kurds, both economically and socially, into the rest of Turkish society.[29] The completion and success of GAP is highly contingent on the well-being of the Turkish economy. No doubt the armed forces will continue to play a major role in suppressing this ongoing insurgency.

The Military

The armed forces continue to play a political role in Turkey as guardians in order that the pre-1980 excesses should not again prevail. The bottom line is that the Turkish military are reluctant participants, ensuring that intervention need not occur in the future, and they intend to disengage willingly from the front line of politics by returning the reins of power to civilian authorities. This is, in part, attributable to the existence of a national ideology, Kemalism, which dominates both military and civil policies. This is in sharp contrast to the Greek military who historically have lacked a strong personality or ideology. This has resulted in the Greek officer corps' continual manipulation by self-serving politicians.

It was Kemal Ataturk's strong personality that shaped, defined, and established principles of behaviour for the Turkish military, and in the end entrusted to them the protectorship of the nation-state. Overall, they have acted as a temporary and progressive political force, taking seriously their self-chosen role as guardians of the constitutional order.

Officership in Turkey is viewed quite positively and considered a very respected profession. The service academies (known formally as the War Colleges) are the basic sources of recruitment of Turkish officers in all three branches of the military. Throughout the four years that a cadet is in attendance, not only is he instilled with professional ethics, but he is also inculcated with the values of Kemalism, learning in detail the history of modern Turkey—a required part of the curriculum.[30]

The military recruits cadets primarily from rural areas—agricultural communities and small towns—as was the case in Greece.[31] Close examination of the data in Table 3.1 shows that the Army favours Central Anatolia, a relatively poor region which provides mobility, security and prestige to the prospective recruit. A stronger argument can be made that Anatolia is closely associated with Ataturk and the revolution, which even today has great appeal to the populace of this region.

TABLE 3.1. *Geographic Origins of Military Academy Cadets, 1982–84*

Region	Army	Navy	Air Force	Total Population
Central Anatolia	44.5	24.2	13.4	29.2
Aegean/Marmara Seas	24.6	56.5	73.7	29.1
Black Sea	12.1	8.5	5.0	12.7
Mediterranean Sea	9.2	4.0	4.1	12.4
Eastern Anatolia	7.6	5.8	2.8	10.4
South Eastern Anatolia	1.8	1.0	1.0	6.3
Numbers	(951)	(718)	(716)	(40,347,719)

Source: The Turkish General Staff, Ankara, Turkey, 16 April 1985.

In the Aegean/Marmara Seas region, cadets' origins are greatly skewed in favour of the Air Force and Navy. This area contains two of the most cosmopolitan cities—Istanbul and Izmir—which are less tradition-bound than other cities and sections of Turkey. In addition, both the air force and naval war colleges, plus numerous major installations of both services, are located here. Lastly, the entire area has a seafaring tradition that perhaps facilitates the Navy's recruitment efforts. It is also evident from the data that both Eastern Anatolia and South Eastern Anatolia are under-represented in all recruitment patterns due to several factors: the geographic remoteness of the areas, economic underdevelopment, and a higher rate of illiteracy than the rest of Turkey. As noted earlier, South Eastern Anatolia is populated largely by Kurds, who, over the years, have generally resisted assimilation because of their traditional orientation and tribal communal structure.

Are there linkages in recruitment from regions where Ataturk initiated the revolution? The nationalist movement was launched at Samsun on the Black Sea in May 1919. In subsequent months, nationalist congresses were held in Erzurum and Sivas. It was also from the Anatolian provinces that Ataturk raised a cohesive army that would go on to defeat the Greeks and ultimately establish the first Turkish republic. Our data reveals that no significant biases in recruitment of cadets have emerged from these regions. In fact, the Army, with its proximity to these historical events, is somewhat underrepresented in comparison to other geographic regions.[32]

Another indication of social background is the occupation of the cadet's father as pointer to social origin. It may also be employed as an indicator for locating an officer's parents at some point on the social pyramid. Data reveals that military personnel, gendarmeries, and civil servants produce the largest percentages of officers for the Turkish armed forces, approximately some 40 per cent or more from each Service.[33] Thus a major aspect of social origin is through familial recruitment—that is, 'sons of the military' and civil servants.

Both these élites hold a significant place in the history of modern Turkey. They have imbued themselves with guardianship responsibilities to the political system and the State, even though they represent a minority of the population.[34] Both have been the primary agents contributing to the political stability of Turkey.[35] Thus the 'guardians of the flame' of Kemalism assure the perpetuation of the revolution through familial recruitment and imply a direct stake in the existing order.

Additionally, farmers' and labourers' sons use this career path as a springboard to upward mobility. Conversely, it is not at all surprising to find that the other professions as a class do not view a military career positively. In general, these background characteristics suggest that the officer corps has a stake in the existing social and political order, and Kemalism is the guiding philosophy for this involvement.

A distinguishing feature of the Turkish military establishment is their 'behind the scenes' role in the political process. At present, the officer corps is institutionally separate from the government. However, a consultative linkage exists at the top between the civilian government and the military establishment as represented by the President of the Republic (Turgut Ozal) and the Turkish General Staff.

Specifically, under the present constitution, Article 118 creates a National Security Council which determines national security policy and coordinates all activities related to such matters. Its membership is dominated by the military and individuals who tend to support the armed forces. It is presided over by the president of the republic and chaired in his absence by the prime minister.[36] By this means, the Turkish armed forces have formal access to the existing civilian government whereby they can legally voice the concerns of the military.

In addition, there exists the Supreme Military Council which is headed by the Chief of the General Staff and includes the commanders of the several services. This body has become an important collective decision-making element for the armed forces, and since 1960 the office of the Chief of the General Staff has acquired paramount importance.[37] Under the existing law, the Council's primary responsibility is the preparation of the Turkish armed forces for war, and their overall administration. In reality, the Minister of Defence and his department play a secondary role. He and his staff are all adjunct to the Turkish General Staff and the Ministry's responsibilities are to oversee personnel, procurement, supplies and the implementation of the budget. Any and all major decisions affecting the armed forces are made by the General Staff and more specifically the Army, which represents about 80 per cent of the armed forces. This supreme body is responsible for most major decisions pertaining to the Turkish military.

There has been no precise method of determining when restraint yields to guardianship, and decisions to invoke the latter responsibility have been painfully made. At the least, such justification would seem to require a lengthy period of failure to deal with urgent problems on the part of the normal political process. If the past is our guide, such a military move would come only after warnings and open indications of military displeasure. Basically, the officer corps, which is generally representative of Turkish society and is held in high esteem by them, is sincere in its attachment to the democratic process and its concern that it should work effectively. Indeed, the officer corps, like the remainder of the Turkish population, appears to accept the principles of multi-party politics and an elected parliamentary assembly as the only legitimate system for governing Turkey. As President Evren states, 'The Turkish armed forces are devoted to democracy and they are its indestructible guard.'[38]

Defence and Economic Considerations

To the extent possible, the Turkish military will avoid direct involvement in domestic affairs which have little impact on the armed forces and will suppress politicisation within the ranks. They will concentrate on the development of a professional, apolitical, well-equipped, and well-trained force. Turkey will continue its efforts to improve the capabilities of its forces, primarily through the modernisation or replacement of obsolete equipment that is rapidly becoming unsupportable. More important, this obsolete equipment, even if supportable, would simply not do the job on a modern battlefield. This task of refurbishment is far beyond the capabilities of Turkey's own limited national resources, and the acquisition of new, sophisticated hardware seems a distant target. Ankara will continue to remain heavily dependent on external sources of military assistance, primarily the United States and the Federal Republic of Germany.

Economic problems are the prime limitation plaguing its defence efforts. Turkey's level of economic development is considerably below that of other NATO members, including Greece and Portugal. The situation is aggravated by large foreign-debt service requirements, high inflation and the strains of modernising an economy sheltered from the world for decades.

No single factor plays as major a role in determining Prime Minister Ozal's tenure in office as his efforts toward economic revitalisation. His blueprint continues to follow the direction he established in the late 1970s while he was overseeing the economic portfolio in Suleyman Demirel's government, before the military take-over.

Throughout his term in office, Ozal's overriding aim has been to turn Turkey into a powerful trading and industrial state. Measures have been introduced to simplify administration and to liberalise foreign trade and capital and exchange transactions. There has also been an emphasis on the development of money and capital markets. As for fiscal policy, greater autonomy given to local administration has resulted in improved public service, while the operation of special investment funds seems to have speeded up investment in infrastructure and housing. Improvements in tax collection following the introduction of a value-added tax in 1985 have helped to keep general government budget deficits to 2 per cent of the gross national product (GNP).[39]

These reforms have brought an impressive stream of benefits for Turkey. The GNP grew at a rate of 6.5 per cent in 1988, and this year it is estimated to expand at about 5.4 per cent, led by both public and private investment and consumer demand. These are impressive growth figures, but they are less than in the previous years. The government still faces a greater challenge in bringing down inflation, which is presently estimated to be about 60 per cent, while the unemployment rate remains high at about 15.2 per cent.[40] The external sector is a challenge, with the need for capital imports continuing side by side with a foreign debt burden of over $37.4 billion.[41] Turkey's economic performance should be sufficient to maintain internal political stability and permit continued growth of capacity with some improvement in standards of living. It will not be sufficient, however, especially with the heavy burden of external debt payments, to eliminate or significantly reduce the need for security assistance, particularly aid from Washington, to accomplish its national defence plans and NATO goals.

In terms of the share of gross domestic product (GDP) going to defence, Turkey, at about an average of 4.5 per cent, bears one of the heaviest defence burdens of the NATO Allies, exceeded only by that of Greece and the United States. Not only is Turkey's GDP the smallest of all NATO members, defence spending *per capita* is the least of all Alliance members—roughly $54 per year—reflecting the underdevelopment of the country and its incapability to sustain large-scale defence spending. In 1990, United States defence assistance was equivalent to about 14.7 per cent of the Turkish defence budget. Overall, defence spending as a percentage of the national budget has declined from 21.4 per cent in 1983 to a 17 per cent low in 1987 (see Table 3.2).

The sharp cut in American security assistance (some 20 per cent)[42] beginning in 1987 added new strains to a traditionally close bilateral relationship that has been cooling over the years (e.g. the arms embargo in 1974). Ankara has criticised the levels of American aid in recent years and has sought greatly increased amounts of guaranteed aid—at least $1.2 billion annually.

For the past decade, the aid to Turkey (as well as Greece) has been linked by the United States Congress to reaction to the Cyprus crises of 1974 and subsequent failures to resolve this problem and other outstanding issues. These differences between Ankara and Athens have been reflected in the sharp disagreements between Congress and the President over military assistance programmes. The former's insistence on the application of the 7 to 10 ratio to security assistance for Greece and Turkey continues to highlight the precarious nature of bilateral defence co-operation.

The President believes that the ratio is an undesirable practice that limits his authority and imposes not only the wrong criteria on determining aid levels, but that the ratio does not accurately reflect a balance between Ankara and Athens in military, geographic or demographic terms.

Turkey sees a direct link between military assistance it receives from Washington and the continued American use of military installations in their country. American bases in Turkey are governed by a Defence and Economic Co-operation Agreement (DECA) which was reviewed in 1980 and extended until December 1990. This extension of the DECA by Ankara probably reflected their expectations that the United States would compensate for the recent aid cuts by easing Turkey's huge Foreign Military Sales (FMS) debt repayment burden and provide a large infusion of surplus American military equipment. For example, in 1987 over $400 million in principal and interest were due, leaving Ankara with less than $200 million in United States security assistance to spend for equipment. Overall, the debt payment for Turkey from 1983 to 1988 was very burdensome, totalling over $1.6 billion. This is less than one-third of the absolute minimum needed to continue force modernisation and to assist operational and maintenance costs. Overall, Ankara feels that the DECA has worked against Turkish interests, since

TABLE 3.2. *Turkish Defence Expenditure, 1983–90*

	1983	1984	1985	1986	1987	1988	1989	1990
Total Defence Expenditure ($ billion US)	.825	1.2	1.8	2.7	2.0	2.4	2.9	3.38
Defence Expenditure as a Percentage of GDP	4.8	4.4	4.5	4.8	3.5	3.3	3.1	3.4
Defence Expenditure as a Percentage of Budget	21.4	20.0	22.3	26.1	17.0	18.3	18.7	19.0
US Military Assistance								
Totals ($ million US)	687.8	856.8	879.0	738.9	594.5	526.0	563.4	497.8
Percentage of Turkish Expenditure	83.3	71.4	48.8	27.4	29.7	21.9	19.4	14.7

Source: Letter from Turkish Embassy, Office of Defence Attaché, dated 17 August 1989; *Defense News*, 13 November 1989, p. 18.

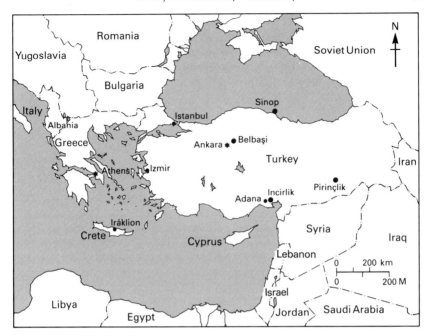

Greek facilities

Iráklion communications station
(intelligence, monitoring of atmospheric testing, support for regional reconnaissance)

Souda Bay complex
(carrier support, NATO port facility, POL storage, NATO firing range)

Turkish Facilities

Belbaşi station
(seismographic monitoring)

Incirlik Airbase
(USAF rotational airbase)

Pirinçlik
(monitoring of Soviet space activity)

Sinop
(monitoring of Soviet space activity)

MAP 3.1. Selected United States Facilities in Greece and Turkey

the United States commitment to the modernisation of the Turkish armed forces has not been fully realised. Turkey not only desires to rid its relationships with Washington of 'extraneous factors' (e.g. Greek and American lobbies in Congress), but also wants the United States to adhere to the basic tenets of economic liberalism which it is promoting and to ensure that the economic aspects of DECA be implemented in a satisfactory manner.[43] Turkey has been particularly displeased with restrictions imposed on its textiles by the Congress.

The 1985 Southern Region Amendment has also benefited Turkey by providing excess military equipment such as M48-A5 tanks, F-4E Phantoms, patrol boats, artillery and anti-tank inventories, radars, and arms and munitions. This programme was seriously constrained by new Congressional requirements in 1988 that the value of the excess equipment provided also corresponds roughly to the 7 to 10 ratio. This has impeded promptness and flexibility in the programme by not allowing provision of any articles to either Greece or Turkey until articles of appropriate value have been identified and made available to the other.

The Federal Republic of Germany (FRG) too is contributing to the revitalisation of the Turkish armed forces. Overall, the total aid provided by the FRG since 1964 is in excess of $2.5 billion and from 1986 to the present the average annual amount is 173 million DM ($96 million US). In addition, the Turkish Air Force has received surplus F-104Gs and other arms and equipment. The FRG is further assisting the Turkish Navy by providing some funding and technological assistance in building MEKO-200 frigates and TYPE-209 diesel submarines in the Golcuk shipyards in Istanbul. During the 1982–87 period, the FRG contributed in excess of $950 million, and both France ($30 million) and Great Britain ($220 million) during that same period modestly contributed military arms and equipment.[44]

Ankara's perceptions of the Soviet Union and its other neighbours to the north (along with Syria to the south) as its primary external security threat is unlikely to change, regardless of the status of American aid. Nor will its recognition that Turkish ties with Washington, along with membership in NATO, are irreplaceable in countering that threat. Nonetheless, Turkish concerns over security assistance levels will persist. Reductions in American security assistance levels may have negative implications for Washington in both political and military spheres. The strongly-held belief that the United States has reneged on its 'best efforts' pledge will make negotiating the renewal of the DECA in 1990 all the more difficult. It is possible that Turkey will be more restrictive in the kind of military access and operational flexibility that Washington will be permitted on these bases, as well as over American transit and overflying rights.

Ankara will continue to question why aid to a NATO ally, Turkey, is cut while assistance to Israel and Egypt is maintained at high levels. Turkey would also react harshly to any Congressional attempts to link American aid to Ankara with aid to Greece or to Turkish concessions on the Cyprus issues, as they would to any United States Congressional resolution condemning Turkey's alleged responsibility for the genocide of Armenians early in this century. An attempt by the United States Senate in February 1990 to designate 24 April as a day of remembrance of the 'Armenian Genocide of 1915–23' was beaten back. If such a resolution were promulgated, it would seriously strain bilateral relations, even more so than the Johnson letter of 1964.

International Relations Dimensions

In contrast to the frequent internal changes on the Turkish domestic scene, Ankara's foreign policy has displayed remarkable continuity. Indeed, Turkey's external relations have been marked by a long-term perspective, by a sense of responsibility, and by a realism that is found in few developing countries and is far from universal even among the democracies of the West.[45]

In the post-Second World War era, Ankara was enthusiastic in its efforts to forge links with the West; yet by the 1960s a large segment of Turkey's population became sharply critical of the United States over Cyprus and other issues, and by the 1970s, *rapprochement* was being sought with the Muslim countries of the Middle East and even with the Soviet Union.

Historically, continuity of foreign policy survived the intense political controversies that shaped Turkish politics even during the 1970s. It was inevitable that details of policy would be shaped by career officials. After 1980 both the military government and later Ozal's government continued to entrust the foreign ministry portfolio directly to career diplomats. Within this framework, Turkey's leaders have tried to reconcile the apparent contradiction in the country's strategic geographic position and its heritage.

Since the late 1940s, Turkey's foreign policy has been inescapably linked with both the United States and the Soviet Union. Relations with the Soviet Union were a cornerstone of Kemal Ataturk's foreign policy, and Moscow consistently reminds Ankara of that fact. However, Turkey remains wary of the Soviet Union in the light of centuries of hostility and warfare, a common frontier that is the longest of any NATO member, and Moscow's undiminished ambition to control the Bosporus and the Dardanelles. When, in 1945, the Soviet Union reasserted its historic expansionist aims against Turkey, the situation culminated, as discussed elsewhere, in Ankara's inclusion in the Marshall Plan and NATO. These actions reassured Turkey's leaders that it had been accepted by the West. From that time, Ankara's and Washington's strategic analysts agreed that Turkey and Greece formed an indispensable barrier to Moscow's moves on the South Eastern flank of NATO.[46] During the 1960s this close relationship began to show strain, and in the 1970s these tensions were exacerbated. As it turned out, the biggest shadow over United States–Turkish relations was cast, not by developments in the Middle East or by Soviet aggressiveness, but rather by Cyprus and the multitude of Aegean Sea issues that continue to fester to this day.

As we saw earlier, unlike Greece, which publicly declares that the greatest threat to it is from the East (Turkey), Ankara leaves no doubt that it believes the principal menace to Turkish security remains the Soviet Union and its surrogate, namely Syria. For its part, Moscow has tended to pursue a dual-track policy in the region. It has sought to maintain access to the Mediterranean and increase its own influence in the area by emphasising closer official bilateral relations with Greece and Turkey. Moscow has paid particular attention to Turkey by attempting to take advantage of strains in the United States–NATO commitment to Turkish security.[47] At times, however, the Soviets have avoided decisive commitments to either Ankara or Athens by tilting toward the Greeks on Cyprus and toward Turkey on the Aegean.

In 1978 the Soviet Union and Turkey signed a political document of 'friendship and co-operation'. The parties agreed not to resort to threats or use of force and not to permit use of their territory for aggression against the other. Although Ankara tried to dampen the West's concern by stressing that the document specifies that the rights of obligations of either country under other agreements are not affected, it was, nevertheless, a distinct diplomatic success for Moscow.

Turkey first sought improved relations with the Soviet Union during the Kennedy Administration. Ankara began to question the seriousness of the United States/NATO commitment after Washington abandoned the strategy of massive retaliation for one of flexible response. Revelations subsequent to the Cuban missile crisis of 1962, that a deal had been struck for the removal of the Jupiter missiles from Turkey, precipitated worries about the possibility that Turkish territory might be traded for time in the event of Soviet aggression against NATO. Turkish efforts to achieve closer ties with Moscow were further encouraged by Ankara's perceptions of United States policy in the region during the 1960s and particularly the 1970s, when Bulent Ecevit's left-of-centre Republican People's Party was in power. Of particular concern to Ankara was President Johnson's letter in 1964. Ten years later, Ankara suspended all United States military activities on Turkish territory after the United States imposed an arms embargo.

The Soviets reacted to the friendly Turkish overtures of this period by tacitly acquiescing in the Turkish intervention on Cyprus and followed that up by leaning towards Ankara's position on Aegean issues. Then, as now, however, cooperation was strongest on the economic level. Turkey became the largest recipient of Soviet economic assistance in the Third World, receiving credits of over $3 billion between 1965 and 1979. Since 1985, trade between Moscow and Ankara has significantly increased and today it comprises some 3 per cent of Turkey's overall foreign trade and is expected to increase in the next several years.[48]

During the period of military rule, from 1980–83, relations between the two cooled. Turkey's previous experience with domestic terrorism and General Evren's strong anti-communist stand gave a boost to traditional anti-Soviet views. Under Prime Minister Ozal, relations between Turkey and the Soviet Union normalised. Several high level delegations' visits have been exchanged, including Ozal's visit to Moscow in 1986. This culminated in an ambitious 25-year trade agreement. There have also been press reports that Presidents Evren and Ozal have urged, and the government is considering, legalising the Communist Party in the light of events in the Soviet Union.

Further evidence of Ankara's unwillingness to antagonise Moscow is the muted protest to Moscow in show of solidarity with Azerbaijan. Though many Azeris, as Shiite Moslems, feel closer to Iran than to Turkey—a point publicly acknowledged by President Ozal—the Turk-in-the-street has come to regard the Azeris as his kinsmen, or even compatriots. President Ozal and Prime Minister Akbulut's passive reactions have offended Islamic extremists and right-wing nationalists who persist in portraying the Azeri-Armenian conflict in Azerbaijan as a religious confrontation, in which the West is siding with the atheist in the Kremlin to suppress innocent Moslems. These actions are aimed at mollifying Moscow,[49] but also these actions strengthen Turkey's democratic credentials in Western Europe.

Meanwhile, Turkey's relations with another neighbour, Bulgaria, worsened considerably in 1989 due to the spectacular migration of ethnic Turks to Turkey. Since the early 1980s, the Zhikov regime had banned the use of the Turkish language in public and had been trying to do away with Turkish names and to restrict the practice of Islam in a renewed assimilation drive. This cast a certain shadow over Turkish–Bulgarian relations. The issue exploded in May 1989, when reports indicated that ethnic Turkish protesters were being gunned down by Bulgarian security forces. In the face of this, Ankara opened her border to ethnic Turks wanting to leave Bulgaria and created a coordinating committee to deal with the reception and resettlement of the refugees. No one could have guessed on the number; ultimately it reached some 300,000.

The problem of accommodating and resettling these refugees has proved very difficult. Turkey's Western Allies, with the exception of the United States, failed to support Ankara. Nor was Turkey satisfied with the reaction of the Islamic Conference. While Moscow's attempts to mediate the issue came to naught. Finally, in September 1989, Ankara accepted the Islamic Conference proposals for discussions between the two protagonists in Kuwait. Several meetings were held and the results were described as 'not negative, but insufficient'. With the change of régimes and the democratisation process blooming in Bulgaria, it appears now that Sofia will restore rights to the ethnic Turkish minority.

This situation, prevailing between Turkey and Bulgaria, is somewhat similar to the ethnic Turkish minority problems in Greece (Chapter 2). The consequence of receding tension between East and West has resulted in Greece and Bulgaria developing common strategies toward Turkey that include military co-operation. This overall co-operation was accelerated by the visit of the Bulgarian Foreign Minister, Bojko Dimitrov, to Athens directly from his meeting in Kuwait with his Turkish counterpart, Mesut Yilmaz at which time Turkey rejected Sofia's offer of a non-aggression pact. With the demise of communism, it now appears that the historical intrigues of bygone days in the Balkans may once again be resurfacing.

When it comes to Turkey's relations with Greece, Ankara is puzzled by Athens' actions since Prime Minister Papandreou came to power in 1981. It is convinced that Greece seeks to undercut Turkey's position in NATO and to delay the normalisation of Turkey's relations with the European Community (EEC), as described in Chapter 2.

In April 1987 Ankara applied formally for EEC membership, although it does not expect full membership until early in the next century. Turkey's reasoning is that, by then, its large and vital economy will make it a suitable member. But the formidable economic problems involved in admitting a large agricultural country into the mainly industrialised EEC (by then Turkey would be the most populous member) are being lengthily debated. Also, the issue of human rights is troublesome for some of the EEC members. The community is already having problems in absorbing Greece, Portugal and Spain, three relatively less affluent and more agriculturally oriented Mediterranean countries. With a geographical foothold in Europe and as a member of NATO, Turkey has not been absolutely refused membership, but difficulties remain, especially on the political front.

The culmination of these political objections was a resolution of the European Parliament in June 1987, calling for 'a political solution to the Armenian question', which contained several clauses that made it even more provocative to Turkey.[50] In Ankara the news of the resolution nearly coincided with the killing by the PKK of 31 people from the village of Pinarcik, many of whom were women and children. The resolution was seen as encouraging terrorism. Shortly thereafter, President Evren made a blistering speech, stating that 'it would be useful to sit down and review once again Turkey's membership in NATO'. However, Prime Minister Ozal's government has not made a major issue of the resolution, restraining its reaction in order to avoid making negotiations with the EEC even more difficult. Recently, the EEC declined to open negotiations with Turkey to join before 1993. The reasons given are the state of the Turkish economy and Ankara's record on human rights and trade union rights.

Related thorny issues that compound the Turkish application are the difficulties that divide Ankara and Athens over the Aegean and Cyprus (Chapter 1). It is conceivable that Greece might use its veto to stop Turkey from entering the EEC if Turkey's entry becomes likely.

In the light of Turkey's associate membership of the EEC, nearly two million Turkish citizens have emigrated to West Europe in search of employment. The associate membership agreement of 1963 envisioned free circulation by 1 December 1986, but the EEC has refused to honour that part of the agreement. West Germany, notably, is against allowing more Turkish workers to join the many Turks already in West Germany. Instead, its tactics are to provide Turkey with increased security assistance, in excess of $96 million per year.

Altan Alpay of Prime Minister Ozal's office commented that although 'cancellation of so basic a principle as free circulation of labour' would threaten 'the whole legal framework of our Association' with the EEC, 'it would be better to reach a wider context of full membership'.[51] Application for full membership keeps the free circulation issue open without forcing a showdown that Ankara knows it would lose.

The greatest single argument for Turkish membership in the EEC is Turkey's security contribution to Western Europe, even though various factors limit Ankara's security contribution. Among these is the belief by West Europeans that Turkey's primary security relationship is with the United States, which is its principal provider of security assistance and the only country that has a significant military presence in Turkey. In addition, most West Europeans have focused their security concerns on the 'Central Front' threat and Turkey appears to them to be geographically too distant and so not germane to their interests.

The Middle East

It was some 10 years ago that Turkey undertook a concerted effort to expand its ties with the Middle East. There are basically two principles that guide Ankara's policies in this area. First, Turkey refrains from taking sides in local disputes. But this principle does not prevent her from acting as a mediator when invited by all parties concerned. In fact, Turkey was an active member of the Islamic Conference mediating the Iran-Iraq conflict. The other ruling principle requires that Turkey's co-operation with the West, especially in the area of defence, does not damage the security interests of Arab states. This principle makes the utilisation of defence installations in Turkey against Arab interests virtually impossible.

Prime Minister Ozal placed special emphasis on trade, viewing Turkey's neighbours as prime markets for its goods and services. Turkey's total trade with its Arab neighbours in 1988 amounted to 26.2 per cent, a bit more than the 24.0 per cent in 1987.[52] Most of the import trade is in the form of oil, while Turkey exports agricultural products. On an individual basis, Turkey, remaining strictly neutral, has maintained close diplomatic relations and lucrative trade with both Iran and Iraq throughout their years of bitter warfare. Turkey's total trade with Iraq in 1988 was about 10.8 per cent, while its trade with Iran is about 6.5 per cent.[53] Overall, trade with both countries is on a downward path reflecting the effect of the price of oil on the world market and the economic toll taken by this conflict on both nations.

Of late, Turkey's relations with Iran have been strained because of explicit Iranian activities supporting religious fundamentalists in Turkey, most especially in the universities. Religious fundamentalism is a very sensitive issue for Ankara and it is an anathema to Kemalism which mandates a complete separation of religion from

political life. Iranian involvement is therefore viewed with seriousness and disdain.[54]

Beyond the economic trade, there are about 125 Turkish contrac-
tors with projects in Saudi Arabia, and some 112 in Libya.[55] The
total value of contracts held by Turkish companies abroad is in
excess of $18 billion, and the number of Turkish workers has
reached 200,000.[56] Of the 311 total projects of Turkish contracting
firms abroad, some 96 per cent are located in the Middle East.

Ankara's relations with Syria, Moscow's closest ally in the Middle
East, continue to be cautious and somewhat distant. Unlike its
relations with Iran, Iraq and Libya (in which the desire to increase
trade is a primary ingredient), Turkey's relations with Syria have
only a minor economic component.

Syria and Syrian-occupied Lebanon have long provided major
training centres for Turkish, Kurdish and Armenian terrorist
groups. More recently, as above, Damascus has also complained
about the giant Ataturk Dam project, which it fears will curtail
Euphrates waters that Syria now uses further downstream for irri-
gating its own north-eastern plain.

In an attempt to lessen the tension between the two nations,
Prime Minister Ozal visited Damascus in July, 1987.[57] This visit
resulted in several agreements enhancing border security and economic co-operation. In the area of border security, both nations
agreed to establish a common security zone to prevent armed bands
from crossing, and Syria also agreed that it would no longer provide
a safe haven for the PKK. So far, however, this understanding has
not occurred.

In the area of economic co-operation, Turkey allayed Syria's concern about how the waters of the Euphrates were to be used and
both governments agreed to a joint project to construct a hydro-
electric dam along their mutual border on the Seyhan and Ceyhan
rivers. This will be a jointly financed and planned project, and the
dam is to be called the 'Dam of Peace' (Saad Al-Salam) to symbolise
co-operation between the two countries. Turkey further agreed to
provide Syria with credits for the sale of Turkish grain and food-
stuffs.

On a much broader scale, in July 1986 Prime Minister Ozal proposed the building of a Turkish water pipeline known as the 'Peace
Pipeline' through Syria and Jordan to Saudi Arabia. Interest on the
part of these three governments has been keen, but without Saudi
Arabia's support and financial backing the plan stands little chance
of success. There is no doubt that if this pipeline is built it will
enhance Turkey's significance in the region.

Surprisingly, Turkish relations with Israel are flourishing

inwardly, while outwardly they are restrained. In 1985, both countries upgraded their diplomatic missions. Since then, their pragmatic relations have embraced more substance under a mutually agreeable, low diplomatic profile. Bilateral economic relations have expanded to about $100 million annually. Also, Israeli tourism in Turkey has increased markedly, with estimates in 1987 set at about 100,000, and the tone of the Turkish press since 1985 has become more positive. This enhanced Turkish–Israeli dialogue is exemplified by Turkey's handling of some 600 Jews fleeing from Tehran in 1987. The Jews first travelled to Istanbul and then by ferry to the Cypriot port of Limassol and then on to Haifa, Israel.[58] Understandably, Turkey is very sensitive about publicising its improving ties with Israel. Not only could this harm her position throughout the Middle East, but it could also bring political forces to the fore which would seek to undermine Turkey's parliamentary institutions and which might seek to establish a government that would be more nationalistic, anti-Western, and anti-secular.

Outwardly, as regards the Arab–Israeli conflict and the Palestinian question, Ankara's position does not appear to differ substantially from those taken by its European allies in the Venice Declaration of 1980. The Turkish Government believes that Washington's handling of the Arab–Israeli problem hinders the achievement of a settlement. It also thinks that the Palestinian problem needs resolving on terms that moderate states in the region can accept. This would mean the end of the continued Israeli occupation of the West Bank and of the present status of Jerusalem as dictated unilaterally by Israel, as well as the creation of a Palestinian homeland and mutual recognition by Israel and the PLO of the other's legitimacy.

In Turkey today there is a general conviction that the country's geographical, historical, and socio-political characteristics not only allow but also require Ankara to pursue a multi-dimensional foreign policy. This trend is particularly evident in Turkey's policy of near neutrality toward the Middle Eastern states. This intensification of its relations with this region, on the one hand, and its role within NATO in this area, on the other, may result in Turkey assuming a greater involvement in the region's affairs. It will naturally create strains in the policy of neutrality that Ankara has followed these many years.

Turkey entered the decade of the 1980s with a balanced set of domestic, regional and international policy objectives. Its experiences, however, taught Ankara not to trust the United States or the Soviet Union; its neighbours to the west and north are viewed with suspicion and uncertainty, while its relationship with Washington has left much bitterness, mistrust and apprehension. Ideologically, Ankara continues to face West. But if political criticisms continue in Western forums and if unreasonable demands are made on Turkey that impinge on its sovereignty, it is very likely that the result will be damaged relations with the West, which could ultimately undermine the crucial role Turkey plays as a barrier to Soviet expansionism in the Middle East.

CHAPTER 4

Competition in the Mediterranean

The Mediterranean is no longer the Southern Flank of the Atlantic Alliance, because in recent years the geostrategic situation has changed. The Mediterranean is part of the Central Front of NATO, while its potential 'Southern Flank' ranges from the Horn of Africa to the Gulf Region.[1]

Lelio Logovia

THE ABOVE statement by a former Italian Defence Minister underscores the fact that the strategic centre of Europe has moved southward, and the NATO countries of the Southern Region are significant to the whole of NATO. This is perhaps more so today than previously. Since tensions in Central Europe have abated, NATO's strategic priorities have now shifted toward the flanks. Furthermore, the events of the late 1970s and early 1980s have increased the geostrategic importance of the Mediterranean with the Persian Gulf.[2] While recent emphasis on improving conventional defences, such as the maintenance of sea-lanes for communication, mobilisation and the need to project power, reinforces the significance of the Mediterranean, it is the United States Sixth Fleet that is the principal symbol of NATO's commitment to the region, and it also serves as the operational bridge to the Persian Gulf. No other Alliance navies in the Southern Region have the capabilities to challenge the Soviet Union's Mediterranean fleet. Any analysis of NATO's security situation in the Mediterranean must therefore examine these two naval protagonists' activities and their potential and actual effect on events.

From a purely military perspective, it is a truism that during any conflict in Europe or the Middle East, control of the Mediterranean would be a precondition of military success for NATO or the Warsaw Pact. This fact is recognised by all affected states, whether external ones seeking political influence, or local ones comprehending the value of what they can offer in terms of promises of neutrality or commitments to act. It is unthinkable, particularly in the event of all-out conflict, that the Mediterranean region should be afforded less significance than the Central Front. The resupply of Western Europe (and the prevention of gains by the Soviets) will depend on NATO's ability to keep open (or closed) the relevant choke points. The Turkish Straits, for example, would be a crucial asset for the Soviets to control (which NATO would strive to prevent), while NATO would be concerned that the Straits of Gibraltar should be secure so that necessary reinforcements and supplies could reach Greece, Italy and Turkey—and, of course, the Soviets would wish to hinder this.

The importance of this region is undeniable. Its military significance to NATO has been underscored by the establishment and maintenance of a Southern European command—Allied Forces Southern Europe (AFSOUTH)—with its headquarters in Naples. It is one of three major commands directly subordinate to the Supreme Allied Commander Europe (SACEUR). American installations extending from Spain to Greece and Turkey are also in service to the Alliance and help support the United States Sixth Fleet whose headquarters are in Gaeta, Italy.

Washington's presence alone is an impressive illustration of the Mediterranean's significance to NATO. Presently there are some 140 NATO military installations in this area, with approximately 40 of these located in Greece and Turkey.[3]

To suggest, however, that the Mediterranean is a NATO lake, while not necessarily completely false, requires a degree of optimism which is difficult to sustain. Such a notion has been rendered increasingly less credible since the 1970s by a quantitative increase in Soviet naval and air power in the region.

It should be remembered that no broad strategic view surfaced during the formative years of the Alliance. In fact, the Mediterranean existed as an almost alien and perhaps unnecessary adjunct. Political turmoil and Soviet pressure on both Greece and Turkey inspired the Truman Doctrine, but the preferred solutions to the problems of those countries have been the result, primarily, of the bilateral efforts of the United States. No doubt NATO recognised that the key to a coordinated defence of Italy, Greece and Turkey was control of the Mediterranean and that the predominance of the Sixth Fleet compensated for many of the vulnerabilities found on the land mass. However, Western Europe was quite content to let Washington play the major and leading role in this region.

In no other area beyond Central Europe proper has the strategic military balance between the United States and the Soviet Union been a factor in international affairs as it has been in the Mediterranean. The nuclear power of the Sixth Fleet has figured intermit-

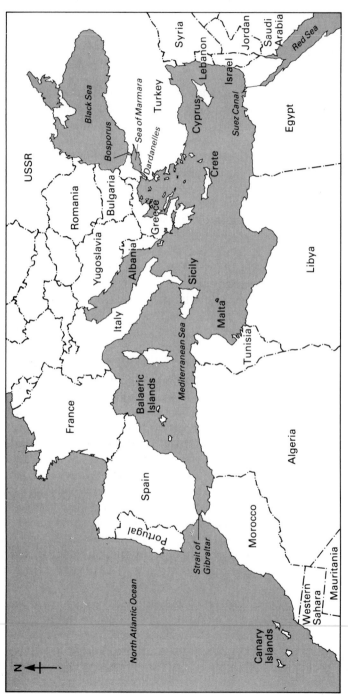

Map 4.1. The Mediterranean.

tently in the SALT talks and has been one of the reasons why Moscow has sought air and naval base privileges among its Mediterranean clients. The Mediterranean is not only the back door to Western Europe but, as Moscow so frequently reminds us, the Mediterranean leads to the Soviet Union's back door, the Black Sea.

Soviet Aims in the Mediterranean

The Soviet Union's involvement in this region has a much longer and richer background than that of the United States, stretching back at least to the Russian attack on Constantinople in 907. Then, the Russian drive for 'warm water ports' was aimed at the Black Sea and not the Persian Gulf. This requirement, in the modern era, can be traced back to the second half of the eighteenth century when Russia was able to take effective action to meet this need. Access to the Black Sea and free passage through the Turkish Straits was needed to export the products of Russia, for which there was a ready demand among the maritime powers in the West.[4] But the Black Sea also provided access to Russia, and in the nineteenth century this access was used increasingly by the maritime powers to dictate the outcome of events—the Crimean War, 1854–55; the Bolshevik Revolution, 1918–19.

In war, 'the Black Sea becomes a grenade in Russia's gut'.[5] It outflanks the defensive glacis to the west, it bypasses the defence of distance, and it turns the large river barriers into avenues leading to Russia's heartland. It also provides entry, directly or indirectly, to potentially rebellious and dissident populations.

The introduction by NATO of long-range sea-based nuclear strike forces means that the Mediterranean is now more than the back door. Moscow is roughly equidistant from the Mediterranean and the Barents Sea, with the important note that a large slice of Moscow's military-industrial complex is found south of Moscow.

This creates for the Soviet Union a direct interest in the Mediterranean basin. But the nature of that interest and Soviet strategic aims in the area have evolved over time, as has the relative importance of the sea when compared to that of the surrounding land mass. This has produced contradictory evidence between evolving Soviet geostrategic interests and political interests that have largely remained constant.

Moscow's concerns and goals in the Mediterranean appear to be primarily defensive and are, for the most part, tangential to NATO. Despite the prominence accorded Southeast Asia, the Middle East and the Eastern Mediterranean in the last decade or so, these areas remain secondary in importance to Moscow when compared to Central Europe, which is still the principal area of strategic concern.

Soviet activity in the Mediterranean region since the Second World War can be divided into four distinct periods. For about a decade after the war, Moscow simply exploited the post-war turmoil and regional strife in Greece, Iran, Turkey and Yugoslavia. Beginning with the controversy over support of the Aswan Dam and the Suez Crisis in 1955, a more pointed and concerted policy took shape as the Soviets began a sustained effort to build positions of influence among countries in the Middle East. Equally important, the Suez Crisis, and especially how the Allies handled it, forged long-term links concerning NATO issues, Middle East conflicts, and the West's relations with Arab states.[6] Between 1970 and 1974 a new phase of Soviet Mediterranean involvement began. As Egyptian-Soviet relations were waning, Moscow's interests and activities shifted to the so-called 'outer ring' states of Aden, Ethiopia, Libya, Somalia, Yemen and, to a lesser extent, Iran. In 1971, almost as if anticipating a rupture in their relations with Cairo in 1972, the Soviets prepared for a fall-back position in Somalia.

The 1973 October war exerted a catalytic effect on the area's issues. It stimulated rapid development of Moslem political radicalism through the remaining years, excited revival of intense Arab nationalism, and transformed both the world energy market and the political and financial significance of the Gulf states. Moreover, it triggered United States–Soviet military posturing and counter-posturing to a degree not seen since the Cuban missile crisis of 1962. But the October 1973 war may have been less notable for what it brought about than for what it did not. The anti-American coalescing of Arab states and the use of oil as a weapon failed to reverse the worsening of Soviet–Egyptian relations. The petroleum exporting states of the Persian Gulf and elsewhere certainly aggravated the economic and political problems of Western industrialised states, as well as those of Third World nations. At the same time, however, they remained for the most part independent of Soviet policy and influence. Moscow could find friends only among political outcasts on the radical fringes of the Arab world—Syria and Libya. Soviet efforts to develop longer term positions of advantage in Iraq, South Yemen, Somalia, Algeria and Ethiopia came basically to naught, especially after 1979 when Moscow invaded Afghanistan.

Yet even before Gorbachev became General Secretary, the Soviet image in the Mediterranean had begun to improve. After the invasion of Lebanon, in the early 1980s, the moderate Arab states became increasingly convinced that Washington would not pressure Israel to withdraw from Arab territories it had conquered. Moscow took the initiative away from Washington by calling for an international conference involving all parties to the dispute. The stage was thus set for further Soviet gains.[7] Since Gorbachev came to power in March 1985, the Soviet Union has improved its ties significantly with all major countries in the area, including Greece and Turkey.[8] Gorbachev's policies have not differed much from those of his immediate predecessors, but political conditions in the region certainly have changed. These changes have led many states, which opposed a greater Soviet role in the area just a few years ago, to welcome greater Soviet involvement or at least to reduce objections to it. Nevertheless, Gorbachev has not, as yet, been able to transform this greater influence into predominance in the Mediterranean and neighbouring environs.

Soviet Forces in the Mediterranean

In the preceding discussion of Soviet interests in the Mediterranean basin, the military dimensions received only passing attention. Since sea power is a major element in United States–Soviet competition within this region, the nature of Soviet sea power in the Mediterranean must therefore be analysed.

The Soviet Mediterranean fleet, the Fifth Escadra or SOVMEDRON, was formed in the late 1950s when Nikita Khrushchev made the political decision to increase Moscow's conventional capabilities to project power abroad. The Cuban missile crisis of 1962 further heightened awareness of American naval superiority and reinforced Soviet policies that were already moving to strengthen and expand Soviet naval capabilities in the Mediterranean. In addition, the presence of the American Sixth Fleet, with its ability to launch nuclear missiles against Moscow, was most disconcerting. While it is true that Soviet submarines were stationed at Valona Bay in Albania from 1958 to 1961, these did not basically perform any important political or military role. In 1961 Albania sided with the People's Republic of China in the first public evidence of a Sino–Soviet dispute, resulting in Moscow's loss of these naval installations.

Beginning in 1965, the Soviets began deploying detachments from their Black Sea Fleet to the Mediterranean, and the size of the Fifth Escadra grew steadily over the ensuing years. Its presence has always been justified by the argument that the Soviet Union is a littoral state; that is, its access to the Mediterranean is directly through the Black Sea, in Moscow's view a distinctive gulf of the Mediterranean. On the other hand, the Soviets view the Sixth Fleet as a 'foreign' presence in the area.

It is clear that the decision by Moscow to deploy a relatively large naval force in the Mediterranean reflected a perceived need to display their flag. Admiral Sergey Gorshkov in 1962 stated that 'the Soviet Navy . . . is obliged to be prepared at any moment and at any point of the globe to secure the protection and interests of our state'.[9] Since this time the SOVMEDRON has served as a participant or a close observer in every major crisis in the Mediterranean area and has become the primary symbol of the Soviet Union's regional presence. The relationship between Soviet political objectives in and around the Mediterranean basin and the status of the Fifth Escadra has been a symbiotic one. Soviet naval forces have played an important role in promoting local Soviet interests, while the cultivation of regional ties has provided the Navy with the access it has required to maintain a standing presence in the Mediterranean, far from its base of support.

The Fifth Escadra has been sized and composed for purposes of political signalling, not as a force to be reckoned with but as a symbolic force to win friends, influence people and intimidate enemies. It has also operated under a number of limitations, including periodic restrictions on shore access, problems of sustainability, extended deployments, the controls imposed by the Montreux Treaty, and the mercurial nature of Moscow's local allies.

The most serious Soviet constraint at sea, in the Mediterranean and elsewhere, has been its modest ability to sustain distant operations. It entered the post-war period with a navy designed primarily for the mission of coastal defence, with a limited blue water capacity. Despite a major fleet construction programme during the past decade or so, the Fifth Escadra is still comprised of warships of limited individual capability and endurance. This is in contrast to the Sixth Fleet, which is superbly capable of operating effectively far from its base of support for extended periods.

As a general rule, Soviet naval forces stay at sea for shorter periods, deploy closer to their logistic points of support, and spend a greater amount of time in maintenance and overhaul than their American counterparts. External deployments in strength at long distances from shore support are difficult.

Faced with problems of sustainability and limited fleet endurance, the Fifth Escadra is structured and sized so that it can be reinforced rapidly under crisis conditions from its principal operating bases in the Black Sea. Such force surges were observed during the Six-Day War (1967), the Jordan crisis (1970), the October war (1973), the Cyprus crisis (1974), the Israeli invasion of Lebanon (1982) and recently in and about Libya (1985–86). This policy of 'valuable presence'[10] was originally adapted as a means of overcoming the dual constraints of poor fleet endurance and the absence of forward bases. While these considerations still influence deployments, the Soviet Union has since made a virtue of necessity by using 'valuable presence' as an instrument for communicating the level and nature of its local involvement.

The Montreux Convention

The main obstacle to the projection of Soviet power in the Mediterranean has remained the terms of the 1936 Montreux Convention which limits the size of the ships that can be brought through the Black Sea into the Mediterranean and which the Soviet Union has attempted to 'stretch' to breaking point. Originally, this convention was welcomed by the Soviet Union as a means of controlling foreign access through the Turkish Straits and into the Black Sea. Several of the Convention's restrictions deserve mention:[11]

> The Treaty requires that any warship of a Black Sea power entering the Straits must give at least eight days' notice before actually beginning its passage. At this time, it must provide its name, type, hull number and date of transit (see Table 4.1).

TABLE 4.1 *Soviet Naval Transits, Turkish Straits, 1975–88*

Year	Auxiliary ships	Surface combatants	Submarines	Total
1975	146	74	1	221
1976	160	85	1	246
1977	164	81	1	246
1978	136	99	1	236
1979	141	87	2	230
1980	139	91	2	232
1981	159	75	4	238
1982	159	78	2	239
1983	145	99	1	245
1984	142	79	2	223
1985	129	64	0	193
1986	120	48	2	170
1987	129	48	1	178
1988	121	65	2	188

Source: *Rapport Annuel sur le mouvment des navires à travers Les Detroits Turcs, 1975–1988.* Data provided to author by the Ministry of Foreign Affairs, Ankara, Turkey.

> All travel through the Straits must be carried out in daylight, no more than nine vessels are allowed to pass through the Straits concurrently, and the total displacement of these ships must not exceed 15,000 tons. The only warships which have been exempted from this rule are single 'capital' ships of Black Sea powers, which can pass the Straits with a limited escort even if their individual size exceeds this limit.
> Submarines are permitted passage only when moving to or from a repair facility. They also must remain surfaced and, like capital combatants, can only sail individually.

Aircraft carriers are not specifically authorized but may enter the waterway at the discretion of Turkey to make local port calls, but may not pass into either the Black Sea or the Mediterranean.[12]
Turkey is permitted to close the Straits to selected powers should it feel threatened in a war or within the context of a local crisis.

Although these restrictions persist to this day and have complicated Soviet planning and deployment policy, the Soviets have nevertheless initiated the practice of 'contingency declarations' stating that a ship would transit, but sending it only if a diplomatic or a military need arose.[13] This permits Moscow to send forces more rapidly into the Mediterranean at the outbreak of a crisis. Furthermore, in time of general war the Soviet Union must assume that passage through the Straits will be denied unless they are able to occupy the areas in and about Istanbul and the Dardanelles, free the Straits of mines, and control the airspace above (see Chapter 6).

Turkey is careful to apply the terms of the Montreux Treaty as rigorously as circumstances permit. Although Ankara is under continuous pressure from Moscow for more 'modern' or 'liberal' interpretations of the Treaty, it must be presumed that it is in the Turkish interests, as well as those of NATO, for Turkey to maintain as tight a control of the Straits as possible. Equally, Soviet policy is to accomplish by 'hook or by crook' what cannot be done overtly. Recently, the Soviets have been successful in introducing larger and more sophisticated warships, including aircraft carriers, into the Mediterranean by carefully defining their characteristics so as to conform to the terms of the Montreux Convention.[14]

Soviet post-war operations in the Mediterranean have been preoccupied with the goal of 'outflanking' the several constraints imposed by geography, fleet sustainability, and the Montreux Convention by establishing permanent bases on shore. Such a presence would permit SOVMEDRON to maintain a comparatively larger standing force in the Mediterranean by greatly expanding their local options and operating flexibility. Considered from this perspective, three periods characterise Moscow's access to shore facilities. The first, the pre-Egyptian period, dates from the establishment of its first permanent naval presence in the Mediterranean Sea in Valona Bay in 1958 until the acquisition of the first Soviet basing rights in Egypt in 1967. Up to this time, the Fifth Escadra was exclusively a symbolic and defensive force. In fact, the Soviets frequently called for the denuclearisation of the Mediterranean and the creation of a peace zone in the region. These concerns reflected the strategic threat posed by the Sixth Fleet and the corresponding incapacity of the Fifth Escadra to offer a credible counter to the United States in the area.[15]

Soviet access was gained to Egyptian and Syrian ports during the 1967 Arab–Israeli War when Moscow sided with the Arab nations. This lead to an immediate and appreciable increase in the level of Soviet naval presence in the Eastern Mediterranean and marked the first time that the Soviets employed a naval force in a crisis situation.

By the time of the Jordanian crisis of September 1970,[16] the SOVMEDRON had grown sufficiently in size (from 40 to 60 ships) to permit it to inhibit the Sixth Fleet's freedom of action. This case is particularly interesting for this study, as it illustrates the dynamic relationship between internal political stresses and foreign policy in the South Eastern Region. It became evident early on that the United States would not be able to make use of Greek and Turkish bases in any Mediterranean operation.[17] This weighed heavily in Washington's assessment of the situation. At a meeting of the Joint Chiefs of Staff (JCS) on 11 September 1970, the importance of base rights in Turkey was made obvious when it was proposed that the United States might be forced to land an army brigade to secure these bases prior to any landing.[18]

It was considered axiomatic that the NATO political leadership would not enforce an American military initiative in the Eastern Mediterranean in support of the embattled Jordanian government. It was also evident to those involved in this crisis that the governments of both Ankara and Athens would find it very difficult to withstand public opinion against allowing United States bases to be used as a staging area for American forces. Finally, the JCS could not be certain that Turkey would close the Straits to Soviet ships in any crisis, despite Turkey's responsibility under the Montreux Convention.[19]

The Middle East Connection

By the late 1960s, the Fifth Escadra was operating regularly out of the Egyptian ports of Alexandria, Mersa Matruh, Port Said, Sollum, and Berenice in the Red Sea and the Syrian port of Latakia. At the centre of these activities was the Soviet naval complex at Alexandria, which featured a command and control centre for the SOVMEDRON, extensive ship repair facilities, and storage and ammunition bunkers. In addition, Soviet access was gained to as many as seven Egyptian airfields, which serviced forces detached from Soviet Naval Aviation, Air Defence Troops and Frontal Aviation. This gave the Soviets maritime strike capabilities and electronic surveillance of the Sixth Fleet. Even more important was the fact that Moscow was able to introduce sophisticated nuclear submarines into the

Mediterranean that complicated the task of the Sixth Fleet and NATO navies. By the beginning of 1972 the Fifth Escadra was maintaining an all-time high, daily strength of between 50 and 55 combatants and support vessels.[20]

The apogee of Soviet naval activity in the Mediterranean in defence of political interests in the Middle East came in 1973, during the October War. Soviet warships began by simply shadowing American ones, but by month's end, after the increase in United States defence alert status, the Soviets initiated anti-carrier exercises against the USS *Independence*, the *FDR*, and the *John F. Kennedy* and their support vessels. To the extent that the threat was credible, it was so only because of the high state of tension that existed between Moscow and Washington at the time and was probably the most intense signal the Soviets have ever transmitted with their naval forces.[21] The risks might have increased substantially if the war had been prolonged.

Soviet–Egyptian relations began to sour by 1972 when President Anwar Sadat decided to nationalise all foreign military installations. By May 1975 Soviet combatants were denied port facilities to the Sollum and Mersa Matruh harbours, and by early 1976 Moscow was formally asked to leave Egypt and remove all remaining units from Alexandria.

The loss of Egyptian facilities had and has continued to have a notable effect on the Fifth Escadra's options, significantly circumscribing its operational flexibility and sustainability. It also effectively eliminated the key support provided by land-based aviation. While this has arguably had an effect on the SOVMEDRON's future combat effectiveness, it has not, however, seriously reduced its value as an instrument and symbol of the Soviet Union's interests and presence.

The third phase of Soviet Mediterranean operations came in the aftermath of the 1972 Egyptian decision to restrict Soviet access whereby Moscow sought to expand its operations to Syria and Libya. This shift to the Syrian facilities of Banyas, Tartus and Latakia in 1972 was facilitated by a decision to develop an elaborate arms transfer policy. From 1973 to 1976 the Soviet Union transferred to Syria MiG 23 and SU 20 fighters, SCUD surface-to-surface missiles, SAM-3s, 6s and 7s, T-62 tanks, modern artillery and armoured personnel carriers. The purpose of these arms transfers was Moscow's desire to show other states the advantage that might accrue to them by providing the Soviet Union with strategic access. This policy proved effective in both Syria and Libya, two major importers of Soviet weapons and other forms of military assistance, much of it provided either free of charge or under well-subsidised credit terms.

Soviet advisers and assistance have rebuilt the Syrian armed forces on four separate occasions.[22]

Since 1973 Syria has been the largest importer of Soviet-made weapons in the Middle East, adding to her arsenal a number of sophisticated Soviet weapons such as the SA-5 long-range SAM, and the SS-21 tactical ballistic missile. Over the years, Soviet material assistance has also paved the way for a growing number of Soviet advisers and an expanded anchorage facility for the Fifth Escadra. Recently, Israel intelligence has reported the construction of a submarine tender at the Syrian port of Tartus which, if expanded, would give the SOVMEDRON an anchorage in the extreme Eastern Mediterranean. This capability is a threat to the Sixth Fleet and NATO navies, and particularly to those of Greece and Turkey.

Libya possesses a force of Soviet-built aircraft which far exceeds that country's reasonable defence needs and which has the potential to affect the entire region. If the Soviet Union deployed a mixed force of TU-22s (BLINDER) and TU-26s (BACKFIRE) bombers, MiG fighers, and SUKHOI fighter-bombers on Libyan airfields, it would considerably shift the balance of power away from the Sixth Fleet and NATO. It is highly likely that Colonel Muammar Quadaffi would grant Moscow the use of these facilities in a NATO–Warsaw Pact confrontation.

The history of Moscow's access diplomacy suggests the difficulty that the Soviet Union has had in maintaining rights to important facilities in the Mediterranean. Since the loss of facilities in Egypt, no significant progress has been made towards finding suitable alternatives and Moscow's presence in both Libya and Syria has not been instrumental in securing permanent and independent access to facilities, despite many attempts to do so in recent years. This remains a stumbling block to Soviet relations with both countries and an important constraint on Soviet regional military options.

For the moment, the Soviet Union has to satisfy itself with a rather modest level of activity in the Mediterranean. It can harass and complicate the task of the Sixth Fleet and NATO navies. The Fifth Escadra can also prevent it from being exactly where it would prefer to be, but an attempt to prevail over the Sixth Fleet would probably be suicidal. The minimum objective for the Fifth Escadra is to prevent the Sixth Fleet from entering the Black Sea. SOVMEDRON is designed principally for anti-submarine and anti-carrier operations. It does, however, possess elements, such as a naval infantry brigade and Spetsnaz units, which are attached to the Black Sea Fleet based at Sevastopol and are trained to seize the Straits and prevent Turkey from controlling or closing them in wartime.

The size of the Fifth Escadra has now stabilised to an average of six surface warships, six submarines and about 28 auxiliary ships.[23] Except in times of crisis, this presence is not very active except for Soviet submarines which are operational about 90 per cent of the time. In fact, the SOVMEDRON spends most of its time at anchor. Its anchorages, as we have already seen, are in protected places in the open sea and off the coasts of various countries. The most important of these located in the Eastern Mediterranean are found east of Crete, Lemnos in the eastern Aegean, and Kithera in southern Greece.[24] The anchorages, however, only partially compensate for the absence of port facilities. In the absence of land-based facilities or protected harbours, the Fifth Escadra must spend a lot of uncomfortable time at sea.

The United States and the Sixth Fleet

No doubt as long as the Sixth Fleet maintains the superiority in the Mediterranean that it now enjoys, it will continue to have the comparative advantage over the Fifth Escadra. For several reasons, however, it can no longer consider itself as secure as before.

Briefly, the Sixth Fleet is both the symbol and the substance of Washington's military presence in the Mediterranean basin. It is highly mobile and effectively projects American power throughout the region and beyond. Though it uses port facilities, the fleet can operate for sustained periods independent of the Mediterranean littoral.

The Sixth Fleet has a fairly secure logistical peacetime network in the Mediterranean, with easy access to NATO bases in Greece, Italy, Turkey and Spain. This is true only in the NATO context. If the Sixth Fleet were to assume *a United States role only*, for example, in support of Israel during an Arab–Israeli conflict, its access to Greek and Turkish bases would be questionable, as these NATO allies would be reluctant to assist the United States in a non-NATO operation except, possibly, for humanitarian reasons. Recall, for example, the refusal of Turkey to assist Washington in its efforts to re-supply Israel in the 1973 Arab–Israeli War. Most probably, technical and logistical support either would not be forthcoming or would be considered on a case by case basis. During the Persian Gulf crises, elements of the United States navy put into Souda Bay to refuel and re-supply. The Greek authorities initially refused their request to be serviced. The problem was finally resolved in such a way that the Greek authorities were not told of the destination of these elements.

Apart from the Sixth Fleet's home port of Gaeta, in Italy, the most critical anchorage in the Eastern Mediterranean is the Souda Bay complex on the northwest side of Crete near Chania. It is a naturally protected anchorage, large enough to hold almost the entire fleet. In addition, the port stores petroleum, oil and lubricants (POL) and ammunition for NATO wartime purposes. Beside the port is an air-field which is used for maritime patrol operations and general supply purposes and can accommodate any naval or air force tactical air-craft, as well as C-141 and C-5A cargo planes. Loss of Souda Bay would deprive the Sixth Fleet of an irreplaceable anchorage. Turkey is now in the process of developing a new naval facility in the Mar-maris region of the Aegean (across from the island of Rhodes) known as Aksaz Karaagac. When completed, it will perhaps rival Souda Bay.

The post-war Mediterranean involvement of the United States may be said to begin with the port call of the battleship *Missouri* at Istanbul in April 1946 as a gesture of support for Ankara against Soviet pressure to control the Straits.[25] In addition to putting pres-sure on Turkey, the Soviet Union was seeking to annex the Dode-canese Islands in the Aegean Sea from Greece, was supplying arms and equipment to Communist guerrillas fighting in the Greek civil war, and was refusing to withdraw Soviet troops from Azerbaijan in Iran. By early 1946 the Cold War was beginning and Washington could observe a broad political and military effort by the Soviet Union to move into the Mediterranean and Middle East. This increasing American concern formed part of Washington's rapidly evolving global involvement to contain Soviet expansionism. Thus, the United States appeared as an heir to the British 19th century role, namely that of a barrier to Russia's drive to gain warm water ports in the Mediterranean and Middle East.

From the early 1950s until the mid-1960s, the Sixth Fleet's ability to project power lay primarily in its nuclear capability.[26] Sub-sequently, the emphasis has been on conventional power projection, although a substantial nuclear capability still remains.

Until about 1965 the Sixth Fleet's position was clearly paramount in the Mediterranean, and up until 1963 there were relatively few Soviet warships, submarines or TU-16s (BADGER) in naval avi-ation that posed a military threat. The probable use of these weapons systems was remote and only to be considered in extreme political circumstances. Nor could they be used as instruments of political persuasion or blackmail. The Sixth Fleet was, therefore, able to move unimpaired within the Mediterranean, flying the flag with confidence that its political effect would have an impact on those it wished to influence. Its principal advantage was its flexi-bility to control the sea-lines of communication (SLOCs) and project power. The Soviet Union's options were limited; a dramatic but unusable strategic attack on the United States and/or Western Europe, blockades of third party shipping, and coastal defence on its own behalf.[27]

The United States has utilised the Sixth Fleet in both overt and subtle ways. For example, on 20 April 1957, when some 1,800 Marines anchored off the coast of Beirut in readiness for a possible intervention in Jordan, the Sixth Fleet concurrently carried out manoeuvres in the Eastern Mediterranean, thereby enhancing Washington's position. Again, in July 1958 the Sixth Fleet assisted in the landing of some 15,000 troops in Beirut 'to support the independence and integrity of Lebanon'.[28] Thereafter the Sixth Fleet was perceived as a deterrent force and a factor that had to be in the calculus of anyone contemplating actions that might adversely affect American interests in the area. By the early 1960s, United States' carrier forces sustained the entire naval contribution to Washington's strategic deterrent and the Eastern Mediterranean was their most advantageous location. But by the late 1960s much of this had changed. The Sixth Fleet's prospective wartime activities were now narrowly defined: air power to support Greek and Turkish forces during the initial stages of an attack; air strikes against the southern part of the Soviet Union; or direct support of the Central Front in case of a Warsaw Pact assault there.[29]

Up until 1979 the Sixth Fleet consisted of about 40 ships, comprised of two carrier battle groups and an amphibious task group supporting some 2,000 marines. While operations sometimes encompassed the entire Mediterranean, the carriers developed a pattern that usually had one carrier battle group in the Central Mediterranean and another in the Western Mediterranean.[30] After 1979 only one carrier battle group operated continuously in the Mediterranean. Following the events in Afghanistan and Iran, Washington decided to redeploy its Sixth and Seventh Fleet assets to the Persian Gulf. Although the present strength of the Sixth Fleet is at the level of the post-Afghanistan period, its overall ability to project power is potent and it continues to serve as a flexible instrument of American power in the Mediterranean available to play major roles as it did in deploying United States marines in Lebanon (1982–84), the Gulf of Sidra incidents (1981 and 1986), and the attack on Libya (1986). No doubt the Sixth Fleet also serves as a constant reminder to Syria that the Soviet presence in that country will not be overlooked by the United States.

If war did break out in Europe or in the Mediterranean basin, it is likely that the Sixth Fleet would manoeuvre throughout the Mediterranean and undertake, from wherever it might be located, a perimeter defence coupled with appropriate counter-attacks against any enemy forces within its reach. Such action would not necessarily mean defence for Central Europe. The probable contributions that the Sixth Fleet could make to NATO forces in the Eastern Mediterranean are twofold. It could bring to bear extremely sophisticated air defence assets (F-14s, F-18s, and E-2C early warning aircraft) to bolster the limited air defence capabilities of Greece and Turkey. Second, it could utilise A-6 attackers to deploy offensive air support over a fairly large combat radius in an all-weather capacity.

Most naval strategists believe that the Sixth Fleet would carry the day in a strictly naval exchange with the Fifth Escadra. But, at present, its capacity to assist in a land battle is limited. The threat from Soviet land-based aircraft from the Crimea, Bulgaria and Libya[31] circumscribes the Sixth Fleet's ability to operate freely in the Mediterranean. Nonetheless, it remains the primary symbol of America's guarantee to its Mediterranean allies. To the extent that the Sixth Fleet is vulnerable, it symbolises American willingness to provide a forward defence for Europe. However, because the Sixth Fleet has obvious missions outside the NATO area of responsibility in peacetime, it is not seen in the same light as the United States commitment in Central Europe and is a source of friction with Greece, Turkey and the other southern allies. Its activities as defined by Washington are much wider than those of any of the NATO countries in the Southern Region. Therefore, its role to the Alliance seems ambiguous. Nevertheless, if the Sixth Fleet were not in the Mediterranean, the advantage would clearly pass to the Soviet's Fifth Escadra.

The importance of sea control in the Mediterranean has been demonstrated. The subject of the next chapter will be an assessment of the conventional force capabilities of Greece, Turkey and the Warsaw Pact and will be followed by a detailed discussion of the land, sea, and air campaigns in the South Eastern Region.

CHAPTER 5

The Military Balance

INTERNATIONAL POLITICS have passed through an historic watershed. By the changes that Mikhail Gorbachev initiated, he has altered the world order as we have known it since 1945. The forces that were unleashed are—and will be—difficult to control. Gorbachev has pried loose the lid on Pandora's box and the elements newly released can no longer be contained. Among the forces so unleashed are the wholesale changes in governments and the process of democratisation taking place in the Soviet Union and Eastern Europe. Already, nascent democratic governments are demanding that Moscow reduce and ultimately withdraw military units from their territory (e.g. Czechoslovakia, Hungary and Poland). Indeed, some movement has already begun. This political turmoil has taken its toll on the Warsaw Pact. It has been transformed from a military alliance created for the dual purpose of offsetting the NATO armies and insuring conformity to Moscow's directives to an increasingly hollow organisation without any clear purpose. Soviet units still comprise about four-fifths of the Warsaw Pact forces and bear some 80 per cent of its costs. Overall, its armies remain intact, but this alliance has been neutralised by popular discontent.

The Warsaw Pact seems now to be in a state of suspended animation with nobody giving orders, much less ones that might not be obeyed. Those ascending to power in Eastern Europe and the Soviet Union have been very careful to isolate the Warsaw Pact military forces from events around them. It is as though by unspoken agreement questions about the role of the military are being left for quieter times. It almost seems that the Warsaw Pact armies have a life independent of the nations that staff them. This cannot last long, given the rejection of communism and the rebirth of nationalism among its members. Moscow recognises this and has adjusted to reality by withdrawing forces behind its borders and reorganising its military under a new defensive doctrine. Eastern Europe is now a buffer between the West and the Soviet homeland, rather than the front line of the Soviet armed forces.

This withdrawal from Eastern Europe has left a major political and military void. The power that possessed the wherewithal to maintain order is no longer capable of or willing to doing so. Even though it is a less threatening environment than we have known these past 40 years, it is conceivable that under circumstances where political and economic instability reign and heightened ethnic awareness is blossoming, evolutionary processes may wane and revolutionary upheaval prevail. This scenario is highly possible throughout Eastern Europe, in particular the Balkan region. Historic irredentism may once again appear, as was the case prior to the Second World War. Already ethnic unrest and minority rights issues have surfaced in Albania (Greeks), Bulgaria (Turks), Greece (Turks), Romania (Moldavians), Turkey (Kurds) and Yugoslavia (Albanians). Also, the Soviet homeland itself has been affected by ethnic strife especially in Azerbaijan, Kirgizia and Tajikistan. These Soviet minorities are Turkic in origin, thereby gaining the sympathetic ear of Ankara (see Chapter 3). Historically, all these nations have formed military alliances and fought wars among themselves. The relations could once again become ever changing, thus affecting the strategic and military calculus.

Moscow's ability to take unilateral military action has dwindled. Its major priority is to revive its ailing economy. Nor does it have the stomach for military intervention and the world criticism that would surely follow. A reunified and militarily strong Germany would be equally unwilling to take intercessory action. Such a move on Germany's part would be viewed disastrously by the international community and seen as a revival of aggressive behaviour, harking back with horror to the great wars that we fought to halt such conduct.

NATO will not disappear. Its new look will result in less force concentration in the Central Region, and more troops and equipment instead will be located on NATO's flanks, especially Norway and Turkey, both of which border the Soviet Union. Troop formations will most likely be more tightly grouped, equipped with more sophisticated stand-off weapons, and trained to be highly mobile. Also, higher priorities will be given to air and naval forces, rather than heavy ground forces and equipment. The inter-German border will no longer be NATO's focus in the post-CFE period.

NATO's success in attempting to intervene in past disputes among Alliance members (e.g. Greece and Turkey) has proved less than effective. No doubt if the Alliance were called upon at some future date to intercede, it would do so, with reluctance. The United States has an enduring responsibility to remain in Europe, and it will do so as a counterweight to the Soviet Union's geographical advantage on the continent. Regardless of the changing landscape in Eastern

Europe, and the negotiations taking place on conventional and strategic weapons (see Chapter 8), the Soviet Union is still the most formidable military power on the European continent. Its only true equivalent is the United States. However, barring a confrontation between these two superpowers—highly unlikely at this point—the United States would be most reluctant to intervene in any regional dispute.

All of this suggests that the political processes sweeping both Eastern Europe and the Soviet Union are irreversible, complicated and fraught with dangers. No doubt, military planners in these countries will continue to monitor and undertake contingency planning. Historical imperatives, the evaluation of force structures, deployments and weapons acquisitions will be part of the calculus in positing wartime scenarios of possible future conflicts. These scenarios, no doubt, will utilise, for contingency planning purposes, the historical routes of strategic geography that are discussed in the following chapter (Chapter 6). What follows in this chapter and in the subsequent two chapters (6 and 7) is an examination of such considerations as might involve Greece and Turkey and their Warsaw Pact neighbours. To this end we will continue to use terminologies with which we have become all too familiar in the post-Second World War period.

The Command Structure

The challenge of establishing a cohesive defence posture in NATO's South Eastern Region of Allied Command Europe (ACE) has not subsided since the early days of the Alliance, although some progress has been made in integrating Greece and Turkey's separate, and somewhat disparate, national defence efforts into a common framework. To all intents and purposes, the defence of the South Eastern Region remains, as noted elsewhere, primarily a national responsibility. Unlike the forces in the Central Front, where the military of several NATO countries are stationed side by side, and would conduct an integrated defence in wartime, AFSOUTH South East is characterised by a juxtaposition of individual defence postures of Greece and Turkey, with the United States present in the form of American generals serving as NATO commanders, and acting as unifying elements (e.g. CINCSOUTH and COMAIRSOUTH).

To understand better the overall problems that the NATO commander faces in this region, a comprehensive description of AFSOUTH's command structure follows. For practical purposes, NATO divides the region it has to defend into specific areas. The Southern Region is the largest, comprising about two million square

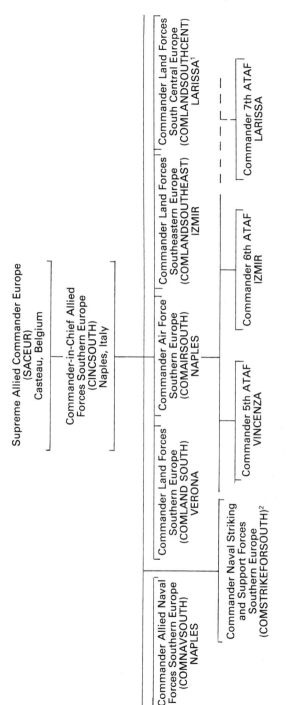

FIG. 5.1 Allied Forces Southern Command: Structure.

Notes:
1. Until 1974, Greek forces were assigned to LANDSOUTHEAST and 6th ATAF; now they report directly to CINCSOUTH in Naples through the Hellenic National Defence General Staff.
2. COMSTRIKEFORSOUTH is the NATO designation for the Commander of the U.S. Sixth Fleet.

miles, and the South Eastern Flank is part of this. The immediate responsibility for the NATO defence of the whole area lies with Allied Forces Southern Europe (AFSOUTH) in Naples, whose overall wartime mission is to defend Greece, Italy and Turkey, as well as the sea-lanes of communications (SLOC) throughout the Mediterranean and the Black Sea. This command has survived a couple of disruptive changes. These have included France's withdrawal from NATO in 1966 and, as detailed elsewhere, the decision of Greece to withdraw from NATO in 1974 in protest over the Turkish invasion of Cyprus. Greece's return to the Alliance's military wing in 1980 was only partial, since a number of key command and control issues have remained unresolved, operationally limiting Greece's military contribution. Five principal subordinate commands of AFSOUTH (one air, two land, and two naval) have been established and follow (see Fig. 5.1):

Allied Air Forces Southern Europe (AIRSOUTH), commanded by a United States Air Force general with headquarters in Naples is responsible for all land-based air operations throughout the AFSOUTH area, a 2,300-mile border stretching from the Italian Alps to eastern Turkey. There are presently two commands under the commander (COMAIRSOUTH); the Fifth Allied Tactical Air Force (FIVEATAF) based at Vicenza, in Italy, and the Sixth Allied Tactical Air Force (SIXATAF) at Izmir, in Turkey. A third command, the Seventh Allied Tactical Air Force (SEVENATAF), will be established at Larisa, in Greece when Greece and Turkey resolve their differences over the military jurisdiction in the Aegean Sea. In peacetime, AIRSOUTH is the only command in AFSOUTH that has NATO forces under its control perpetually in peacetime, with the primary role of maintaining air-defence capabilities.

Land Forces Southern Europe (LANDSOUTH) is commanded by an Italian four-star general with headquarters in Verona, Italy, and is responsible for NATO's defence of north east Italy.

Land Forces Southeastern Europe (LANDSOUTHEAST), commanded by a Turkish three-star general with headquarters at Izmir, has the task of protecting the Turkish flank, and particularly the 375 mile border with the Soviet Union, which Moscow might decide to cross if ever it wished direct access to Middle East oil supplies. A comparable command for Greece, which is still a subject for negotiations, is Land Forces South Europe (LANDSOUTHEAST) commanded by a three-star Greek general with headquarters at Larisa. (LANDSOUTHEAST and 6th ATAF at Izmir are the only AFSOUTH headquarters in which Greek personnel do not participate.)

Allied Naval Forces Southern Europe (NAVSOUTH) has responsibility for six geographical areas and is commanded by an Italian four-star admiral with headquarters in Naples.[1] It is responsible for the defence of the SLOCs from Gibraltar to the Black Sea, as well as naval maritime air operations. Although no ships are permanently assigned to NAVSOUTH in peacetime, a multi-national naval task force is activated twice a year for month-long exercises. One of its more important tasks is the coordination, on a 24-hour basis, of the surveillance of the movement of maritime forces (primarily Soviet) within the Mediterranean. This is effected from its surveillance coordination centre in Italy. In wartime the commander of NAVSOUTH assumes control of seven subordinate naval commands.

Last, NAVSOUTH works very closely with the subordinate command designated as Naval Striking and Support Forces Southern Europe (STRIKEFORSOUTH). This is the NATO designation for the United States Sixth Fleet, commanded by an American Vice Admiral, with home port at Gaeta, in Italy. As we discussed previously, essentially it has two missions: to establish sea control of the Mediterranean and to 'influence' the outcome of the land battle ashore. STRIKEFORSOUTH has three subordinate commands at its disposal: Task Force 502 (Carrier Striking Force), Task Force 503 (Amphibious Forces) and Task Force 504 (Landing Forces).

Although NAVSOUTH and STRIKEFORSOUTH have similar areas of action, in practice NAVSOUTH would be responsible in wartime for the safeguard of supply lines in the Mediterranean while STRIKEFORSOUTH's mission would be directed more toward the projection of power ashore. In general, NAVSOUTH is geographically focused—it must assure the security of the Mediterranean through anti-submarine warfare and the protection of convoys. STRIKEFORSOUTH is functionally oriented—it must be prepared to undertake various measures to defeat the 5th Escadra and other Soviet assets in the Mediterranean and assist in the land battle in Europe.

Because of the region's geographic and political fragmentation, AFSOUTH's ability to develop a southeastern-wide strategic concept for its defence, integrating land, air and naval operations is undermined.[2] Other factors that contribute to this disarray include the division of this flank into three areas of operation: Thrace (Northern Greece/Western Turkey), Eastern Turkey and the Mediterranean Sea and present commanders with unique problems of planning and strategy. Communications throughout this region are extremely thin, partly because Greek and Turkish systems remain inadequate, and also because those that exist are not perfectly compatible. Further, NATO is at a disadvantage as its ability to move ground forces throughout the area is limited; thus the Soviet and Warsaw Pact forces are able to present a significant threat to them. Recent exercises suggest that Soviet strategy to gain access to the Middle East and the Indian Ocean probably includes plans to overrun the Turkish First Army in Thrace, and to take the Bosporus with a minimum of some eight to ten divisions supported by air and sea elements and reinforced by tank regiments staging from Varna and Burgas.[3] The aim would be to split the Greek and Turkish units and leave the defence of the Straits and the west coast of the Bosporus exclusively to Turkish forces (detailed in Chapter 6).

NATO Strategy

Any defence of this region must be designed to ensure that the Warsaw Pact cannot realistically believe that it can outflank the NATO forces in a drive to the Middle East or disrupt Allied control of the Mediterranean. Given these divided theatres of possible battle, it is clear that the initial defence must be national. Both Greece and Turkey must be able to resist aggression at least until NATO can sound its first warning of its determination to fight by

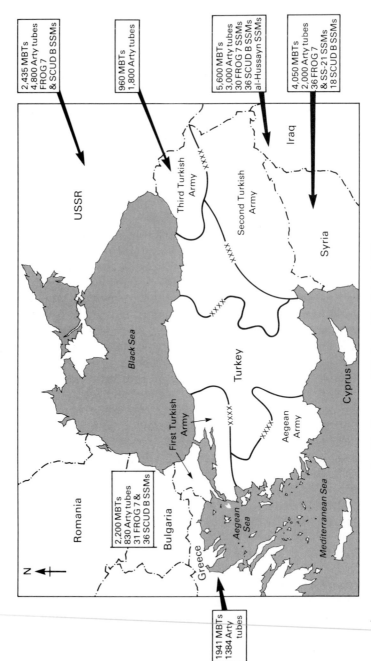

MAP 5.1. Greece and Turkey—The Potential Threats.

sending in the ACE Mobile Force (AMF), accompanied by a further warning to the aggressor that continued action could lead to the use of nuclear weapons.[4] Established in 1960, the AMF's purpose is to come rapidly to the aid of NATO states in the Flanks, namely Denmark, Greece, Norway and Turkey.[5] Realistically, it is not truly a fighting force; it is intended 'to show the flag'. It should not be considered a force capable of providing reinforcements, but rather as an immediate reaction unit to signal concern. With its headquarters in Heidelberg, in West Germany, few of the AMF troops are permanently on station. Indeed some elements are not winter equipped. The Force might be able to deploy rapidly once assembled, but this deployment would take time. AMF is not fully integrated into the general defence plans of either Greece or Turkey, and current AMF exercises are hampered by the fact that Greece has not participated fully in NATO exercises since 1974.

In recent years NATO exercises have increasingly emphasised the ability of the Alliance to reinforce Turkey. The AMF has been regularly staging major field training exercises in Eastern Turkey (e.g. ADVENTURE EXPRESS in 1983, AURORA EXPRESS in 1987) and in Turkish Thrace (e.g. ARCHWAY EXPRESS, 1985 and ALLY EXPRESS, 1988). For Exercise DISPLAY DETERMINATION 84, the United States Army dispatched a battalion task force of the 82nd Airborne Division from the continental United States to Turkey on a non-stop flight culminating in an airdrop over the exercise area. During DISPLAY DETERMINATION 87, the United States exercised its capability to deploy to Turkey, by sea, elements of the 24th Infantry Division (Mechanised) garrisoned at Fort Stewart, Georgia, equipped with M–1 Abrams main battle tanks. Current AMF exercises are hampered by the fact that Turkey does not allow the AMF to mix with the local population nor do they allow the AMF to work as closely with Turkish forces as they would deploy in a wartime contingency. This type of participation would be useful training for the AMF, given its possible utility in an immediate reaction role.

Furthermore, NATO reinforcements of Turkey in a crisis would be constrained by inadequate reception facilities, poor road and rail networks (particularly in the more remote regions of eastern Anatolia), and shortfalls in ammunition and fuel storage capacity. These, and similar infrastructure deficiencies in Greece, should be partly eliminated by the mid-1990s as a result of the substantially higher level of infrastructure funding allocated to the South Eastern Region in the 1985–91 infrastructure plan approved by NATO's Defence Planning Committee in 1984.

At sea, NATO's position is, of course, quite strong, given the presence of the United States Sixth Fleet. However, it would be psychologically helpful if more Alliance members contributed to the naval mission in the Mediterranean. Apart from the AMF, NATO's only other immediate reaction force is the Naval On-Call Force Mediterranean (NAVOCFORMED), which provides a deterrent and quick intervention capacity and is composed of combatant warships of several NATO members, usually Italy, Turkey, the United Kingdom and the United States. Other NATO states may provide support when this force is exercised. NAVOCFORMED is called together for training purposes biannually for a thirty-day period. Responsibility for detailed planning of these exercises rests with COMNAV-SOUTH. Unfortunately, the disputes beween Greece and Turkey have prevented NAVOCFORMED from becoming a standing force and have made it impossible to create a more multilateral permanent maritime presence for NATO in the Mediterranean. This is most disheartening. A standing force could work more efficiently with elements of the Sixth Fleet and serve as a strong signal for collective Alliance concerns. Clearly, the priorities must continue to be focused on improving Greek and Turkish defence capabilities and their ability to integrate reinforcements efficiently.

NATO Force Deployments

Greece

Currently, two of Greece's 11 infantry divisions and three of its armoured brigades are stationed in Thrace opposite the Turkish border. In addition, some 32,000 men are assigned to the military commands on six major Aegean Islands (Rhodes, Kos, Samos, Chios, Lesbos and Lemnos).[6] The present disposition of Greek military forces reflects the 'New Defence Doctrine' of 1985, which formalised the reorganisation and re-deployment of the Greek army that took place following the Cyprus invasion by Turkey in 1974. Prior to this incident, Greek Army forces were spread out primarily along the borders of Albania, Yugoslavia and Bulgaria, and only one division was stationed near the Turkish border (Alexandroupolis). In 1976 Greece created a fourth army corps—'D' Corps—to defend the border with Turkey, and it is this corps that is at nearly 100 per cent combat readiness, whereas Greece's three remaining corps 'A', 'B', and 'C' are relatively weak in manpower and material although their forces are aimed toward the north and what was once the Warsaw Pact threat.[7]

The Greek Army's main field organisation, known as the Hellenic First Army, is responsible for defending about 60 per cent of Greece and controls about two-thirds of the Greek land forces, including most of the armour and artillery units. The Athens Military Command is basically a training and supply organisation that provides manpower from the heavily populated regions of Greece in wartime. The third major command is the Higher Military Command Interior and Islands which controls the infantry division on Crete and the six military commands on the Aegean Islands.

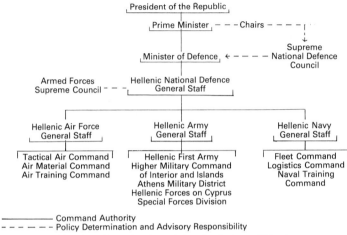

FIG. 5.2. Organisation of the Greek Armed Forces

The Greek Navy is divided into three commands. The Fleet Command has operational control over all ships and maritime patrol and anti-submarine warfare aircraft and is divided into a submarine squadron, three destroyer squadrons, an amphibious force, a landing craft squadron and a fast patrol boat force. The Logistics Command is responsible for the administration of shore-based support facilities and the Training Command is responsible for most training requests. The Greek Navy's assets are primarily located in the Athens area (Piraeus, Salamis and Poros) with a secondary naval headquarters at Souda Bay on Crete.

The modernisation of the Greek fleet through acquisition of modern submarines (diesel TYPE-209s), MEKO-200 frigates and fast patrol boats armed with EXOCET and PENGUIN surface-to-surface missiles has greatly enhanced her naval capabilities. For the most part, the Greek Navy's major surface combatants, (of which there are some 16), have equipment that has been modernised or that has recently been purchased. Nevertheless, it still remains a coastal navy very well-suited for operations in the Ionian and Aegean Seas, conducting patrol, escort, anti-submarine and mine warfare. It can also conduct amphibious operations to a limited degree in support of NATO missions in the Aegean and Ionian Seas. However, the Greek Navy would require substantial Alliance assistance in order to conduct sustained combat operations. It would be hard pressed to counter the threat posed by Soviet naval aviation, surface ships and submarines.

TABLE 5.1. *The Greek Armed Forces*

ARMY	
Manpower	160,000
Divisions	14
Independent Brigades	6
Tanks (MBTs)	1,941
Armoured Personnel Carriers	2,283
Anti-tank Missile Systems	400
Artillery	1,384
Air Defence Systems	600
NAVY	
Manpower	20,500
Destroyers/Frigates	21
Submarines	10
Fast Patrol Boats	35
Amphibious Ships	13
AIR FORCE	
Manpower	28,000
Combat Aircraft	259
Reconnaissance Aircraft	46
Trainers	85
Transport Aircraft	75

Source: *The Military Balance, 1989–1990* (London: The International Institute for Strategic Studies, (Published Brasseys (UK)), 1989), pp. 65–7.

The Greek Air Force also is divided into three major commands. The Tactical Air Force controls all aircraft except trainers, surface-to-air missiles (SAMS) and the air defence radar. The Air Material Command and the Air Training Command are responsible for all logistics and major maintenance support and training, respectively. The Tactical Air Force is organised into eight combat wings with 16 squadrons and eight training groups while the Training Command has two training wings.

Besides the major airfields on the mainland (Thessaloniki, Larisa, Nea Anchialos/Volos, Tanagra, Elevsis, Araxos, Andravida, and Kalamata) and on Crete (Souda Bay), new ones were constructed and became operational in the late 1970s, located on a north-south axis crossing the central Aegean (Chryssoupolis/Kavala, Skyros, Thera and Karpathos). Of the 260 combat aircraft that Greece possesses and with the recent purchase of 40 Mirage 2000s and 40 F-16 Fighting Falcons, only some 50 aircraft can be judged to be obsolescent or obsolete or are known to be in poor condition because of age.

The lack of modern weapons systems to equip its new aircraft will detract from Greece's inability to fight against the Warsaw Pact. Especially lacking are electronic countermeasure equipment which makes the Greek Air Force vulnerable to surface-to-air and air-to-air missiles.

Turkey

Turkey maintains the second largest standing army in the Alliance, second only to the United States. Unlike Greece, which views Turkey as its principal enemy, Turkey's defence policy is shaped by its perception of the Soviet Union and Warsaw Pact (principally Bulgaria and to some extent Romania) as the primary threats to its national security and territorial integrity. It faces this threat of attack from two separate directions. Together these two frontiers amount to 37 per cent of NATO's borders with the Warsaw Pact. Turkish threat assessments must also take into account its neighbours to the south and south-east: Syria, Iraq and Iran. These countries could pose various dangers to Turkey's national security (see Chapter 3).

Mirroring the New Defence Doctrine of Greece, Turkey has now altered its security outlook and has adopted the 'Mask Doctrine', which envisages Greece as one of the major threats to Turkish national security. (Iraq and Syria is also accorded high priority.[8]) Realistically, the Turkish General Staff does not consider Greece as a viable military threat, but this doctrine places emphasis on Greece's efforts to turn the Aegean Sea into a 'Greek Lake'. This affronts Turkish national pride. The naming of an annual exercise for the Aegean Army's 'Primary Target' lends substance to the 'Mask Doctrine'.

Currently, Turkey earmarks about 75 per cent of its approximately 528,000 Army personnel to NATO-committed units. The Turkish land forces are organised into four field armies (see Fig. 5.3). The First Army, with headquarters in Istanbul, consists of ten divisions and four brigades and is the best equipped of the four field armies. Its formations are heavy in armour (primarily M48-A5 MBTs) and are organised for mobile operations in the rolling terrain near the Bulgarian border and along the coast of the Black Sea. It has responsibility to protect the Straits and Turkish Thrace. Under the original terms of NATO, the First Army was to have cooperated with the Greek 'C' Corps along its western flank in defensive operations against attacks from the north.[9] However, since 1974 Greece has not cooperated in joint efforts and Turkey's First Army has therefore been obliged to assume full responsibility for the defence of its sector.

The Second Army at Malatya consists of ten brigades and is respon-

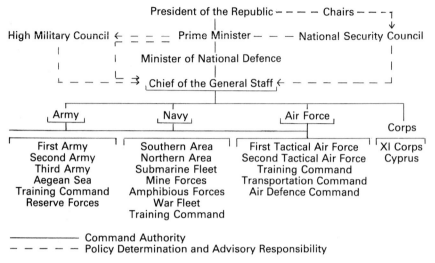

FIG. 5.3. Organisation of the Turkish Armed Forces

sible for protecting Turkey's volatile borders with Syria, Iraq and Iran. At any time, these countries could pose dangers to Turkish national security. Iraq and Syria, a well-armed client state of the Soviet Union. Syria has had a long-standing dispute with Turkey over the Sanjak of Alexandretta, and today she poses the greatest danger to Turkey. In fact, Syria has never accepted this territorial loss (in 1939) and Syrian maps still show this area as part of Syria. They share a common 600 kilometre border. Syria's geographic proximity to the important NATO and Turkish installations of Iskenderum, Incirlik, and Mersin makes these prime targets for Syrian missiles [SCUD-B (modified) with a range of 310 kilometres]. Syria is also known to train and arm PKK terrorists who continually infiltrate into Turkey and cause havoc.

In the light of a less threatening Warsaw Pact, Turkey has reorientated her defence strategy toward the south. Both the 6th and 66th infantry divisions were disbanded in the Western Thrace region, and three new highly mobile mechanised brigades were created for operations in South Eastern Turkey. The Third Army, covering the Soviet Trans-Caucasus border and the historic invasion routes from the east, is deployed throughout the rugged mountains and deep valleys of Eastern Anatolia. Its headquarters is at the strategic centre of Erzincan. Made up of four divisions and eight brigades, the Third Army stands at a readiness of about 40 per cent, facing Soviet forces that are also at a low state of readiness (Category C units). This region lies at the extreme limit of NATO's overall area of responsibility and it flanks Soviet routes to the Persian Gulf and the Middle East.

The Aegean Army is a recent addition to Turkey's ground forces complement. It consists of two brigades and has its headquarters at Izmir. Its sector of responsibility is the vast area facing the Aegean coastline, a region which extends from the Dardanelles in the north to the southernmost Greek island. This army has three basic missions: peacetime training for infantry and artillery conscripts; the command and control of its two infantry brigades and other army, navy and air force elements in any limited conflict with Greece in the Aegean; and, finally, in a conventional war, serving as the principal mobilisation training force in Turkey.

TABLE 5.2. *The Turkish Armed Forces*

ARMY	
Manpower	528,500
Divisions	16
Independent Brigades	23
Tanks (MBTs)	3,727
Armoured Personnel Carriers	3,300
Anti-tank Missile Systems	247
Artillery	2,100
Air Defence Systems	1,090
NAVY	
Manpower	55,000
Destroyer/Frigates	22
Submarines	15
Fast Patrol Boats	48
Amphibious Ships	80
Mine Warfare Ships	33
AIR FORCE	
Manpower	67,400
Combat Aircraft	385
Reconnaissance Aircraft	27
Trainers	116
Transport Aircraft	84

Source: *The Military Balance, 1989–1990* (London: The International Institute for Strategic Studies (Published Brasseys (UK)), 1989), pp. 76–78.

The XI Corps, deployed on Cyprus, consists of about 24,000 men and possesses top-of-the-line equipment (e.g. M48-A5 tanks). The exact number of personnel fluctuates depending on the level of political and military tension on the island and the Turkish General Staff's (TGS) confidence in its ability to reinforce rapidly. This Corps reports directly to the Turkish General Staff, due to its highly visible and sensitive mission. Neither the XI Corps nor the Aegean Army is part of Turkey's contribution to NATO.

The Turkish Navy is the smallest of the three Service components, numbering approximately 55,000. It is organised into seven commands with an assigned NATO role to COMNAVSOUTH (see Fig. 5.1). In the event of general war, COMNAVSOUTH in Naples is responsible for protecting lines of communication through the Mediterranean and the Black Sea and for anti-submarine operations in the event of general conflict. However, the Turkish Navy's share in this mission is less clearly defined than, for example, are the roles of the other Turkish Services. Inasmuch as the United States Sixth Fleet is the primary naval element employed to counterbalance the Fifth Escadra in the Mediterranean, Turkey's role is somewhat restricted to the support of the regions of the Black Sea and the Bosporus and Dardanelles. With some 25 per cent of the Soviet Union's naval forces located in or assigned to the Black Sea area, Soviet control of the Straits during the early stages of any NATO/Warsaw Pact conflict is essential to the effectiveness of Soviet naval power in the Black Sea and the Mediterranean. Control of access to, and movement through, the Straits is therefore the paramount NATO mission of the Turkish Navy.

While the age of the ships in the Turkish Navy is a subject of some concern, the Navy has been more successful in its quest for modernisation than the Army or Air Force. Much of this is attributable to Turkey's important domestic capability for production of naval vessels at Golcuk naval yard, notably MEKO-200 frigates and TYPE-209 diesel submarines.[10] In early 1989, the United States announced that four frigates would be transferred to the Turkish Navy under a five-year lease agreement.[11] Although these vessels are nearly 20 years old, they have been refurbished and upgraded. Overall, Turkey's surface combatants can be classified today as either equipment modernised or improved via retrofit or refurbishment programmes or equipment that was recently purchased new from the manufacturer.[12]

The future core of surface warships for the navy will be the MEKO-200s and the fast patrol boats that are now coming on line. Their state-of-the art equipment will enhance the Navy's anti-surface and anti-submarine capabilities. The guided missile, patrol force, armed with HARPOON and PENGUIN surface-to-surface missiles is relatively potent and well-suited to the narrow waters of the Straits and along the island-dotted Aegean coastline. To enhance this capability further, the Navy has acquired anti-ship missiles (e.g. SEA SKUA) for use on its Augusta-Bell 212 helicopters. It is, however, the submarine force that has become the Navy's most effective combat arm. Its primary limitation thus far is the age of the fleet overall in comparison to Soviet anti-submarine proficiency. This force constitutes the only NATO force likely to be available for pre-alert reconnaissance, search and rescue, and anti-shipping operations in the Black Sea.[13] It would also be tasked to counter the threat of Soviet aviation, surface ships and submarines. All in all the Turkish Navy would require substantial assistance from NATO to conduct sustained operations during combat.

The Turkish Air Force, organised into two tactical air forces, symbolises the national desire for recognition as a contender in the world power equation.[14] At the same time, the high cost of technological modernity has placed a heavy burden on the country's economy. The Turkish Air Force's missions are air defence of territorial integrity and airlift of troops and supplies, as part of NATO's SIXATAF headquartered at Izmir[15] (see Fig. 5.1).

In the late 1970s, most of the aircraft and the air defence missiles in the Air Force were obsolescent models discarded by other NATO countries, mainly the United States. A very ambitious programme was launched in the late 1970s to modernise the Air Force through the acquisition of technology through a joint-venture programme with the United States to build 160 F-16 FIGHTING FALCONS. Around 50 of these have already been delivered to the Air Force, and the remainder will be operational by the early 1990s. The F-16 squadrons will greatly enhance the Turkish Air Force's defence close air support, interdiction and nuclear strike capabilities. Four squadrons are scheduled to be operational in each of these two roles. Older aircraft such as the F-104G STARFIGHTER and the F-4E PHANTOMS II will retain a ground attack mission and reconnaissance capability. The upgrading of some of the F-4s with avionics and engine packages will enhance the operations. Overall, the Turkish Air Force can be characterised-today as being fairly modern with most of its equipment modernised, improved, or refurbished—and newly purchased, as in the case of the F-16.

Warsaw Pact Force Deployments

The Soviet Union's military perceptions of the Alliance must be viewed in the context of its overall vision of areas of potential conflict outside the country. Therefore, Moscow organises its military forces and its operational planning around theatres of war and theatres of strategic military operations (TVDs) which correspond to its own strategic priorities and administrative needs. Each of the TVDs falls within a theatre of war and each, naturally, has a different level of potential military importance to the Soviet Union. This is reflected in the category and readiness of Soviet and Warsaw Pact forces responsible for these areas. From Moscow's perspective, the overall Southern Region of NATO falls within two different theatres of war and three TVDs.[16] For our purposes, the most important are the South Western and Southern TVDs. The expanse of the South West

TABLE 5.3. *The Soviet-Warsaw Pact Forces*
(The Balkan Sub-theatre)

	Bulgaria	Romania	Soviet Union	Total
ARMY				
Manpower	117,500	171,000	250,000	538,500
Divisions	8	10	16[1]	34
Independent Brigades	5			5
Tanks (MBTs)	2,200	3,200	2,435	7,835
AIR FORCE				
Combat Aircraft	198	295	750	1,243
Reconnaissance Aircraft	35	15	145	195
NAVY				
Major Surface Warships	3	5	45	53
Submarines	4	1	34[2]	39
Naval Aviation	0	0	90	90[3]

Notes: [1] Of the total of 16 divisions, nine are from the Odessa MD and seven are from Kiev MD.

[2] Includes elements from both the Black Sea and Mediterranean Squadrons.

[3] This includes bombers (BADGERS and BLINDERS) and fighters (YAK-38s and SU-17s).

Source: *The Military Balance, 1989–1990* (London: The International Institute for Strategic Studies (Published Brassey's (UK)), 1989), pp. 45–46, 50–51, 60–61.

TVD (SWTVD) is about 3,000 kilometres from east to west and about 2,500 kilometres from north to south. It is broadly orientated toward Northern Italy, the Balkan sub-theatre of Greece, Turkey and the Mediterranean. It is the portion of the SWTVD sub-theatre that includes Greece and most of Turkey's Western Anatolian plains that is of interest. The Soviet side of the area comprises Bulgaria, Hungary, Romania, and the Odessa and Kiev Military Districts. The Eastern Anatolian region of Turkey and the region where Turkey also shares its borders with Moscow's client state Syria falls within the Southern TVD (STVD).[17] Eastern Anatolia extends about 600 kilometres between these two potential enemies.[18] Since any Syrian move must take Israel into consideration, the most pressing Turkish security concern in STVD rests along its border with the Soviet Union, a frontier approximately 620 kilometres long. Turkey must therefore look both east and west to the SWTVD and the other to the STVD.

The immediate threat (see Table 5.3) to both Greece and Turkey from elements of the SWTVD would include predominantly Soviet forces from the Odessa Military District and perhaps the Bulgarian Army, and follow-on forces possibly from Romania and the Kiev Military District. Greek and Turkish defences aligned against the

SWTVD consist of some 26 divisions, primarily infantry. The SWTVD forces are largely mechanised motor rifle divisions and are equipped with a total of 6,845 MBTs more or less. They are on terrain suitable for armoured offensive operations and could be reinforced by amphibious forces and airborne or air mobile divisions. Of these 34 divisions, some 20 are deployed forward and are considered at a high state of readiness. There are an additional 20 Soviet divisions which could be committed against Eastern Turkey equipped with 4,300 MBTs, of which 12 divisions are deployed forward with 2,435 tanks.[19] These forces could also be reinforced by airborne and air assault/mobile divisions. The Turkish Third Army maintains four divisions and eight brigades in this area.

TABLE 5.4. *NATO-Warsaw Pact Force Comparisons*
(The Balkan Sub-theatre)

	NATO	WARSAW PACT
ARMY		
Divisions	30	34
Independent Brigades	29	5
Tanks (MBTs)	5,668	7,835
AIR FORCE[1]		
Combat Aircraft	644	1,243
Reconnaissance Aircraft	73	195
NAVY[2]		
Major Warships	63 (43)	53
Submarines	30 (25)	39

Notes: [1] This data does not include any elements from other NATO Air Forces.
[2] The US Sixth Fleet's warships and submarines are included as part of this data. The figures in parentheses represent the Greek and Turkish elements.
Source: Compiled by author from Tables 5.1, 5.2, and 5.3.

Our data suggests that the NATO forces in the Balkan sub-theatre overall do not compare favourably with those of the Warsaw Pact, with the exception of naval forces and this is due to the presence of the American Sixth Fleet (see Table 5.4). In addition, the geographic separation of the Balkan sub-theatre and Eastern Turkey from each other and the remainder of NATO makes reinforcements, resupply and effective coordination between these two theatres difficult, particularly when lines of communication are under attack.

Comparison of the opposing air forces and navies is more difficult. The range of some of the modern Soviet aircraft [e.g. BACKFIRE (TU-26), BLINDER (TU-22) bombers, and SU-25 fighter bombers] is such that they have the potential to operate anywhere in the Mediterranean,[20] possibly affecting the security of sea lines of communications of vital importance to this theatre of operations as well as land targets throughout the area. The geography of the Mediterranean emphasises the interaction between maritime, land and air situations. The NATO naval forces and the Fifth Escadra would most likely face opposing land-based and naval aviation. Naval operations would, in turn, greatly influence land and air operations in the Balkan sub-theatre. External air reinforcements from the Alliance could be of crucial importance, since the Greek and Turkish air forces are presently equipped primarily with F-104, F-4 and F-5 aircraft which have somewhat limited capabilities to intercept low-altitude attack aircraft or provide effective close air support to ground forces. The qualitative disadvantages will not be so great after 1990, when Greece and Turkey have their full complement of MIRAGE-2000s and F-16s.

The imbalances in conventional forces that have been noted on closer examination may not be as great. NATO is a defensive alliance; typically, the attacker must possess at least a 3 to 1 ratio of forces over the defender. Such an imbalance does not presently exist. Further, Greece and Turkey have acquired modern, capable tanks which provide a qualitative and quantitative edge over both Bulgarian and Romanian ageing tanks.[21] While the Soviet Union may enjoy a numerical edge over both Greek and Turkish armour, qualitatively both sides are about evenly matched and the terrain in Eastern Turkey somewhat favours the defence.[22] In order for the Soviet forces to accomplish a break-through in this region, Soviet advantage would have to be increased to 4 or 5 to 1.

In addition, a potentially significant factor in assessing overall Warsaw Pact strength in the Balkan sub-theatre is the political unreliability of non-Soviet Warsaw Pact forces, most particularly in the light of present events. The reliability of the Bulgarian forces is partly related to a territorial issue with historic antecedents. Bulgaria never recovered small sections of Madeconia (now in Greece and Yugoslavia) and irredentist claims, from time to time, continue to affect relations between Athens and Sophia, while ethnic tensions between Turkey and Bulgaria date back to the Ottoman Empire.

In assessing the forces capabilities of NATO and the Warsaw Pact in the Balkan sub-theatre and Eastern Turkey, and their implications for deterrence, crisis management and defence, the greatest need is to examine a number of geographically specific scenarios between all of these protagonists—which will be the subject of the next chapter.

CHAPTER 6

The Strategic Geography: Land, Sea and Air Campaigns

CONSIDERATIONS AT the operational level of war are given very little prominence in Western writtings on security, but they haappen to be very useful for our purposes. As we noted earlier, it is important for military planners to go back o first principles and examine the options in light of geography, politics and the llessons of history. The insights gained are of immense value. The strategic geography of the Balkans and Easttern Turkey are historically rich for both ooooffensive and defensive operations. Conflict among these peoples is a historical truism, and each war left its mark on anothher generation of military planners. This chapter will be examining the geoography of these regions which should allow us to make educated guesses concerning whhat NATO, the Soviet Union and the individual countries affected would stand to lose or gain in possible conflicts and by exercising their contingency options and specific threat scenarios. More importantly, in light of the Conventtional Forces Europe (CFE) negootiations (Chapter 8), such geographic considerations are of immense importance and can be very telling when arranging troop withdrawals and realigning force structures for offensive and defensive deploymentss.

In planning offensive operations against Greece and Turkeyy, no doubt Soviet planners have identified the strategic geography that must be surmounted in order to attain these military obbjectives which are critical for victory. What follows is a detailed discussion of these.

Soviet and Warsaw Pact contingency options against the South Eastern Flank cover a spectrum of progressively more ambitious campaigns, fanning out from the Turkish Straits to encompass the entire South western TVD (SWTVD) and portions of the Southern TVD (STVD).[1] For example, a limited campaign launched by the

Soviet Union in the SWTVD might include, as a minimum, an assault on the Bosporus and the Dardanelles, accompanied by a ground offensive from Bulgaria inn Turkish Thrace to seal off the Black Sea and prevent counteer offensive operations by the United States Sixth Fleett and United States Air Force against targets in the southern Soviet Union, Bulgaria and possibly Romania. In this scenariio, Warsaw Pact forces in Bulgaria might adopt a defensive posture opposite Greek forces in the hope that Greece would be isolated or persuaded to adopt a position of non-involvement or withdraawal from NATO. In fact, Moscow made efforts to de-couple Greece from NATO during the 1980s. The Bulgarians have also normalised relations with Greece, while at the same time heightening tensions with Turkey.[2] One can certainly see advantages for Moscow in securing Athens' non-involvement during an offensive elsewhere in the region.

In such circumstances the bulk of the Warsaw Pact foorces would be allocated to an operation into Turkish Thrace and the Straits. Simultaneous ground operations would not necessarily bbe taken into Eastern Turkey. The Warsaw Pact position in the Straits, if once captured, could be a difficult one, however, since it would be constantly threatened by Turkish, United States and possibly Greek air power.

A more ambitious campaign might involve simultaneous air attacks through the depth of Greek and Turkish landmasses as far south as Crete to eliminate the ground infrastructure necessary for the performance by Allied air forces of offensive counter-air and tactical air support to maritime operations, without the accompaniment by offensive ground operations further inland, at least not until the later stages. As an option, the Soviet Air Force could also launch air attacks on Italian bases to neutralise NATO offensive counter-air capabilities, again without necessarily involving simultaneous ground operations against Italian forces.

Accompanied by amphibious assault landings and airborne/air assault operations on the Greek islands in the Aegean, Warsaw Pact operations into Central Greece and Western Turkey would aim at establishing a defensive perimeter which would eventually extend from the mainland of Peloponnesos to Crete and across to the Turkish landmass. From captured airfields in Greece such as Larisa, Preveza, and Tanagra, Soviet long-range bombers could threaten NATO assets in the Mediterranean, especially in Italy. From safe havens on the Aegean littoral and under the cover of Soviet land-based aviation, the Soviet Navy could conduct sea denial operations throughout the Mediterranean with a more reasonable expectation of success.

Considerations such as the timing of the operations, the requirements to achieve operational, if not strategic, surprise, the behaviour of other nations, and the susceptibility of Greece and Turkey to Moscow's psychological warfare—all would affect Soviet contingency planning and force allocation decisions as much as objective assessments of relative military capabilities.

Although the probability that the Warsaw Pact would initiate a conflict with NATO in the SWTVD is very low, it is conceivable that the Alliance could be confronted in the STVD with a lesser contingency than general war. One option might involve a deliberately limited Soviet attack in Eastern Turkey where Turkish forces stand guard alone and the local infrastructure for receiving NATO reinforcements is very deficient. Such an attack would confront NATO with a *fait accompli* before the Alliance could react militarily, thereby undermining the mutual defence guarantees extended under the North Atlantic Treaty. In addition, such an operation could be used by Moscow to create a diversion in the WTVD to attract NATO reinforcements in the STVD which might otherwise have been deployed to the Central Front.[3]

Turkey has, from time to time, expressed concerns regarding the vulnerability of its eastern and southern borders to limited aggression by Moscow or a surrogate, such as Syria, in circumstances which may not elicit a prompt and collective military NATO reaction. It is debatable whether the Soviet Union or Syria, for that matter, would be willing to risk provoking NATO in any circumstances short of a general European conflict.

If the Soviet Union and its allies were successful in defeating NATO forces in Greece and Western Turkey, Moscow would obtain uninhibited air access to the Mediterranean, which would facilitate its sea denial activities against STRIKEFORSOUTH and other NATO naval units. It would also enhance the Soviet Union's ability to establish an air bridge to north and West Africa. If successful, this would raise the possibility of utilising both air bases and naval installations to circumvent NATO's North Atlantic air defence and anti-submarine barriers. More directly, the Soviet Union primarily could utilise Greek and Turkish naval facilities to resupply its Mediterranean fleet, especially its submarines, thereby facilitating its sea denial campaign in the Mediterranean.

Anything short of this would be of small value to the Soviets unless they could achieve reliable maritime access from the Black Sea to the Mediterranean. This would necessitate securing the Straits and the Aegean Sea. As long as NATO forces hold the Straits and key Aegean Islands (Lemnos, Lesbos, Chios, Ikaria, Kos, Crete) or mine deep water choke points, reliable passage to the Mediterranean can be prevented. If Soviet naval forces were to gain access to the Mediterranean, NATO would then be required to conduct a sea denial campaign of its own against the Fifth Escadra.

The Warsaw Pact enjoys flexibility in the allocation of its ground forces and air assets (close air support and battlefield interdiction potential) and possesses battlefield mobility. NATO forces overall are at a disadvantage since effective movements must be carried out by sea and air. This is the biggest problem facing NATO in the Mediterranean, especially for international operations. In contrast, the Warsaw Pact in the Southern Region has wide communications by land, sea, and air, which gives Soviet strategists the ability to marshall their assets more effectively. Furthermore, in order to counter a Warsaw Pact offensive, ACE must redeploy air assets and commit its Mobile Force early on in the conflict.

Overall NATO objectives in the event of a general war include: preserving the territorial integrity of the South Eastern Region nations; maintaining access to key ports for reinforcement and resupply; guarding the exposed flank of NATO operations in Central Europe; and lending air and naval support to those operations. Clearly, the viability of NATO strategy in this sector will depend heavily on its ability to allocate assets to this region from other theatres.

The Campaign on Land

Both Greek and Turkish forces in Thrace can be easily isolated.[4] The extensive fortifications and the mountainous terrain that runs along the border between Greece, Turkey and Bulgaria benefit the defender. After an invading army breaches these, the terrain turns mostly into open plains. The situation from Thessaloniki eastward is precarious due to the limited strategic depth afforded the defender. Successful penetration in one of the several attack corridors would largely isolate part of Greece from the whole of Turkey and from other NATO forces and permit the attacking forces direct access to the Aegean.

Strategic geography and specific threat scenarios that might be employed by the Warsaw Pact in the SWTVD and STVD and specifically against Greece and Turkey follow in some detail. Considerations of this kind are given little prominence in studies of the South Eastern Flank and yet cover a spectrum of possibilities.

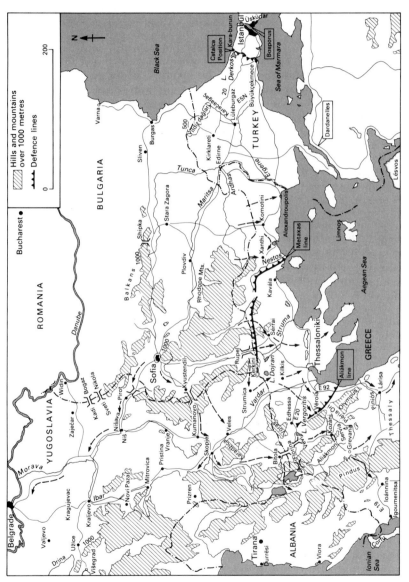

MAP 6.1. Macedonia and Thrace, showing potential military thrust lines.

The North Aegean-Thrace-Direction

The views of the Warsaw Pact regarding North Aegean-Thrace and the Bosporus-Dardanelles operations are inextricably intertwined for two reasons. First, even if Soviet forces successfully seized control of the Straits, Soviet naval forces would still need to transit some 600 kilometres between the Dardanelles to the open Mediterranean. Second, the easiest access to the open rolling terrain of Turkish Thrace is found on the Greek side of the Evros (Maritsa) River.

Regardless of the political overtures made by the Warsaw Pact toward Greece, the main attack on the Bosporus-Dardanelles direction is likely to swing south of Edirne across Greek territory to avoid the Turkish defences west of Edirne. One tactical axis at Kesan would turn east toward Istanbul and another south toward the Dardanelles (Gelibolu Yarimadasi).

Other elements (and most likely Bulgarian forces)[5] would drive south along the plain of the Evros River toward the city of Alexandroupolis to acquire the rolling Aegean coastline. If the Warsaw Pact engaged the Greek forces on this axis, the objective would be the city of Kavala. Additional forces from Bulgaria would probably drive southward toward Serre. This position serves as an outer defence for Thessaloniki. To move along this axis would require extensive combat by *Spetsnaz* and air mobile forces and also require air superiority to overcome the defences in and about Thessaloniki.

The responsibility for the defence of Greek Thrace and Thessaloniki rests with 'C' and 'D' Corps. Their theatre of operation is somewhat mountainous, but along the Aegean coast it is quite open for some 300 kilometres, and what geographical obstacles may exist have little more than a temporary canalising effect, given the high mobility of Warsaw Pact mechanised forces. The least tenable ground to defend is a long-drawn out strip—the corridor between the Evros River west, which has an average width of about 50 kilometres and lacks strategic depth. (East of this line, defensive responsibilities rest with the Turkish First Army, as discussed elsewhere in this chapter.) This terrain poses the threat of encirclement for 'D' Corps located at Xanthi, and isolation from the remaining Greek forces, should the attacking forces move down the Strymon River against Thessaloniki (seat of CINCSOUTH's wartime forward command post). In this scenario the tactical axis from Bulgaria would likely split at Lake Kerkinis once the difficult ten kilometres stretch from the border had been breached. One axis could move south along the floor of the Strymon River valley to Serre, where it would turn east to Drama, and then back south to Kavala to link up with the axis moving west from the Evros (Maritsa) River.

Since fortifications have been constructed on the right bank of the Strymon River and the routes through the Bertisko Mountains provide little room for off-the-road manoeuvres, the main tactical axis from Bulgaria to Thessaloniki is likely to follow the rail route south past Lake Doiranes and the city of Kilkis to the wide open plains leading directly to the Aegean. This route never narrows to less than three kilometres in width and could also be supported by an additional thrust cutting through the south-east corner of Yugoslavia at Idhomeni (providing the Warsaw Pact enjoys unopposed passage through Yugoslavia).[6] Such an operation could move into Greece along the Axios River valley. Historically this route has proved the Achilles' heel of Thessaloniki's defence.

Offensive forces attempting to seize Thessaloniki would probably reflect Moscow's decision to occupy the entire country. The route south of Thessaloniki is blocked at the edge of Western Macedonia by the fortifications of the Aliakmom Line which runs from Lake Vegorritis south-west to Veria to the Aegean coastline. There are limited points of penetration through the Aliakmon Line.[7] The line of attack would then follow the main highway from Thessaloniki south to Athens through Larisa, headquarters of the Hellenic First Army and Tactical Air Command, to the Plain of Thessaly east of Lamia to Thivai and on to Athens.

The Western Coastline

Another stretch of the Greek frontier, namely the border with Albania from the Pindus Mountains to the Ionian Sea, is dominated by parallel ridges and river valleys which follow a pronounced north-west to south-east direction. Presently this region appears to be non-threatened by any Warsaw Pact offensive, but it is notable that the recently completed coastal route bends inland by way of Ioannina, which is by no means immune from attack from the east. An attacking force moving south from Ioannina would meet little resistance from 'B' Corps forces in its march south toward Patras, an important ferry passage at the western exit of the Gulf of Corinth.

A full scale invasion of Greece probably would be structured as part of a larger operation aimed at the whole of the Eastern Mediterranean. After the capture of Athens, the next immediate objective would no doubt be the Corinth Canal. This barrier would provide the Greek forces the most readily defensible line should the offensive have to be halted to support the diversion of reserves elsewhere. The subsequent objectives in Greece would require airborne and

Spetsnaz operations and assault landing operations against Crete and selected Aegean Islands.

The Bosporus-Dardanelles Direction

Within the SWTVD the most important strategic area is the Turkish Straits. The territorial significance of this region to the Soviet Union is no different today than when the Ottomans were in power.

> . . . The Slav people, led by Russia, had been committed for a long time in wars with Turkey. The struggle for domination over the Black Sea, occupation of the Straits and freedom of the Balkan people from Turkish domination continued until the 20th century.[8]

Planning an offensive operation against the Turkish Straits must include three elements: the Bosporus, which is about 30 kilometres long with its northern entrance beginning at the Black Sea, but only about two kilometres wide; the Sea of Marmara, a broad inland sea which is 200 kilometres in length and at its widest part some 70 kilometres; and the Dardanelles (Strait of Canakkale), which are about five kilometres wide and lead for 70 winding kilometres to the Aegean Sea.[9]

NATO's grand strategic interest is in blocking the Straits to the Soviet Union's Black Sea Fleet,[10] which must divide its main forces between the Black Sea and the Mediterranean, as well as provide naval aviation coverage of the Caspian Sea.

The Bosporus and the Dardanelles are eminently suitable for mining, and much of the hydrography of the Straits favours the operation of small naval submarines. The Dardanelles are, in fact, an anti-submariner's nightmare, for a strong outflowing current of fresh water overlies a layer of salt water making acoustics badly distorted.

The chief danger to the Straits, however, comes not from direct naval assault, but from airborne, *Spetsnaz* and amphibious forces' action on either side of the narrows. Assault from the Black Sea would, in all likelihood, surge against the sandy Thracian beaches with air support from the attacking forces. These elements would then be in place to link up with the columns advancing overland from Bulgaria.

The Asiatic side is more formidable for amphibious forces because it lacks landing sites. Airborne and *Spetsnaz* operations along with helicopter support would be required if a pincer strategy was employed in the Bosporus.[11]

Although the Warsaw Pact would undoubtedly prefer to husband their resources for the Central Front, the temptation to fulfil the historic Slavic dream might be too strong to postpone until the conflict in the WTVD was successfully resolved before initiating an offensive in the Black Sea-Bosporus area. Part of their planning calculus would depend upon the attitude of Athens and the NATO resources available to support the forces in this theatre.

The first sign of an impending move on this front is likely to be a large-scale passage of troops and equipment by sea and air from the Soviet Union to Bulgaria. Perhaps as many as 34 divisions might be involved in the initial attacks. Almost certainly these would be directed along two main axes: (1) one would be a drive south along the Maritsa (Evros) River to the Aegean, thus dividing the Turkish and Greek forces; and (2) the preparation or support of a second offensive—a narrowly focused attack of some eight to ten divisions, aimed at Istanbul and the Straits.

The responsibility for defence lies with the Turkish First Army, and more specifically the 5th Corps at Corlu. This theatre of operation is far smaller and more open. The only natural asset is the way that Turkey (Europe) is hemmed in toward the east between the Black Sea and the Sea of Marmara. The border with Bulgaria is 270 kilometres long, but the frontage narrows to less than 50 kilometres on the approaches to the Bosporus. This dampens the ability of mechanised elements to maximise their offensive capabilities.

Turkey's main strategic outpost is the city of Edirne. It is likely that the offensive forces would bypass Edirne driving south to Kesan. At this juncture one axis might head toward the Dardanelles while another could drive east toward Tekirdag. A secondary axis would likely be directed at Kirklareli from the north. While the low wooded Yildiz Daglari constitutes a defensive barrier, once penetrated, the terrain to the south and west is excellent for armoured units. Furthermore, the east-west transportation network of Turkish Thrace supports a direct advance on Istanbul. There are very few natural defensive positions for the the Turkish forces to defend effectively in Turkish Thrace. The last line for the defence of Istanbul is at Catalca and runs for some 20 kilometres as the isthmus narrows and small lakes and the arms of the sea can be exploited. Unfortunately, the Black Sea coast east of Catalca provides the attackers with ample opportunities to outflank these defences with amphibious and airborne assault landings[12] supported by naval combatants and naval aviation.[13]

As noted, 'the Soviets are cognisant of both Turkish fixed defences, such as fortified areas near the Bosporus, and NATO plans for a mobile defence of the Thracian beaches.'[14] The Soviet Union is also aware that success in the defence of Turkish Thrace and Istanbul is dependent on the timely arrival of ACE Allied Mobile Force reinforcements and the involvement or non-alignment of Greece. Given the open terrain that the First Army has been given to defend, the challenge to NATO to deploy the Allied Mobile Force in timely fashion is formidable.[15]

The Eastern Anatolia Front

As discussed previously, Eastern Turkey is part of the Soviet Southern TVD, and in lectures given at the Voroshilov General Staff Academy, this part of Turkey is linked with the defence of NATO's 'oil sources against threats from the north',[16] and the 'interruptions in oil and other raw material shipments will place the economy and armed forces of West European countries in a very difficult situation'.[17] This strongly suggests that the Soviets view Turkey as both a Middle East regional power and an important NATO member making crucial contributions to the security of Western Europe.

Not only does Turkey share a common border with the Soviet Union, it also shares common borders with Iran, Iraq and Syria. All of these, as discussed in Chapter 5, are potential enemies, with the latter—Syria—being the most formidable. The area bordering on Iran, Iraq and Syria is important to Turkey's national security concerns and is accentuated by Ankara's insisting that it should be excluded from the CFE negotiations.

Even more unfortunate for Ankara, however, is the fact that most of NATO perceives Eastern Turkey as an impenetrable mountain bastion. Although the mountains and steep river valleys make going difficult at times, extensive plains and plateau would facilitate the ability of Soviet forces to seize key terrain features that restrict rapid movement.[18]

While the terrain in Eastern Turkey is very difficult and the defensive advantage lies with the Turkish forces, it is still not impossible for the Soviet Union to surmount these natural barriers. As history has shown, 'it is frequently possible for an attacking force to discover hill tracks or neglected valleys which lead around the flanks of locally strong defensive positions',[19] but 'the chief obstacle to progress has always been the winter, which descends with literally killing cold, and blankets much of the level ground with snow for about half the year' (from October to April).[20]

As we noted (in Chapter 5), in an attack against Eastern Turkey, the Soviets would be likely to employ forces from the North Caucasus and Transcaucasus Military Districts, possibly as many as 20 divisions equipped with about 4300 MBTs, of which 12 divisions are deployed in forward positions and supported by some 800 tactical aircraft. The Turkish defenders (Third Army) consist of four div-

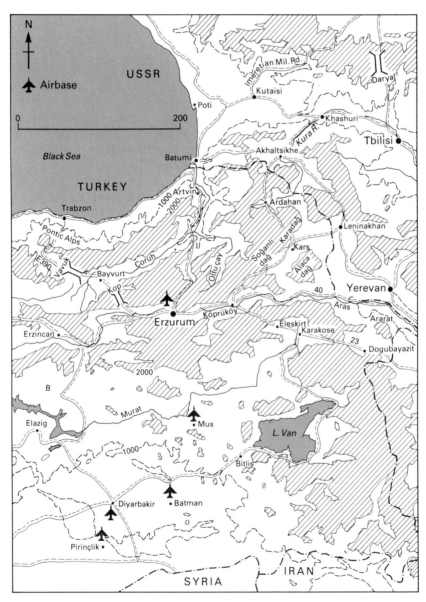

MAP 6.2. Eastern Anatolia.

isions and eight brigades with some 1,000 MBTs (M48-A1/A2s) and supported by about 300 tactical aircraft.

There are three possible scenarios that Soviet forces could undertake in Eastern Anatolia that affect Turkey and NATO, and each is amplified below.

The Coastal Approach

The coastal tactical axis from Batumi to Hopa in Turkey is some 20 kilometres which require no small effort to keep open even in peacetime. High cliffs overhang the coastal road, which is immediately on the edge of the sea and is closed periodically by natural rock slides. With little effort the Turkish forces could easily block this road or create mammoth engineering requirements in support of any attempt to move along it. At Hopa, the road turns back east to Borcka and subsequently follows the Coruh River valley to Artvin and beyond to Erzurum. This passage has numerous locations for the defenders to choke off an advancing force. The Black Sea coast is a difficult route for purely overland attack, for it is intersected by numerous valleys descending from the Kuzey Anadolu Daglari range. This topography provides the defenders with ample opportunities to withdraw back up the valleys, only to reappear subsequently and counter-attack. West of Hopa, none of these valleys afford the Soviets a practical route until Rize, about 130 kilometres from the Soviet border. At Rize a road runs 25 kilometres southwest that links the Solaki River valley and a lesser road up the Kara River valley. Both provide an easily interdicted axis over the mountain range. The coastal road to Trabzon and east to Terme (a bit before Samsan) is easily blocked, but no doubt the task of the attacker becomes easier when the ground forces are supported by elements of the Black Sea fleet and amphibious forces.

The North-Eastern Approaches

Soviet forces attacking from this direction would have two primary objectives in mind: the cities of Erzurum and Kars. In order to achieve these goals their operational bases should be just inside the Soviet borders at Akhaltsikhe and Leninakam and further south at Yerevan.

One axis of attack could be at Ardahan where the Soviets move up the Kura River valley—essentially unrestricted terrain—to Gole. As this axis leaves the Kura Valley, a significant number of choke points present themselves until the Penek River valley opens up into the Oltu River valley.

It is some 20 kilometres south-west of Oltu that two tactical axes meet, one from the north emanating from Artvin (the Coastal Approach) and the other from Ardahan. The last 60 kilometres to Erzurum is over terrain that provides several choke points, and the Soviets would here encounter the last restricted terrain—a set of interlocking fortifications about 25 kilometres north of the city. Once these barriers were cleared, the joint forces could quickly close in on Erzurum and cut the rail link east to Kars.

Erzurum serves today as a major transportation hub and the focal point for overland communication between Europe and Iran. Moreover, major concentrations of NATO and United States air bases and intelligence-gathering facilities (Diyarbakir, Batman, Mus, Pirincli) are to be found in Southern and South Eastern Anatolia, a fact which lends major strategic significance to Erzurum. Furthermore, nuclear weapons stores for Turkish-operated nuclear capable delivery vehicles and a modern NATO airfield lie nine kilometres west of the city. Behind the city, one axis leads north-west to Trabzon and is easily blocked at the Kop Pass and the Vavuk Pass in the Kuzey Anadolu range. West of Erzurum are the road junctions that lead to Erzincan (Third Army Headquarters) and Sivas and southwesterly to Elazig. The former two cities have historically been considered the 'keys' to Central Anatolia.

The city of Kars would pose a major obstacle to Soviet forces. The inland fortress is situated in a basin of generally open downland. Its chief strength rests with its outer defences—the fortifications on the steep Karadag heights just to the north, the rearward positions on the Soganli range, and the Alaca heights to the south.[21] It is only to the east that Kars is exposed to a direct advance from Leninakan in the Soviet Union.

From Kars south-west, both rail and road routes move over open ground to Sarikamis, where the terrain becomes somewhat restricted and the appearance of tree cover facilitates the possibility of close combat of armoured formations and dismounted infantry. A corresponding thrust west from Yerevan, following the Aras River valley (extremely restricted in places), and the possibility of linking with elements from Kars at Horasan, would set the stage for an attack on Erzurum. This invading force could continue to follow the Aras River valley until the river bends south outside of Pasinler. There, commanding heights have been fortified by the Turkish Third Army, making penetration highly difficult and costly for an invader bent on capturing Erzurum.

Beyond these scenarios the Soviet aircraft would also need to undertake actions against other NATO facilities in both Greece and

Turkey if their campaign in the South Eastern Region is to be overall successful.

These would include the crippling and/or destruction of the following:

NATO headquarters of LANDSOUTHEAST and 6th ATAF in Izmir.

The forward operating NATO AWACS bases in Preveza, in Greece and Konya, in Turkey. These are important facilities since the NADGE sites throughout both countries do not provide adequate and timely notice of low-level Warsaw Pact attack aircraft.

The Iskenderun naval logistical complex near Adana, Turkey, located some 40 kilometres from Syria and a fuel depot for the US Sixth Fleet. In addition, Incirlik Air Base (outside Adana), a few minutes flying time from Syria, is home base for US's F-16 (Fighting Falcon) rotational squadron from Italy. Incirlik is also a key staging area for American transport aircraft and a communications centre for South-West Asia.

Souda Bay, Crete's magnificent anchorage that is capable of accommodating most of the Sixth Fleet, and its shore facilities. Also, the associated airfield which is used by American air force and naval planes, including P-3 maritime patrol aircraft on rotation from Italy.

Irakleon Air Base (Crete) which receives KC-135 aerial tankers on rotation from the FRG and also serves as an electronic listening post for Soviet activity in the Eastern Mediterranean.

The important Gournes ELINT base some 20 kilometres east of Irakleon, which monitors the Mediterranean and the Middle East.

Finally, Akrotiri and Dekelia, Cyprus which are important SINGINT installations and air bases for the United Kingdom. A detachment of F4 PHANTOM and TORNADO strategic aircraft are stationed here.

Effective deployment of Greek and Turkish forces would be constrained by weaknesses in their communications and electronic warfare (C^3I) capabilities.[22] The Soviet Union and its allies have an advantage in reliable, secure tactical communications and have few fears of efforts by NATO forces to jam their communications.

On the ground they have an advantage in armoured vehicles, antiarmour assets, artillery, attack helicopters and ammunition stocks. The Soviet Union's ability to concentrate its forces against either Greece or Turkey dramatically increases ACE's difficulties and ability to cope with the threat. A more basic problem is that Greek and Turkish aircraft on ground attack missions might simply fail to survive or might be unable to operate. Present aircraft are generally not equipped with very modern electronic and infra-red countermeasures. Against attacking forces that are concentrated, as they would be on the main attack axes, close air support would most likely experience high loss rates, unless countermeasures could be effected against enemy radar aid air defence systems. Ultimately, NATO's capacity to provide air support for the ground forces would depend upon denying the enemy air superiority and keeping its air bases open (discussed below). Even if NATO air forces in the South Eastern Region possessed air superiority and were not deficient in munitions, communications, electronic countermeasures and secure bases, it is highly unlikely that they could compensate fully for the Soviet Union's theatre-wide advantage in ground combat potential.[23]

NATO's conventional countermeasure to an attacker's armoured offensive in Greece and Turkey is the commitment of reinforcements from outside the region. Proposed reinforcement planning suggests that ACE will be able to exert only a minimal influence in the course of the conflict, but psychologically it would greatly boost the morale of Greek and Turkish personnel. At present, NATO's Rapid Reinforcement Plan proposes that ACE Mobile Force would arrive in Greece and Turkey soon after hostilities broke out (once committed) and would subsequently be followed by elements of the 82nd Airborne Division and a Marine Amphibious Brigade. Note that these elements in terms of combat power are like infantry units and do not supplement the deficiency of Greek and Turkish forces in armour. Furthermore, it is the author's understanding that elements of both the 82nd Airborne Division and the Marine Amphibious Brigade are designated for specific sectors of the conflict, whereas the Soviet forces enjoy a much higher degree of flexibility in the allocation of its forces and how it engages the enemy.

The Campaign at Sea

S. G. Gorshkov, the architect of the modern Soviet Navy, stressed that naval forces must enter the Mediterranean to meet and defeat STRIKEFORSOUTH and American ballistic missile submarines. He argued that this is a continuation of the navy's historical role:

> As is seen, historically, it has turned out that when a threat arises of enemy encroachment on the territory of from the south-west, the Russian Navy has moved into the Mediterranean Sea where it has successfully executed major strategic missions in defending the country's borders from aggression.[24]

Most of the historical naval campaigns that Gorshkov describes above involved interdicting Turkey's line of communication. In subsequent discussions he suggests that cutting NATO's sea lines of communications is essential to the success of the Warsaw Pact land operations against Allied Command Europe.[25] Thus, from Gorshkov's perspective, a Soviet victory in the South Eastern Region would require destroying or crippling STRIKEFORSOUTH and cutting the Mediterranean's LOCs, both air and sea, thereby hindering NATO's ability to reinforce and retain operational flexibility.

A corollary to controlling the Mediterranean lines of communication is denying their use to the Fifth Escadra. This would prevent Moscow's access to potential allies in Africa and the Middle East and would sever the Soviet Union's principal peacetime route to the Indian Ocean. Sea denial begins forward in the Black Sea and the Turkish Straits and continues through the successive Aegean islands.

It is conceivable that Soviet naval units would attempt to interdict NATO's SLOCs by mining, although this would be a very costly enterprise.[26] The sea lines of communications for both Greece and Turkey are possibly vulnerable because of the small number of major ports. On the Greek mainland three exist (Piraeus, Thessaloniki, Volos), and on Turkey's Mediterranean coastline there are only four (Izmir, Mersin, Iskenderun, Antalya);[27] all are susceptible not only to air attacks but to mining.

Rather than mine these ports the Soviet Union could conceivably mine deep-water choke points such as the Peloponesos-Kithira-Crete-Karpathos line and the Mykonos-Ikaria-Samos line. Mining either of these two chains would probably require more mines than mining all the ports in both Greece and Turkey.[28] Unfortunately, both the Greek and Turkish navies are lacking in equipment to undertake effective mine-clearing operations.

A much larger threat to the reinforcement and resupply of NATO forces are Soviet submarines. Estimates of the wartime submarine threat in the Mediterranean range from ten to as many as 18, all armed with surface-to-surface missiles (SS-N-12s) and with both conventional and nuclear torpedoes. To counter this Soviet effort, STRIKEFORSOUTH would be required to launch anti-submarine warfare platforms (escort vessels, helicopters, and long-range maritime patrol aircraft) in order to protect shipping.

Just as Soviet submarines can utilise the Mediterranean choke points to increase their probability of interdicting NATO reinforcement and supply shipping or the carrier battle groups,[29] NATO's anti-submarine warfare forces can also utilise these same choke points to increase their probability of encountering Soviet submarines or discouraging them from patrolling there. The choke points would seem to be ideal for employing some of the 14 new TYPE-209 diesel submarines that Greece and Turkey now have in their arsenals.

There is no doubt that the Fifth Escadra has as its highest priority target the NATO aircraft carriers. Survival of these is paramount to the battle of the Mediterranean. If they were able to survive the initial onslaught of hostilities we might surmise that the SOV-MEDRON had depleted its munitions (SSMs), thereby allowing STRIKEFORSOUTH to destroy or cripple this Soviet force with relative ease. The submarine risk would remain and is a long-term threat requiring continuous anti-submarine warfare operations on the part of STRIKEFORSOUTH.

Another formidable challenge to STRIKEFORSOUTH is Soviet naval and air aviation from the Black Sea Fleet and elsewhere. BACKFIRES, BADGERS and BLINDERS have the capabilities to acquire ship targets on radar and to launch their stand-off missiles at a range of about 160 nautical miles. This is beyond the range of NATO shipboard surface-to-air missiles. If the AEGIS fire control system is available, many of these incoming missiles would be destroyed although some would no doubt reach their targets. All of these Soviet aircraft have the capability to fly from their bases from as far north as the Baltic Fleet at Kaliningrad, attack STRIKEFOR-SOUTH, and return without refuelling. Because of the long range of Soviet aircraft, an attack against a carrier in the Eastern Mediter-ranean could come from almost any direction, but fragmentary infor-mation from NADGE radar (the British radar on Cyprus and NATO Airborne Early Warning Aircraft [AWACs]) could provide STRIKE-FORSOUTH with valuable clues about incoming Warsaw Pact air-craft. There are, however, enough gaps in radar coverage in the area to raise the possibility of an attack from various fronts. Of course early warning aircraft (E-2Cs) from the carriers and AWACs would assist fighters from the aircraft carriers and provide air cover far enough out to impose heavy losses on the Soviet bombers, but the threat of air defence saturation remains. Unfortunately, a single carrier group cannot sustain, in the author's opinion, an adequate airborne early warning and combat patrol posture. Ultimately, the effectiveness of the Soviet aircraft will depend on penetrating not only land-based air defences, but those of the carrier group.

While NATO has a sea control problem in the eastern Mediter-ranean, the Soviet Union likewise has one in the Black Sea. As Gorshkov reminds us, control of the Black Sea helps protect the Soviet Union. The Warsaw Pact would not be dependent on the Black Sea SLOCs unless Romania denied transit privileges to them. Soviet capabilities to ferry cargoes to Bulgaria and, above all, to land amphibious forces on Turkish soil, give it valuable flexibility. The ferry line to Varna and Burgas in Bulgaria relieves some of the pressure on rail lines, whose efficient operations are dependent on Romanian co-operation. The possibility of amphibious assaults has the beneficial effect of tying down a substantial portion of the defend-ing Turkish First and Second Armies.

NATO's sea denial campaign in the Black Sea, as well as in the Aegean, includes attack aircraft armed with anti-ship missiles (HARPOON), shore-based long-range anti-ship missiles (TOMA-HAWK), TYPE-209 diesel submarines and high speed patrol craft armed with anti-ship missiles. Both the Greek and Turkish navies are well-adapted to fight in the Aegean. A serious air threat from NATO aircraft would also require the Soviets to keep MiG-31 (FOX-HOUNDS) orbiting over the Fifth Escadra for its protection or choose to keep it in port. Ultimately, all the above combinations make Soviet naval operations in the Mediterranean—or for that matter the Black Sea—very risky.

The Campaign in the Air

The Warsaw Pact employment of air power places emphasis on independent air operations, in particular the employment of air power during the conventional phase of the conflict in order to reduce NATO's theatre nuclear capabilities and disrupt conventional defences. The recent modernisation and expansion of the Soviet Union's medium-range bomber (BACKFIRES, BADGERS, etc.) and fighter-bomber fleets (FLOGGERS, FULCRUMS etc.) enhances this capability.

The integrity of the South Eastern Region's air defence systems is critical to the integrity of the whole of NATO's air defence capabilities. Any weaknesses in air defence puts the ground forces at risk, their supplies and munitions, storage facilities, air and sea ports of disembarkation, reinforcement and resupply convoys, air bases and STRIKEFORSOUTH.

No doubt the attacker's principal aim would be to close down NATO air installations, either by widely distributed selective targeting or a sequence of highly concentrated attacks. They cannot, however, be effective in achieving these ends by spreading their efforts across the entire region, nor would they be able to achieve these ends by conducting a rolling campaign, concentrating on Greece one day, on Turkey the second day, a third country the third day and then back to Greece (the first country) again. By mobilising military and civilian resources, NATO should generally be able to repair a base in 18 hours without rapid runway repair kits and interference from delayed action bombs, runway cratering bombs, mines, or persistent chemicals.

Selective targeting by Soviet aircraft could achieve important results: temporarily closing down most of the long-range attack aircraft bases, most ground attack bases, and most interceptor installations.

The success of these sorties would be dependent on the existing air defence systems and the presence of NATO AWACs. In sharp contrast to the Central Front, this area has no semblance of an air defence barrier. The NIKE-HERCULES air defence system is chiefly deployed in Greece and Turkey.[30] Its weaknesses are the ease by which it can be underflown, outflown and jammed. By selectively choosing its targets in Greece and Turkey, Soviet attack bombers, in one-day's sorties, might close less than 40 per cent of the 33 NATO bases in this area. This estimate would be considerably lower if NATO practised effective dispersal of its aircraft.

The burden of hindering or preventing penetration of Greece and Turkey by the attacker's aviation will rest with the NATO interceptor force, which would most likely be launched after detection by radar or AWACs of incoming aircraft. Unfortunately, air command, control and communications (C^3) networks are less than effective in targeting. The weakness in the overall system is the number of NADGE fixed ground radar sites that are not only vulnerable to physical attack and jamming but are susceptible to low-level penetration. Many of these sites, as well as airbases, are located in forward positions very close to the lines of intercept that require defending either by combat air patrols or ground-based air defence. Certainly an attacker, under the above circumstances, would seek to destroy selective command and control sites in order to establish corridors of penetration to permit attacks on selective targets, shipping in the Mediterranean, and interdiction of air lines of communications (ALOCs) by intercepting strategic lift aircraft in flights. This would be done by FLOGGERS (MiG-23s), FULCRUMS (MiG-29s) and FOXHOUNDS (MiG-31s) operating from forward bases in the SWTVD region, plus the possible use of Libyan bases.[31]

All these potentially troublesome threats are manageable for NATO as long as Greek and Turkish air defences remain intact and interceptor forces[32] are strengthened, especially in Eastern Turkey. In addition, the acquisition of modern air-to-air missiles (AIM-9Ls, MLRS, AMRAAMs) would mitigate NATO's qualitative disadvantages.

What are the prospects for reducing the air threat by attacking Warsaw Pact bases? Overall, NATO could expect to face FOXHOUND and other fighter aircraft and suffer heavy losses if deep penetration was undertaken as far as Somlensk and Vinnitsa Air Army bases. The only aircraft that NATO has in this area capable of penetrating that far are F-111s that would be temporarily deployed at Incirlik. There are, however, some potentially vulnerable targets close to the NATO's south-eastern borders: the Naval Aviation bombers in the Crimea, forward deployed fighters and close air support forces consisting of FROGFOOTS (SU-25s) and attack helicopters. These elements could become primary targets for the F-111s and F-16s from Merzifon[33] whose success rate would depend on knowing when and where the Soviet aircraft are exposed, and responding effectively with required intelligence to catch them on the ground, while surviving the air defences that they are likely to encounter.

Conclusions

Assessing the outcomes of the scenarios and campaigns described in this chapter is a great challenge because the likelihood that the Warsaw Pact would define a war outcome in this region the same way that NATO or the United States would view it is remote. For example, the successful outcome of an offensive operation into Thrace might conceivably be viewed by the Soviets as a very successful outcome in the SWTVD. In contrast, NATO would have to consider the loss of the Straits as a 'phase', but an important one surely, of a larger and longer conflict spanning the breadth of the European theatre—a protracted conflict and an uncertain outcome. Other outcomes, such as a concerted attack on Greece to isolate Turkey from the Alliance, could conceivably have, in the long-term, far greater adverse consequences for NATO and ACE than the loss of the Straits.

In addressing likely outcomes in this region and how they might be defined and analysed, it is important to realise that the outcome of a conflict between NATO and the Warsaw Pact cannot be assessed in terms of a 'zero-sum' game, and the geographical configuration of the area virtually precludes symmetry in NATO and Soviet views of how 'outcomes' may be defined.[34]

In attempting to influence the outcome of a campaign, Soviet and NATO strategies are quite the opposite. While the Soviet concept of operations is geared to reinforcing success where the adversary's forces have been defeated by concentrating numerically superior capabilities, NATO's concept of operation is, of necessity, geared to preventing failure across its front lines by allocating its limited assets. At the level of ACE, this asymmetry may have dire results for NATO as it attempts to keep a balance in the allocation of these assets between all sectors of the Alliance.

Some defence experts maintain that the successful defence of the South Eastern Flank is critical to the successful defence of the Central Front. Yet, while recognising the contribution that Greece and Turkey make in a contingency by 'tying-down' Soviet forces that might otherwise be diverted to the WTVD, it is not axiomatic that defeat of Greece and Turkey would necessarily lead to an inescapable NATO defeat in the Central Region or to the collapse of the Alliance. Certainly, the loss of Greece and Turkey and part of the Mediterranean would be a political disaster for the Alliance and be seen by the Soviets as a major shift in the overall balance in the conflict. The relative ability of the two alliances to 'tie-down' opposing forces in this area which might otherwise have been deployed elsewhere in Europe, and the resulting advantage achieved, is one of the keys to assessing the balance of forces in the South Eastern Region and its implications for deterrence, crisis-management, and defence.[35] The South Eastern Region provides unique opportunities for NATO for potentially 'counteroffensive' actions against the Soviet Union and its allies' capability in a possible East–West confrontation.

CHAPTER 7

Conflict Between Two Allies

THE PREVIOUS discussion centred, in some detail, on a possible confrontation between NATO forces and the Warsaw Pact in the South Eastern Flank. There is, however, another possible conflict scenario in this area headlining those ancient adversaries Greece and Turkey. As has been noted elsewhere in this volume, there are several outstanding issues that divide the two NATO allies; the Alliance thread linking these two neighbours in a common defence could unravel quickly. In the recent past there have been several events that had the potential of initiating such a confrontation. In March 1984, during Turkish exercises, a Turkish destroyer fired upon a Greek destroyer in the Aegean Sea. In 1985, there were shooting incidents on the Thracian border between ground forces of the two countries. Also in 1985, Greek and Turkish aircraft staged respective interceptions because of alleged air space violations. In June 1986, a Turkish warship fired warning shots near a Greek Cypriot cruise ship east of Rhodes.[1]

The most serious crisis between Athens and Ankara occurred in March of 1987 over oil exploration rights in the north-eastern Aegean off the island of Thassos (near the Gulf of Saros). Greece granted the North Aegean Petroleum Company (NAPA) a concession which required it to drill in international waters off Thassos before 1 April 1987 or forfeit its rights in the area. If Turkey permitted these explorations to take place, her position on the highly volatile Continental Shelf issue would have been substantially weakened. Both Greek and Turkish forces were placed on alert, and for a short period the Papandreou government suspended operations at Nea Makri (intelligence station near Athens) and appealed to Bulgaria for support. Ultimately, both nations exhibited restraint. Athens assured Ankara that it had not intended that NAPA should drill for oil in international waters, and Ankara responded by not sending the exploration vessel *Sismik I*, with its military escort into the disputed area. Who blinked first? Who cares?[2] This incident demonstrates how fragile are the relations between these two NATO allies and how ever-present are the sources of friction that divide them. Against such a background, effective military cooperation between Athens and Ankara can scarcely be assumed should conflict with an adversary arise. Given a similar future unpleasantness, 'cooler heads' of state in both capitals might not be available to legislate such a reasonable outcome, thereby opening a channel for further confrontation.

If a war between Athens and Ankara were to occur, it would likely be fought primarily near their common land and sea borders, specifically along the Maritsa (Evros) River in Thrace and in the vicinity of the islands in the Eastern Aegean. The major objective for Athens would be to maintain its current position, that is to defend its territory including the Eastern Aegean islands. On the other hand, if Ankara chose to challenge Greek claims and change the Aegean *status quo*, Turkey would probably resort to military means in the Aegean and in Thrace. Greece would then need to be capable enough to forestall a Turkish offensive, but it need not be powerful enough to wrest Turkish Thrace or the Anatolian coast from Ankara's control.[3] If history is any indicator, there would undoubtedly be political and military leaders in Athens who would wish to resurrect the *Megali Idea* of annexing territories once inhabited by Greeks in Asia Minor (Istanbul and in and about Izmir). If such a view prevailed, Greek forces would most likely attempt to drive into Turkish Thrace and, if possible, onward to Istanbul.[4]

In assessing the relative quantitative and qualitative strengths and weaknesses of each military force, it would appear that at the present time rough strategic parity exists between Greece and Turkey. Whatever form Greek–Turkish fighting presented, a conflict involving more than small-scale skirmishes would almost certainly be short and costly on both sides. The duration of the strife would depend largely on fuel and ammunition supplies on hand at the start of hostilities. Both sides are known to have inadequate stores of ammunition, fuel, spare parts, air-to-air and surface-to-surface missiles, and weapons reserves. Thus, without external resupply, Greece and Turkey would have difficulty sustaining intensive combat for more than several weeks. Hostilities could last substantially longer than if the two sides limited the scope of fighting to an air war of attrition, hit-and-run operations, and/or border skirmishes.

The Cyprus Conflict

On Cyprus there is no doubt that the Turkish Army's XI Corps and the Turkish Cypriot forces clearly have the upper hand. They outnumber the Greek and Greek Cypriot forces by a margin of about 2 to 1;[5] they have the only viable tank force on the island (mostly M48-A5s); and given the proximity of the island to the Turkish mainland, they have relatively greater resupply and reinforcement capabilities and a superior regional air support capability. The Greek Cypriot National Guard, supported by Greek forces, has strengths as a defensive force, but little offensive power due to their lack of armour and a tactical air force. The Greek Cypriot National Guard's defensive capabilities are its potential to mobilise its 40,000 man reserve force, recent purchases of multiple rocket launchers and 105mm howitzers from Yugoslavia, Soviet SA-7 shoulder-fired surface-to-surface missiles, armoured reconnaissance vehicles from Brazil and recent purchases of armoured equipment from France.[6]

TABLE 7.1. *Greek and Turkish Forces in Cyprus*

	Greek Greek Cypriot	Turkish/ Turkish Cypriot
Manpower	16,950*	28,000
Tanks	24	275
Artillery/Mortars	540	450
Air Defence Guns	100	84
Armoured Personnel Carriers	129	200

Note: *This figure includes some 3,950 personnel from the Greek armed forces.
Source: *The Military Balance, 1989–1990* (London: The International Institute for Strategic Studies (Published Brassey's (UK)) 1989), pp. 67, 78, 85.

In addition to tanks and the support of tactical aircraft based in Turkey, the Turkish Cypriot forces major advantage is the preponderance of manpower and the combat readiness (close to full strength) of both the units of the XI Corps and the Turkish Cypriot forces. On balance, the Turks could most probably dominate their opponents in an island clash, particularly if they launched offensive operations before the Greek Cypriots had time to mobilise their reserves and if air superiority was maintained. If restricted to relatively low-level actions along the Green Line separating Greek and Turkish forces, the conflict might then develop into an artillery/mortar duel with minor infantry thrusts across the Green Line. A larger confrontation, involving major pushes along the Green Line, could quickly escalate into a broader war involving both air and naval assets in the Aegean Sea and ground and air operations in Thrace.

Thrace

If Turkey attacked Greek positions in Thrace its objectives, in addition to attempting to cross the Maritza (Evros) River and seize territory,[7] would be to tie down the Greek forces and prevent Athens from reinforcing the Aegean Islands or launching a counteroffensive to seize territory in Turkish Thrace. Greece's primary objective would be to stop a Turkish offensive, while extracting as high a mortal toll as possible.

TABLE 7.2. *Greek and Turkish Ground Forces Available for Combat in Thrace**

	Greece	Turkey
Corps/Army Involved	'C' & 'D' Corps	1st Army
Personnel	80,000	210,000
Tanks	765	1,030
Artillery	410	865

Note: *This data is an approximation of the number of forces and equipment deployed in Thrace.

Source: *The Military Balance, 1989–1990* (London: The International Institute for Strategic Studies, (Published Brassey's (UK)) 1989).

No doubt Turkey could bring numerically superior ground forces to bear in Thrace, but to do so they would need to redeploy forces currently located near the borders with the Soviet Union, Iran, Iraq, and Syria. The Greeks, who would rely on well-prepared defensive positions and offensive operations by the Greek Air Force, could probably make the price too costly.

A key tactical advantage for the Greek forces lies in the nature of the terrain they would be defending. The geography in North-Eastern Greece provides manoeuvre room for mechanised warfare, but the attackers would first have to traverse the Maritza River where the Greeks can be expected to mount their major defence. West of the Maritza, near the city of Soufli and west to Komotini, mountain ranges dominate with some narrow plains, making feasible a defence in depth by the Greek forces, on high ground with the river to their front.

The Turkish First Army, especially the 5th Corps at Corlu, would be the primary forces engaging Greece's 'D' Corps, headquarters at Xanthi and backed up by 'C' Corps in Thessaloniki. These corps are the best trained and equipped with upgraded M48-A5 tanks, 105mm guns and improved fire-control systems. The Greek forces are well-placed defensively and have sheltered stockpiles of supplies and munitions in this region. The Turkish forces, in contrast, would face

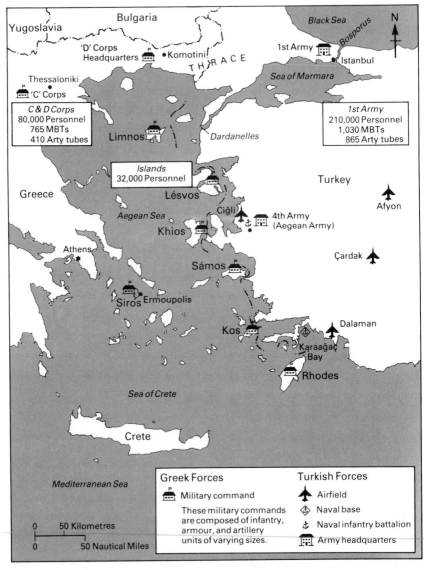

MAP 7.1. Greek and Turkish Forces in the Aegean Area.

a long supply trail extending back across the Maritza River into rear echelon depots.[8]

Similarly, if the Greek forces were to defend successfully and then attempt a border crossing, they would face serious difficulties trying to wrest territory from the larger Turkish forces, who also have well-prepared defensive positions. Given the array of forces, the geography, and the posture of each side, fighting in Thrace would most likely develop into a bloody stalemate with heavy losses on both sides.

The Aegean Front

Turkey would be at a decided disadvantage here and would find it quite difficult to invade one of the six well-defended and armed major islands (Lemnos, Lesbos, Chios, Samos, Kos, Rhodes). The Greek forces would be operating from prepared defensive positions on familiar terrain. In addition, ground control intercept radar on the islands would provide the defenders at least limited warnings of likely targets for Turkish air strikes.[9] Furthermore, Turkey would require several days to marshal an amphibious task force, allowing the Greek forces time to detect these preparations and take defensive measures on the islands. The Greek Air Force would most certainly try to disrupt the Turkish invasion force and inflict serious casualties. Given these conditions, it would appear that the Greek forces might foil a Turkish invasion against one of the major Aegean islands.

TABLE 7.3. *Greek and Turkish Air Forces*

	Greece	Turkey
Combat aircraft	261	385
Fighters	76	224
Fighter-bombers/attack	185	161
Reconnaissance aircraft	34	28
Transport aircraft	75	84

Source: *The Military Balance, 1989–1990* (London: The International Institute for Strategic Studies, (Published Brassey's (UK)), 1989), pp 66, 78–79.

If, however, the Turkish military met with success Greece, would require a substantial force to retake an island. This undertaking might prove difficult, if not impossible, since Greece does not have the ships or aircraft necessary to carry out such counter-attacks on a large scale. Add to this the geographic proximity of the islands to the Turkish coast and the Greek outlook appears bleak.

If operations in the Aegean were confined to aerial combat, the advantage would of course go to the country that was able to achieve air superiority. Both Greece and Turkey have added MIRAGE 2000s and F-16s to their inventories which suggests some parity between the two forces on an equipment level. For the Greek Air Force to establish supremacy over the Aegean islands' air space, it would be crucial that they operate from Aegean airfields, since bases on the Greek mainland would cut down the time spent in combat patrols over the region. If, on the other hand, the Turkish Air Force achieved superiority, they could patrol the Aegean almost at will. Greek Air Force F-4s have all-weather capability and possess both MAVERICK air-to-ground missiles and SIDEWINDER air-to-air missiles.[10] While the Turkish aircraft are overall a bit older and do not completely possess all-weather capability, the Turks do have more aircraft and would be operating closer to their bases and could thus spend more time over target.

Turkey might also be able to tip the balance if they could entice the Greeks to operate over mainland Turkey where the Turkish advantages are most pronounced. If aerial combat escalated into both naval and ground operations, the Greeks' first priority would be to reinforce their island garrisons and keep open their sea lines of communication. In order to prevent this eventuality, Turkey would counter with air and naval attacks to disrupt Greek supply lines from the mainland. If the Turkish Air Force dominated the air war, the Turkish General Staff might be tempted to try an assault on one of the Greek islands in order to buttress Ankara's position in any negotiations following the fighting.

TABLE 7.4. *Greek and Turkish Naval Forces*

	Greece	Turkey
Destroyers and frigates	21	22
Submarines*	10	15
Mine warfare ships/crafts	16	39
Patrol craft	37	46
Amphibious ships	13	18
Maritime patrol aircraft	12	22
Helicopters	17	9

Note: *Greece posseses eight diesel TYPE 209/1100s; Turkey's inventory includes six diesel TYPE 209/1200 submarines.

Source: *The Military Balance: 1989–1990* (London: The International Institute for Strategic Studies, (Published Brassey's (UK)) 1989), pp. 65–67, 76–78.

Neither country enjoys an edge in naval capability although the Greek Navy may possess somewhat newer ships. Both submarine fleets represent the élite of their navies, each possessing a preponderance of the new German diesel TYPE-209s. However, both navies have only limited anti-submarine capabilities, rendering each fleet vulnerable to attack.

The Greek Navy is at a geographical disadvantage. It would need several days at least to assemble a task force and get it underway, and it would take a minimum of two days sailing time to reach the islands in the Aegean. Although Turkey would also require time to marshal a task force, it would be operating closer to home from the outset and would be able to move out to confront the Greek task force before it reached its destination. While Greek ships are armed with SSMs, including the EXOCET (a formidable but increasingly outdated weapon), Turkish patrol boats are equipped with HARPOON surface-to-surface missiles, which have a somewhat longer range than the Greek SSMs.

Alliance military coordination in the Aegean, particularly in air defence, has been almost non-existent since the 1974 Cyprus invasion, and NATO's greatest challenge in the south-eastern area will continue to be seemingly intractable hostility between Greece and Turkey. As in all confrontations, in any locale and at all times, the outcome is dependent on which combatant has the more effective forces and equipment and utilises these elements most efficiently. In this case, whatever the ensuing confrontation, it would assuredly prove costly and deadly to both parties and in the end permanently fissure the South Eastern Flank of the Alliance.

CHAPTER 8

Conventional Arms: Negotiations, Modernisation and Defence Industrial Development

IN MARCH 1989 the 23 countries that make up NATO and the Warsaw Treaty Organisation (WTO) launched a new arms control forum in Vienna on reducing conventional forces in Europe, known as the CFE talks.[1] In the official mandate for these discussions, both sides agreed that the agenda would only cover their ground and air forces based on European territory, in the region stretching from the Atlantic to the Urals (ATTU region).[2] The area covered by the ATTU talks in the East includes all of Eastern Europe, plus the Soviet military districts that lie west of the Urals, the Ural River and the Caspian Sea.[3] In the West, the ATTU region includes all the territory of NATO countries in Europe, plus Iceland and most of Turkey excluding the territory of Turkey south and east of the following line: 'the point of intersection of the border with the 39th parallel, Muradiye, Patnos, Karayazi, Tekman, Kemaliye, Feke, Ceyhan, Dogankent, Gozne, and thence to the sea'.[4] Within the corresponding ATTU proposals, both NATO and the WTO have subdivided this area into zones, with corresponding alliance-wide limits for each of the conventional forces in each zone (see Fig. 8.1).

The official objectives of the CFE talks, as agreed by both sides, are:

'The establishment of a stable and secure balance of conventional forces . . . at lower levels;
'the elimination of disparities prejudiced to stability and security; and
'the elimination, as a matter of priority, of the capability for launching a surprise attack and for initialing large-scale offensive action.'[5]

In aiming for these objectives, the CFE mandate reflects a long-standing NATO view that Warsaw Pact superiority in numbers of

Zones Proposed by the WTO	Zones Proposed by NATO

Zones Proposed by the WTO

Extended Central Zone (Zone 1)
NATO: Belgium, Denmark, FRG, France,
  Luxembourg, Netherlands, UK
WTO: Czechoslovakia, GDR, Hungary,
  Poland, Baltic, Byelorussia, Carpathia,
  Kiev MDs

Rear Area (Zone 4)
NATO: *Iceland*, Portugal, Spain
WTO: *Southern Leningrad*, Moscow,
  Ural, Volga MDs

Northern + Southern Flanks
(Zones 2 + 3)
NATO: *Italy*, Norway, Greece Turkey
WTO: Bulgaria, Romania, Northern
  Leningrad, Odessa, North & Trans-
  Caucasus MDs

Zones Proposed by NATO

Intermediate Zone (Zone 2)
NATO: Belgium, Denmark, FRG, France,
  Italy, Luxembourg, Netherlands, UK
WTO: Czechoslovakia, GDR, Hungary,
  Pol, Baltic, Byelorussia, Carpathia
  MDs

Rest of Zone 3
NATO: Portugal, Spain
WTO: Moscow, Volga, Ural MDs

Rest of ATTU

NATO: *Iceland*, Norway, Greece, Turkey
WTO: Bulgaria, Romania, Leningrad,
  Kiev, Odessa, North & Trans-Caucasus
  MDs

Note: Countries in italics indicates points of difference between WTO and NATO proposals.

FIG. 8.1. ATTU Zone Proposals.

ground forces—particularly in armoured divisions—poses the greatest risk of war in Europe and the greatest risk of a surprise attack. As noted elsewhere, in terms of force quantity, quality and structure, the Warsaw Pact and most especially the Soviet Union has for 20 years made every effort to enhance its ability to conduct strategic operations and to sustain them at a conventional level as long as possible. The steady increase in firepower, mobility, flexibility, air attack potential and logistic sustainability has created an offensive potential which cannot be regarded as 'not threatening'—whatever might be said by way of qualifying the meaning of force ratios, or about the diminishing probability of deliberate aggresion. NATO's overall security objective has been to prevent any kind of war in Europe effectively and reliably.[6] NATO, in its initial proposals, held that tanks, artillery, and armoured troop carriers (ATC), in terms of mobility and firepower, are the elements most relevant to surprise attack and large scale offensive actions. In NATO's perspective, numerical superiority in these systems remained the key element of WTO's invasion capability and the 'substantial disparity in the numbers of these systems . . . most threatens stability in Europe'. Since this proposal was made, both sides have also agreed to include, as part of the CFE negotiations, discussions limiting aircraft, helicopters, personnel, and specifically Soviet and American forces stationed in the territory of foreign states in Central Europe to a common ceiling of 195,000. The United States may also station

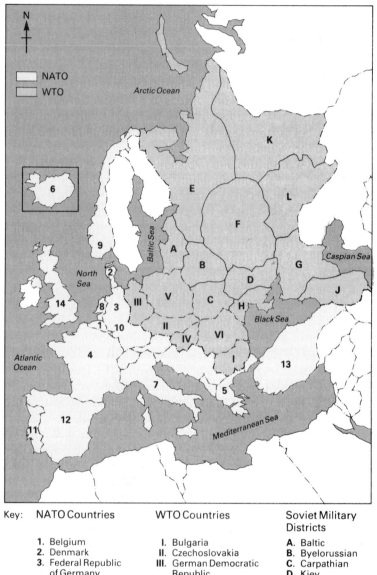

Key:

NATO Countries	WTO Countries	Soviet Military Districts
1. Belgium	**I.** Bulgaria	**A.** Baltic
2. Denmark	**II.** Czechoslovakia	**B.** Byelorussian
3. Federal Republic of Germany	**III.** German Democratic Republic	**C.** Carpathian
4. France	**IV.** Hungary	**D.** Kiev
5. Greece	**V.** Poland	**E.** Leningrad
6. Iceland	**VI.** Romania	**F.** Moscow
7. Italy		**G.** North Caucasus
8. Netherlands		**H.** Odessa
9. Norway		**J.** Trans-Caucasus
10. Luxembourg		**K.** Ural
11. Portugal		**L.** Volga
12. Spain		
13. Turkey		
14. United Kingdom		

Map 8.1. The Atlantic to the Urals (ATTU) Region, NATO and WTO Areas.

another 30,000 in the peripheral areas of Europe (e.g. Greece, Turkey, Italy, Spain).[7]

In seeking 'a stable and secure balance . . . at lower levels', and 'the elimination of the capability . . . for large scale offensive actions', the official mandate invites further cuts on both sides; and it opens the door to cuts in air forces with the potential for long-range offensive action.[8] These passages in the mandate suggest that the CFE talks could eventually lead to truly deep cuts in the conventional forces of both sides, and to stabilising defence-oriented restructuring of the forces that remain.[9]

In a curious role reversal, and for different reasons on each side, the military leaders of the two alliances have avoided discussing the implications of the 'military balance' from a military point of view; and political leaders have avoided discussing, except in general terms, the relationship between the relative size of military forces, their character and capabilities, the intentions with which they are maintained, and the situation in which they might be used. As a result, it appears as though the political and military concerned with conventional forces all agree that maintaining equal number of forces of various types in Europe is a political and military recipe for stability, security and peace.

This convenient fiction rests on the centuries-old notion that in any given area, an equal number of military forces of any kind, between potential adversaries, is likely to provide the greatest stability in terms of crises. This simplistic assumption permeates the CFE talks. Additionally, another basic view that affects these East–West talks is that the 'balance' of conventional forces is not precarious, because the risk of conventional war is extremely low; and that far from requiring closely equal numbers, stability will probably endure through fairly substantial quantitative changes in forces favouring one side or the other, over a wide range of force ratios. If this is correct, it means that the CFE discussions concern political issues as much as or more than military ones. This makes a 'political' approach to cuts appropriate, even though it may seem far-fetched on strictly military grounds. Indeed, it supports Michael Moodie's elegant comment that 'conventional arms control is a political transaction conducted with military currency'.[10]

It is widely assumed that the political will is available for a conventional forces reduction treaty, and that this could be agreed shortly. To date the negotiations have made rapid progress and an accord will most likely create parity in all the key elements of offensive military power. Specifically, NATO suggests that overall parity should be fixed at up to 15 per cent below its own current level, with the exception of manpower which embraces the same principle, but applies only to the United States and the Soviet Union and at a level of 10 per cent.[11] The WTO, on the other hand, has argued for much lower manpower levels, involving all states. It is agreed that these should be limited to the total holdings of individual countries, to holdings stationed in other countries, and to holdings in the several zones.[12] Both sides are likely to accept much deeper manpower cuts in future negotiations.

The CFE discussions have brought forth disagreements among NATO members. This is most evident and troublesome in the South Eastern Flank between Greece and Turkey. Greece historically, as discussed in earlier chapters, mistrusts her NATO ally Turkey. This colours Athens' interpretations of most NATO-CFE proposals and especially those that affect levels of force structure. On the other hand, Ankara's misgivings are more politically motivated focusing on the effect that the CFE discussions will have on Turkish foreign and defence policies, especially Ankara's links to Europe and the EEC.[13]

In considering the effect that the CFE discussions will have on both Greece and Turkey, recall that in Chapter 5 obvious discrepancies of force structures favouring the Warsaw Pact exist. The CFE negotiations and discussions follow the zonal proposals as presented by both sides (Fig. 8.1). Although it is difficult to extract the exact cuts by NATO and WTO in this region, some specific information is available on the South Eastern Flank area that is worth examining. Both Tables 8.1 and 8.2 suggest that NATO and WTO are fairly close in their proposals on levels of MBTs and aircraft allowed in this sector. The WTO will be most affected by fairly substantial asymmetrical cuts.

In the case of Greece and Turkey, the NATO proposal anticipates MBT cuts of about 1,500 while at the same time Warsaw Pact MBTs need to be cut by some 5,500. The WTO proposal requires that Greece and Turkey cut their main battle tanks by some 2,400 and the Warsaw Pact by some 8,000.[14] The cuts in MBTs suggested by WTO may be motivated by the need to lessen their logistical burden, since most of the Bulgarian and Romanian tanks are older types (e.g. T-62, T-64A and B models) and pose problems of interoperability. On the other hand, both Greece and Turkey's armoured forces are quite modern, having been upgraded in the last few years (M48-A5s). The present WTO proposal affects NATO in the South Eastern Flank negatively. The overall regional impact of the agreement on equipment towards which the two alliances are moving has one disturbing effect. The Central zone will continue to have the lion's share of concentration of tanks while the Southern (and Northern) Flanks and rear areas will be reduced by a more than proportionate amount.[15] There is also the difficulty of dealing satisfactorily with what might be called the 'swing forces' (e.g. Soviet troops in the Kiev Military District) which could be committed either to the Central or South Eastern fronts and Soviet Central Reserve forces. The Soviet Union will no longer have the freedom nor the flexibility in where it stations its forces in Eastern Europe. Recently, the newly elected governments of both Czechoslovakia and Hungary have requested Moscow to remove its forces from their territories. Poland will also make such a request very shortly. Perhaps a renegotiated Warsaw Pact Treaty is in the offing and will be modelled after the NATO Alliance. Thus, the individual members will have a voice as to when, and under what circumstances, forces are permitted on their soil.

TABLE 8.1 *Greece/Turkey ATTU Deployments after NATO/WTO Proposed CFE Cuts*

| | NATO Proposal | | | | | WTO Proposal | | |
	Greece	*Turkey*	*Total NATO*	*Net Cuts*	*Net Cuts*	*Total WTO*	*Turkey*	*Greece*
MBTs	1,615	2,332	3,947	−1,521	−2,344	3,976	2,400	1,567
Aircraft	357	503	860	−135	−639	451	226	225

Source: *Cutting Conventional Forces* (Boston: Institute for Defense and Disarmament Studies, 1989), Appendices 5C-1, 5F-2, 7E-1&2, 7F-1&2.

Reducing levels of NATO and Warsaw Pact aircraft is one of the most controversial issues of the CFE talks. Problems of definition plague both sides. As usual, the negotiating positions of both reflect the longstanding differences in their strategies and perceived interests. The original NATO proposal calls for both sides to cut all their aircraft in Europe by 15 per cent below current figures. For both Greece and Turkey, under this plan, this would mean a cut of a total of 150 aircraft while for the Warsaw Pact the number would be about 600. On the other hand, the WTO places emphasis on attack-capable planes (including attack helicopters). Their proposal, therefore, would require both Greece and Turkey to cut their levels by some 650 planes while the Warsaw Pact cuts would amount to about 450 aircraft.[16] The WTO proposal prevailed. The effect is more destabilising as it heightens the asymmetry in combat aircraft.[17]

Additionally, the threat posed by aircraft, attack helicopters, air mobile, naval and amphibious forces, rather than MBTs, suggests that a differentiated approach in separate sectors of the ATTU might be desirable. For example, in the South Eastern Region, Turkey is concerned about the Straits, and the potential threat that such units pose.

TABLE 8.2. *Country and Military Districts ATTU Deployments After NATO/WTO Proposed CFE Cuts*

| | WTO Propsals | | | | | Net Cut | Net Cut | NATO Propsals | | | | |
	Bulgaria	Romania	Odessa MD	Transcauc.	Total WTO			Total NATO	Transcauc.	Odessa MD	Romania	Bulgaria
MBTS	650	1,041	1,032	1,418	4,131	−8,089	−5,458	4,552	867	632	1,979	1,074
AIRCRAFT	182	316	178	605	1,281	−433	−579	1,052	514	141	254	143

Source: *Cutting Conventional Forces* (Boston: Institute for Defense and Disarmament Studies, 1989), 55 and 63.

Specifically, Greece tends to object to CFE proposals that might possibly affect its military balance *vis à vis* Turkey. One of the Greeks' initial objections concerned Turkey's demand to exclude from the CFE region the areas adjoining its borders with Iran, Iraq and Syria which includes the Turkish port of Mersin (opposite Cyrpus).[18] A resolution of the Mersin issue was delayed when NATO, led by the United States and United Kingdom, persuaded Turkey to accept language which defined the boundary of the exclusion zone as '. . . Gozne [north of Mersin], and thence to the sea.' The United States and other NATO members assured Turkey that all understood that Mersin would be outside the zone. After Turkey agreed and this language was included in the final agreement, Athens began to make clear that she in no way accepted such an interpretation of that language. Greece continues to hold its reserved position on the exemption of Mersin from the CFE negotiations. It is still an open question, and one that remains to be satisfactorily resolved. Any acceptable solution will be very difficult to negotiate. Athens wants the port of Mersin inside the zone because this is the port from which operations and support for Turkish troops on Cyprus are primarily conducted. By raising this issue, Greece is also attempting to isolate Ankara further from NATO since this issue has no meaning for the rest of the Alliance members. Other troublesome issues over which Greece has been most concerned have to do with attack helicopters and limitations to the size of military manoeuvres. NATO's proposal would require that manoeuvres be announced 42 days in advance, if 40,000 troops were called up and if 1,200 APCs, 400 artillery pieces of 600 MBTs were used.[19] Athens' objection on this proposal is that the limits set are too high and that without advanced notification, Turkey could conduct manoeuvres that might threaten Greece's security. Athens would like to include a provision that notice should be given on smaller manoeuvres. Similarly, any decision reached at the CFE talks setting limits on APCs that would give Turkey a substantial numerical advantage (coupled with advantages in MBTs, artillery and attack helicopters) would be perceived by Athens in terms of Ankara gaining in mobility and firepower—elements most relevant for a surprise attack.

Ankara views the CFE discussions with some alarm and from a much broader dimension than Athens. This stems from the perception that Turkey will lose her strategic importance within NATO. Such developments no doubt affect both the economic and military aid that Turkey receives, and could ultimately jeopardise Turkey's desire to be part of the EEC. Ankara's fundamental problem is how to accommodate her security interests in an era of lessening tension (real and/or perceived) between NATO and the WTO, while Turkey's immediate environment, most especially the area excluded by the CFE discussions, is ever threatening.[20] In fact, some restructuring of her armed forces is now taking place. No doubt, as the threat from the East lessens, pressures will mount in NATO capitals to cut defence budgets. This is already evident in the recent cancellation of billions of dollars in weapons systems. Can Turkey continue to argue, as it has throughout the post-Second World War period, that it is in the interests of NATO and the West to support her national security needs because of her strategic importance? There are elements in NATO capitals today that are quite prejudiced towards Turkey. Not only is Turkey geographically removed from Central Europe, but more importantly, in the eyes of these groups, Turkey is ethnically, socially and religiously quite different from Western Europe, and her human rights record has not been outstanding.[21] Furthermore, Turkish workers in many NATO nations have not integrated well with the indigenous population and this further amplifies the above differences. A lessening of the military threat could conceivably bring to the surface these ever-present issues which could eventually force Turkey to make some very hard choices: remaining in the Western Alliance or possibly leaving it. The challenge that Turkish leaders face today is how to accommodate the new international environment with Turkish traditional defence and foreign policy objectives. Perhaps this is the time and the occasion for Ankara to affect a new look at its world position, a rather longer reach Westward, or to enunciate views less relevant in the context of East–West tensions. If this challenge is not met, Turkey will find herself isolated from the West (not particularly accepted by the Arab world) and, in the end, may become another Middle Eastern country buffeted by superpower diplomacy.

The CFE negotiations within the Alliance still may prove very troublesome. Potentially the most difficult issue will be to decide how the mandated arms cuts will be allocated between the Alliance members. When it comes to Greece and Turkey, this will inevitably be a very sensitive issue in its actual and/or perceived implementation. Both will view any cuts within the framework of their bilateral relations, while Turkey will also be concerned with how they affect its geostrategic position. There can be no doubt that the ever-increasing political and economic issues facing both countries portend stubborn negotiations.

Another issue for Turkey has to do with the status of the Soviet equipment withdrawn from Central Europe. Will this equipment be destroyed or stockpiled in regions where it will constitute no less a threat to Turkey than it did in Central Europe? Finally, Greece and Turkey would like the Alliance members to shift some of the equipment earmarked for destruction or withdrawal from the Central Front to Ankara and Athens. These arms can replace equipment that is obsolete or at least marginally effective. This proposal is fraught with problems. Specifically, for Greece and Turkey, any transfer of arms to Ankara would upset Athens into demanding equal equipment for itself or at least the maintenance of the 7:10 ratio. Arrangement to do so would be complicated by a maze of national laws governing weapons transfers and sales. Can legal means be found to achieve these transfers? The most likely solution would be a series of bilateral agreements between those nations that agree to equipment transfers. Other questions complicating such transfers would include the cost of destroying the equipment and the costs of shipping arms and equipment from one country to another, as well as retraining personnel to operate and repair this equipment.

In spite of the CFE discussions and a fading Warsaw Pact threat, Western military planners are still pressing ahead with force modernisation plans for the 1990s. No doubt the CFE discussions could reduce or slow down weapons purchases, but promises of cutbacks by the Warsaw Pact are carrying little weight in current NATO thinking on necessary upgrades, especially in armour, for the Alliance.[22]

Modernisation Programmes

Greece

Greece's long-term force planning is driven by two imperatives: the need to respond to NATO Force goals that are designed to enhance its capabilities to meet a Warsaw Pact threat, although this possibility has greatly diminished; and, more important to Greek eyes, the need to increase its capabilities against Turkey. In its NATO role, the Greek military's primary responsibilities in a confrontation with the Warsaw Pact would be to insure the country's territorial integrity and to defend, along with Turkey, the Turkish Straits and the sea lines of communication in the Aegean and Eastern Mediterranean.

Planning a strategy for a military confrontation with Turkey, on the other hand, as discussed in Chapter 7, requires a reorientation of Greek military forces that would detract from the ability to adhere to NATO plans and objectives. Briefly, the Army would concentrate on defending Greek borders with Turkey in Thrace and reinforcing and defending the Aegean islands. The Navy would concentrate on transporting reinforcements to the islands and preventing the Turkish Navy from controlling the Aegean. The Air Force's operational plans would be to maintain air superiority over the Aegean Islands and Thrace, interdict Turkish naval operations in the Aegean, affect airfield operations in Turkey, and transport troops to the islands, if necessary.

Over the next 10 years, the focus of Athens' weapons modernisation programmes will continue to implement Greece's NATO Force Goals, because any advances in weapons technology will enhance the qualitative side of the Greek-Turkish force balance. On the other hand, Athens' decisions on force deployments and manpower allocations are driven primarily by any renewed drive to respond to the Turkish threat. Indeed, Greece today has focused its defence planning efforts and resources in dealing with this threat.

Army

Progress in modernisation over the last 10 years had brought a number of new weapons systems into the Army and enhanced its combat effectiveness. The primary focus has been on modernising its armoured forces, further mechnising its infantry units with additional armoured personnel carriers (APCs), and bolstering its force support capabilities with improved anti-tank, artillery and short-range air defence systems. To date, for example, over 600 American M-48 tanks have been up-gunned and given more reliable engines and improved fire-control systems. In addition, some 300 late-generation French and German tanks have been purchased.

The Greeks have also increased their APC inventory by buying and upgrading over 900 American M-113 models with more powerful engines and improved armour protection. They have also manufactured, under Austrian licence, some 300 Leonidas APCs. Further, they have procured small numbers of TOW, COBRA, and MILAN anti-tank guided missiles (ATGM) systems. Artillery modernisation has focused on replacing old vintage towed guns with modern self-propelled weapons. Self-propelled systems still make up only about one third of the Army's larger calibre (over 105mm) weapons.[23] In the air defence area, the Army has replaced old anti-aircraft guns with newer radar-equipped gun systems and the American improved HAWK SAM system. However, small unit air defences are still limited by inadequate numbers of short-range SAM systems.

The plans to modernise its armoured forces include not only the continued upgrading of existing MBTs but also the possibility of Greece co-producing, with West Germany, some 800 LEOPARD II MBTs.[24] Further, Greece has purchased some 10 ground attack helicopters (AH-1 COBRA with TOW) and heavy-lift transport helicopters. Other planned modernisation programmes identified by Athens include new shorter range anti-tank weapons and additional longer ATGMs, more self-propelled artillery and air defence guns, and continued participation in improving the HAWK SAM programme.

Moreover, the Greek Army suffers major deficiencies which are not addressed in its current force plans. These include serious shortages in ammunition stock levels, particularly of anti-tank, artillery and air defence munitions, and inadequacies in armour and in anti-armour capability; small unit defence assets are limited; and shortfalls exist in nuclear, chemical and biological defence equipment.

Air Force

In the 1970s, the Greeks made several purchases of aircraft, primarily to respond to the growing perception of the threat from Ankara. As a result, the Greek Air Force, that formerly had only a limited all-weather attack capability, is now capable of all-weather air defence, ground attack, and anti-ship missions against either Turkey or the Warsaw Pact.

The modernisation programme since 1974 has seen the delivery of F-4E fighters[25] and A-7H attack aircraft from the United States, procurement of MIRAGE F-ICG interceptors from France and the transfer of F-104G from the FRG and the Netherlands. The most recent acquisition consists of 40 American F-16s and 40 French MIRAGE 2000s[26]—the most current generation of aircraft—will round out the Air Force's programmes for the mid-1990s. Most likely the Air Force will request that these latest aircraft should be equipped with large fuel tanks, increased capability landing gear and with drag chutes, so that they will be operationally capable over the Aegean and equipped to land on Aegean Island airfields.

Furthermore, they have substantially upgraded their munitions inventory with third-generation versions of SIDEWINDER air-to-air missiles, radar homing AAMs, MAVERICK air-to-surface missiles, and electro-optical and laser guidance kits for general purpose bombs. The Air Force has also improved its air defence radar network[27] and has integrated its installations with NATO's NADGE, thus providing effective cover for most of Greece. In addition, modern air defence guns and short-range air defence missile systems (SHORAD) for airfield defence[28] have been purchased. Furthermore, Greek early warning capabilities against the Warsaw Pact have improved with the deployment of NATO AWACS aircraft at Preveza. In addition to the purchase of new equipment, the Greek

Air Force has made various improvements to their air bases, especially those on the Aegean Islands.[29]

In spite of these improvements, the Greek Air Force still has shortcomings in air-to-air missiles and precision guided munitions and lacks defensive capabilities against nuclear, chemical and biological attack. The number of reconnaissance aircraft they possess which are capable of night/all weather missions is limited.

Navy

The Navy began a major modernisation programme in the mid-1970s to replace or extend the life of its Second World War vintage fleet. With an eye toward the perceived threat from Turkey, they have concentrated on acquiring small warships, such as fast attack craft, to meet their surface and anti-submarine requirements. As a result, the Navy is quite capable of supporting the defence of the Aegean Islands. However, it is not capable of conducting sustained combat operations. The obsolescence of its ships and the lack of modern weapons renders it vulnerable to submarine and air attack.

In addition to modernising its fleet and expanding its inventory of fast-attack craft, the Navy's frigate force has been substantially upgraded with the purchase, thus far, of seven new ships, armed with HARPOON SSM, and ASW torpedoes.[30]

Other key modernisation plans include procurement of West German attack submarines (FRG T–209/1100), (eight of these are presently operational) upgrading of the naval air arm by the acquisition of AB–212 helicopters, and the expansion of the capabilities of their mine clearing force, which is essential for keeping NATO's SLOC's open during wartime and minelaying to prevent the Soviet Navy from exiting the Black Sea into the Aegean.

The Navy still faces serious deficiencies that limit its ability to perform its NATO mission. These shortcomings include its major surface warships being vulnerable to Soviet naval aviation during a full scale attack and the lack of modern air defence systems on these ships; modern ASW sensors and weapons systems are lacking to counter Soviet submarines attempting to transit the Aegean Sea;[31] a severe shortage of ammunition, especially anti-submarine torpedoes, limits the Navy's ability to mount sustained operations; and, the lack of mine-hunters and inadequate port air defence systems affects their capacity to ensure the safe arrival of reinforcements and re-supply ships.

Of the three Services, the Navy will be most dependent on outside military assistance to accomplish its modernisation objectives, because its share of the budget is so small,[32] and replacement units are quite costly. Greece will enter the 1990s with a Navy that will do well in combat against the Turkish Navy. However, it will have serious difficulties countering a Soviet naval threat.

Turkey

Ankara, in the next decade, will concentrate on the development of well-equipped and well-trained forces, primarily through the modernisation or replacement of obsolete equipment that cannot be properly supported. As noted elsewhere, this momentous task is far beyond the capabilities of Turkey's own limited resources, which are barely sufficient to maintain and operate what it now has, let alone acquire new sophisticated hardware. This immense hurdle is being addressed by the modernisation and expansion of Turkish defence industries as well as the assistance which Ankara receives from NATO members.

Army

The modernisation efforts over the past decade have enhanced the Army's combat effectiveness. The principal programme has been the complete upgrading of its M48 series MBTs to the M48–A5, with a conversion of some 1,600. This upgrading and deployment provides the Turks with armour that is far more capable than most of the Soviet T54/55 MBTs which they face in Thrace and Eastern Anatolia. In addition, the FRG[33] will deliver to Turkey shortly some 150 upgraded LEOPARD tanks (A3T models) which will further enhance the Army's capabilities. Modernisation programmes also include the purchase of some 1,500 mechanised infantry fighting vehicles, improving the Army's anti-tank and artillery capabilities, low altitude short-range air defence systems (SHORAD), fire control radar, enhancing command, control and communications (C^3), acquiring multiple-launched rocket systems, and the purchase of attack helicopters. Further, they have also purchased small numbers of AH-1S COBRA helicopters and TOW, and MILAN ATGMs. Artillery modernisation has focused on replacing old vintage guns with some MLRS systems.[34] Self-propelled systems still only make up about one-half of the Army's larger calibre (over 105 mm) inventory.[35] In the air defence area, the Army is now replacing old anti-aircraft guns with some newer radar-equipped systems, 35mm guns by Oerlikon-Buhrle. However, small unit air defence is still lacking, with inadequate numbers of SAM systems.[36] Turkey is presently negotiating with NATO for the co-production of some 2,000 STINGER missiles.[37] The Turkish forces recognise the need to augment their airmobile capability, especially in the light of the counter-insurgency operations now taking place in South Eastern Anatolia, and are in the process of co-producing some 200 UH–1H. This is one of the top five priority items for Turkey's army.[38] The need to acquire helicopters designed for anti-armour roles such as the AH–1 COBRA with TOWS is not possible at present, because of their exorbitant cost.

Moreover, the Turkish Army suffers major deficiencies in ammunition stock levels, particularly anti-tank, in anti-armour capabilities and small unit defence assets. It has a non-existent capability in nuclear, chemical and biological defence.

Navy

The Navy will continue to be required to carry out its primary mission of controlling the Turkish Straits with a fleet of mostly antiquated major surface warships. The submarine force has become the Navy's most effective combat arm, thanks to the six new TYPE 209/1200 submarines (out of a total of 15). The Turkish Navy would like to obtain an additional six but naval modernisation is being given lower priority than the ground and air forces, and funds are unlikely to be available in the near future. Also, four MEKO 200 class frigates have entered the fleet replacing Ankara's Second World War vintage destroyers. Two additional frigates are planned but Ankara will continue to place greater emphasis on acquiring a fleet of smaller, fast patrol combatants (FRG Luerssen-57 and Jaguar). This patrol force armed with HARPOON and PENGUIN SSMs is relatively potent and very well suited to the narrow waters of the Straits and along the island-dotted Aegean coastline. The Navy hopes to augment this capability by acquiring SEA SKUA anti-ship missiles for use on its six AB212 helicopters.

Turkish amphibious and mine-warfare capabilities are barely adequate and will improve marginally in the near future because scarce resources are earmarked for other priorities. Anti-submarine warfare capability is also limited with the exception of the new TYPE 209s. Attempts to refurbish the squadron of naval air S-2E Tracker aircraft does not appreciably strengthen this capability.

Air Force

The Turkish Air Force's air defence and nuclear strike capabilities were greatly enhanced by the acquisition of some 50 F–16s by the end of 1989 out of a projected 160 by 1995. All-weather air defence will remain a serious deficiency until suitable AAMs are acquired for the F–16. Although the F–104G STARFIGHTERS and F–4E PHANTOMS will be phased out of their nuclear strike and air defence roles respectively by the mid-1990s, they will continue to retain a ground attack mission. The F–104 force will continue to increase as Ankara acquires second-hand aircraft from NATO partners.[39] Ankara will also seek to increase its F–4 fleet in order to enhance its ground attack and reconnaissance capabilities. The RF–4 will be the mainstay of the Air Force's reconnaissance force, but it will be acquired in too few numbers to fulfill the probable need.

Although fairly modern, the Turkish Air Force's shortcomings are still numerous: air-to-air missiles, air-to-surface missiles, the non-existence of nuclear, chemical, and biological warfare defence, and a limited number of reconnaissance aircraft capable of night and all-weather missions.[40] The need for a tanker capability to complement the procurement of the F–16s will become more pressing by the mid-1990s.

Overall, the Greek and Turkish economies are less than vibrant. Domestic economic stringencies make it unlikely that all these expensive programmes—as presently envisioned—will come to fruition without foreign assistance, especially from the United States and other NATO members.

Complicating matters will be the bilateral negotiations that will take place between the United States, Turkey and Greece in renewing their DECA agreements. In the case of Greece, economic considerations will be the compelling reasons to renew the agreement. In fact, with the continued deterioration of the Greek economy, Athens will use these discussions to extract more aid and economic concessions. Athens is also likely to press hard for reinstatement of more grant aid as compared to FMS credits and for the establishment of trade and investment schemes designed to boost the ailing Greek economy.

The Turkish economy is still the weakest among those NATO members incapable of supporting large scale defence spending. The defence spending issue is further complicated because of Turkey's FMS debt dilemma (see Chapter 3). No doubt, Ankara would react harshly to any United States Congressional attempts to link American aid to a resolution of the Cyprus imbroglio or to any attempt by the Congress to condemn, directly or indirectly, Turkey's alleged responsibility for the genocide of Armenians early in this century. Furthermore, if Turkey should find the levels of aid have become insufficient, even after receiving surplus American equipment, it will enter into bilateral defence agreements outside the NATO context and any other agreements which Ankara feels to be in the best national interest. As a last resort, although unlikely, a Greek or

Turkish decision to abrogate their DECA agreement cannot be ruled out entirely.

Defence Industrial Development

In the light of economic trends, less security assistance, shrinking defence budgets and fading East-West tensions, both Ankara and Athens are viewing defence industrial development as an alternative means of securing military improvements, while at the same time gaining independence from their traditional suppliers of weapons system. Further, developing indigenous defence industries is seen as a means of expanding trade relations with lesser developing nations and acquiring the economic benefits that accrue to the supplier. In addition, both Greece and Turkey are very interested in broadening their commercial defence relationships. This is part of the reason why heavy emphasis is placed on the offset agreements that flow from weapons acquisitions as in the weapons systems themselves.[41]

The modernisation requirements of Turkey's large armed forces provide a substantial market for its emerging defence-industrial capacity. Moreover, it has an abundance of labour and a coherent national strategy for defence-industrial development. Greece, on the other hand, is very much behind Turkey in this respect. The seeds of a more effective defence industrial base have been sown, but the Greek defence industry continues to suffer from charges of corruption,[42] disorganisation, and excessive politicisation.

Greece

To lessen dependency on foreign military suppliers and to develop an industrial base for local military needs, Greece officially established an arms industry organisation in 1977 with the creation of the Defence Industry Directorate (DID) within the Ministry of Defence. Its primary purpose is to develop and coordinate a modern defence industry, and to ensure low costs associated with acquisitions. Unfortunately, it has not been able to fulfill its mandate. Politicisation of DID and the whole defence industry have rather limited Greek efforts to develop a coherent national strategy for defence-industrial development. Nevertheless, since 1977, Greece has become a regional military supplier of small arms and an exporter of tanks and other armoured vehicles. The defence industry has been divided into separate branches for aerospace and small arms production.

Hellenic Aerospace Industry (HAI) was established in late 1976 as a government-owned firm to provide a domestic industrial base for aircraft maintenance, repair, and overhaul facilities. A $300 million plant, located at Tanagra, presently employs over 3,000 people, with a total annual sales of $90 million. By 1985, it had support and overhaul contracts with the United States, Egypt, Jordan, Nigeria and the United Arab Emirates, as well as support and co-production agreements with international companies such as Airbus Industries and Dassault-Breguet.[43] These arrangements covered services, including the manufacture and installation of aviation components, and technical support and training. It is HAI that is playing a major role in the co-production of some parts of the 40 F–16s and the 40 Mirage 2000 aircraft that the Greek Air Force purchased in 1984.

The growth of international demand for regional defence industries and increased competition for defence business have been beneficial to the embryonic aerospace industry in Greece. The terms of contracts for the supply of aircraft and equipment to Greece, military and civilian, have stipulated that offset agreements are expected. The suppliers are expected to use Greek industry either to supply component parts for the aircraft or provide other services. For example, HAI is managing offset programmes which include production of door frames for the Airbus 300, parts for the Dassault-Breguet MIRAGE F–1 and 2000, and fuselage section for Agusta A–109 helicopters.

As part of the MIRAGE–2000 deal, HAI will manufacture wing and fuselage sections and assemble the SNECMA M53 turbofan engine which powers the aircraft. In addition, the Greeks will participate in producing Thomson-CSF radar components, and Matra Magic missiles. Overall, Dassault promised offsets worth 60 per cent of the purchase price, of which 30 per cent must go to the Greek defence companies. The offset package also includes the import of 3 billion Francs-worth of Greek products over a 15-year period.

As part of the F–16 contract, General Dynamics, General Electric and Westinghouse are setting up a business development company for implementation of their offset agreement. The companies will provide $50 million in capital over 10 years, with some 5 per cent of the shares to be held by the Greek Government. This development company will be responsible for implementing investment, trade and technology programs.

Hellenic Arms Industry (EBO) was established in 1977 as a state-owned corporation consisting of three factories located at Aiyion, Lavnon and Kimi, manufacturing small to large calibre guns, small arms, explosives, propellants and fully integrated weapons systems. EBO has the capability and capacity to produce a broad range of weapons not only for domestic consumption but for export to earn hard currencies.[44]

EBO has developed the Artemis–30 twin anti-aircraft gun which has an all-weather capability and is used by the Greek Army on the Aegean Islands. This system also appears to have found an international market.[45]

While there are several large shipyards in Greece, the major builder of naval vessels is the Hellenic Shipyards at Scaramanga. After labour and financial difficulties forced the shipyard to close, it was purchased by the government. The yard has built the French La Combattants III class fast attack missile craft and is presently assembling the last three of four MEKO 200 frigates and building Osprey–55 patrol boats. The shipyard also does a great deal of repair work.[46]

In 1979, the Greek Government purchased the Austrian firm Steyr Hellas, now known as the Hellenic Vehicle Industry (ELVO). The company produces military trucks, jeeps, diesel engines and, most significantly, armoured personnel carriers. ELVO produced 100 LEONIDAS–1 APCs under licence for the Greek Army. Recently, it received a new order for 292 LEONIDAS–2 APCs, worth approximately $140 million. ELVO has also supplied more than 7,800 trucks to the Greek Armed Forces. The production range covers 8.5-ton to 38-ton trucks. In addition, it now has a contract to produce some 18,000 jeeps for the Greek Forces.

Although Greece has yet to become a net exporter of arms, the economic effect of the developing defence industry is significant. In 1985, sales amounted to over $130 million or about four per cent of Greece's total exports. The growth of the defence-related companies and their performance since 1977 means that Greece has become a regional arms producer in spite of the industry's politicisation.

Turkey

The defence industry in Turkey is in an embryonic state of development at present, but the government's policy for a coherent national strategy for defence-industrial development is well established. Historically, the Turkish Government's policies toward this sector of the economy were monopolistic in nature, given to slow modernisation of the infrastructure and preventing foreign companies from investing in it. This all came to an end in 1985 when the government created the Defence Industrial Development and Support Administration (DIDA).[47] It came about as a result of events in the 1970s. First, the United States arms embargo and its negative implications for United States-Turkish relations, followed by the expenditure of huge sums of money on arms purchases, which resulted in the depletion of scarce foreign exchange reserves. A need for self-sufficiency became paramount. Another by-product of the creation of this industrial base was to alleviate the burden on the defence budget, by providing funds through military sales. It was originally the Turkish Government's intention to include, as part of the co-production contracts, indirect offset agreements to enhance its domestic economic base. For example, the agreement with General Dynamics to co-produce F–16s included, as part of the indirect offsets, investing in and the building of hotels, transferring in a wide and diverse range of technologies and for marketing Turkish marble, tyres, boric acid, wall-to-wall carpeting, and to promote tourism to Turkey. DIDA is now emphasising direct offsets[48] as opposed to indirect ones. According to Vahit Erdem, Under-Secretary for DIDA, 'direct offsets bring greater long term benefits since the most common form is a joint venture, creating a long term industry and manufacturing plant.'[49] Erdem also indicated that it was too difficult for the government to follow up their implementation. 'I cannot say we are managing the offsets for the F–16s very well.'[50]

Specifically, DIDA's mandate is to encourage the modernisation of existing defence industries and assist in the creation of new ones. DIDA was intended to be an efficiently run department that would make decisions in an expeditious manner, unlike many other Turkish organisations. This, however, has not been the case. To assist in underwriting various projects, monies accrue to DIDA from a variety of sources outside the national budget (e.g. special surcharge on the sale of tobacco and alcohol; gaming machine profits, and funds from military service foundations). It is estimated that DIDA presently has in excess of $1 billion for the underwriting of projects. [51]

At another level Turkish society does not possess enough qualified skilled workers to meet the needs of anticipated joint venture projects. More importantly, the lack of skilled workers mitigates an ability to maintain a high level of quality control for high-tech projects. These two deficiencies, along with gnawing economic difficulties, affect the speed by which Turkey will be able to implement and digest highly modernised and technically advanced defence industries.

As a result of these factors, it has taken DIDA some three years before it awarded its first joint venture contract. This was with FMC of Chicago and the Ankara-based Nurol Group for $1.07 billion for the purchase of 1,698 armoured combat vehicles with an option on another 1,500. Full production was begun in 1990. There are several other proposals being studied by DIDA and the Turkish General

Staff. A memorandum of understanding[52] was signed recently by the Missile and Electronic Group of LTV Corporation of Dallas and two Turkish firms ENKA Holding and Makina Ve Kinya Endustrisi Kurumu (MKE) to coproduce multiple launched rocket systems (MLRS). Turkey anticipates purchasing about 160 of the MLRS units at a cost of $1 billion. It will also co-assemble with Spain some 50 light turbo prop transport aircraft, the contract totalling about $700 million. Other major procurement contracts being reviewed include co-assembly of 200 attack helicopters (e.g. UH–1H), at an estimated cost of $1 billion, to enhance the Turkish forces air mobility, fire control radars and computers for the Oerlikon-Buhrle air defence gun, and a mobile air defence radar system.

The largest joint venture, thus far, for Turkey has been the F–16 programme. This is an arrangement between the Turkish Government and General Dynamics to build 160 F–16 C/D aircraft for delivery to the United States Air Force who in turn will deliver them to the Turkish Air Force. The completion of this project is scheduled for 1995, and thus far some 50 have been built. The vehicle for this joint venture is TUSAS Aerospace Industries of which 51 per cent is owned by the Turkish Government and the remainder by General Dynamics (42 per cent) and General Electric (7 per cent).[53] The investment cost for building the F–16 is estimated at $4 billion, plus 'indirect offset' investments of $1.27 billion within 10 years.[54]

ASESLAN was established in November 1975, under the control of the Turkish Ground Forces Foundation which controls 70.1 per cent of the shares, with the aim of supplying the Turkish Armed Forces with modern electronic equipment. It produces VHF/FM combat radios, digital encryption equipment, telephone scramblers, data terminals and printed circuit boards. ASESLAN is a very modern facility matching anything comparable in Western Europe and could easily compete in world markets. In fact, ASESLAN and MKE are now part of the six-nation EUROMAV consortium producing image infra-red variant components for the STINGER-POST and MAVERICK missiles.

MKE is the largest and oldest industrial organisation in Turkey, dating back to the days of the Ottoman Empire; a state monopoly that reports directly to the Ministry of Industry and Commerce. With a labour force of some 18,000 employees MKE operates some 20 factories throughout Turkey. Its primary focus is the production of arms (G-3 rifles, 81 and 105 mm mortars, 20 and 30 mm Oerlikon anti-aircraft guns, tank gun barrels, etc.) and a variety of munitions ranging from .50 mm cartridges to 8 inch howitzer ammunition. Although the array of items that MKE produces is quite large, this industry, as is true of most Turkish state monopolies, is inefficiently run, and its overall manufacturing capacity and facilities are quite old. If MKE is to be competitive on the international scene, it must modernise its equipment and facilities.

There are two major shipyards in Turkey. Golcuk Naval Yards in Istanbul, a part of the Fleet Command of the Turkish Navy, is an excellent facility that has built, under co-production agreements with HDW of Kiel and Blohm and Voss of Hamburg, three TYPE 209/1200 diesel submarines and four MEKO 200 class frigates respectively.[55] These systems are the pride of the Turkish Navy. In addition to its shipbuilding capabilities, Golcuk also produces naval shipboard equipment such as fire control systems and communications security systems.

The Taskizak Shipyard located on the Golden Horn is smaller than Golcuk and, like MKE, dates back to the Ottoman Empire. This yard once built and maintained most of the vessels in the Ottoman Navy, although today it does not play such a significant role. It is under the technical management of Turkish Naval Headquarters in Ankara. Its primary function is the repair and overhaul of about 190 vessels per year. Taskizak's shipbuilding capacity is limited although in the 1970s it built eight fast patrol craft and a number of very fast 170 ton Type SAR–33 coast guard boats.

The ARIFIYE overhaul facility for tracked vehicles is a modern factory which initially used West German technical and material support. Subsequently, American aid has further refined its capabilities so that today it not only rebuilds and overhauls tracked vehicles but it is responsible for the overhaul and upgrading of most of Turkey's MBTs to M48–A5s. In addition, ARIFIYE has the capacity to upgrade self-propelled weapons systems and to produce spare parts for the equipment it repairs.

Turkey's desire to export systems it co-produces will grow increasingly important in the future as Ankara asserts itself as a regional arms supplier. Pakistan has expressed serious interest in co-operation with Turkey on M48 upgrades and F–16 maintenance, not to mention possibly purchasing Turkish-built F–16s. Pakistan has also shown interest in the MEKO–200 class frigates and the TYPE 209/1200 submarines being built at Golcuk, and possible Turkish co-production of West German LEOPARD 2 tanks. The Pakistani economy impedes pursuit of these co-operative ventures. Turkey has also agreed to explore arms co-operation possibilities with Egypt, Kuwait and Saudi Arabia.

While Turkey's defence industry has developed significantly over the past decade, the country is still largely reliant on imported arms to fulfill its major equipment requirements. For the five-year period from 1983 to 1987, Turkey imported in excess of $2.5 billion worth of arms, a 67 per cent increase over the previous five years. Meanwhile, $370 million in arms exports for 1983–1987 represent a 602 per cent increase over 1978–1982. For 1983–1987, arms imports accounted for an average of 4.9 per cent of total imports, while arms exports accounted for an average of about 1.2 per cent of total exports.

Turkey recognises that foreign capital and expertise are vital for the long-term growth and modernisation of Turkish defence industrial development. Market factors, such as the availability of labour and sales opportunities, make co-operative joint ventures very attractive. On the downside, foreign investors will continue to be wary and cautious in their appraisal of investment opportunities as long as the balance of payments and inflation rates continue to have a negative effect on the economy.

CHAPTER 9

Summary and Conclusions

AT THEIR December 1989 meeting on the island of Malta, United States President George Bush and Soviet President Mikhail Gorbachev cleared away much of the ideological debris left over from the Cold War and moved to put relations between the superpowers and their allies on a businesslike footing. Gorbachev declared that the Cold War 'epoch' has ended: 'We are just at the beginning of our road, a long road to a long-lasting peaceful period.'[1]

One might date the beginning of this process of rapprochement with the signing of the INF Treaty in December 1987. A year later (7 December 1988) President Gorbachev declared that between that date and 1991 the Soviet Union would reduce its armed forces by half a million men. These cuts would affect Soviet forward-deployed forces in East Germany, Czechoslovakia and Hungary. These reductions would be exclusive of the ATTU negotiations taking place in Vienna. Although it is not intended to discuss the details of these changes in this book, nevertheless, events in Eastern Europe and the Soviet Uion have developed an unprecedented scope and tempo, culminating in the evaporation of monolithic communist control in the Warsaw Pact countries. They cannot fail to have far-reaching effects upon the defence of the West.

Even though surface movements appear sharp and evidence of a new order is emerging, the old system is not entirely dead.[2] Since the United States and NATO are losing the luxury of building strategy around a single enemy, political and military balances are perhaps even more crucial now than before for the maintenance of stability and the avoidance of conflict. It should be noted that, in spite of these changes, the Soviet Union has given little indication at this point concerning the future of the Warsaw Pact as a military alliance. No doubt, as more Warsaw Pact countries elect new governments and are free from Moscow's domination, it is likely that that alliance will go through a process of transformation. This evolutionary process will provide the individual members' freedom to decide when and where Soviet forces will be deployed.

157

NATO too has decisions to make regarding the stance it should assume in the face of a greatly diminished threat from the Warsaw Pact and the possibility of a more powerful and perhaps neutral Germany. The likelihood of all-out conflict between the United States and the Soviet Union—that is between NATO and the Warsaw Pact—is probably lower now than at any time in the post-Second World War era. NATO Secretary-General Manfred Woerner stated that the Alliance 'is the core of our security and remains essential in a world still marked by instability and massive military deployments.'[3] The potential for a new era of unplanned violence continues to be ever present. The world could well become more unpredictable, and military threats to both the United States and NATO might come from a far wider range of sources. As Prime Minister Margaret Thatcher states, 'When the ice breaks up . . . it can be very dangerous.'[4]

This maxim is most apropos for South Eastern Europe and its environs. As noted in Chapters Two, Three and Five, historic interstate rivalries among the nations of this region still persist. The fine details of geography and historical interests may become of greater relevance than at any time since the 1930s. For both Greece and Turkey, relations with their Warsaw Pact neighbours have long been thorny, with a tradition running back a few millennia now of warfare, hostility, and suspicions while Turkey's neighbours to her south are also ever troublesome.

The relations between Ankara and Athens continue to be worrisome. Greece has publicly declared that the greatest threat to her security emanates from the East (Turkey). Turkey, on the other hand, believes the principal menace to her security remains to some extent the Soviet Union but more importantly her southern neighbours. These tensions between Ankara and Athens have proved to be a source of annoyance to both the United States and NATO. Yet in spite of these differences, conflict between these two Alliance members has been avoided with the exception of the Turkish invasion of Cyprus in 1974. Will this unsteady peace continue during this era of *détente* between East and West? Highly unlikely! Any kind of coherent partnership within a more loosely structured international environment will be more difficult to manage.

The historical issues that divide Greece and Turkey continue into the present. They will not dissipate, in the foreseeable future. The 'Davos Spirit' is void. In political and economic terms, each country faces serious problems with possible resultant instabilities, thereby adding fluidity to an already pliable context. The military balance between the two neighbours does not give either a decided advantage. Yet, as noted in Chapter Seven, the 1987 Aegean Sea crisis demonstrated how fragile are the relations between Ankara and Athens, and how ever present are the sources of friction that divide them. Given similar unpleasantness in the future, reasonable outcomes may not be in the offing. Confrontation might be unavoidable. Against such a backdrop, effective military cooperation between Greece and Turkey can scarcely be assumed, should conflict with the Warsaw Pact or one of its members arise.

Nevertheless, collective security will continue to demand centralised crisis management during the period of the 1990s, and it is only through NATO that this will be attained. The Soviet Union, and to a lesser extent the Warsaw Pact, must remain the focus of United States and NATO military strategy for the foreseeable future. NATO's strategy on the South Eastern Flank in the post-CFE period is to strengthen its troop and equipment commitments, a shift in focus away from the inter-German border. In addition, increased priorities will be given to air and naval forces, rather than ground troops supported by heavy equipment. Continued cooperation between Greece and Turkey in defence of the all-important Turkish Straits and on maintaining the security of the Aegean Sea will be necessary; for Soviet strategy demands control of these sea lines of communication and reinforcement of their Mediterranean Navy with units from the Black Sea. As observed earlier, the Black Sea itself is critical to Soviet land strategy in this area, since it represents the focus of Soviet vulnerability and provides the principal rational for Soviet interest in the Mediterranean. Maintaining sea control throughout this area will also continue to be a key element in the United States' and NATO's strategy. In particular, the Alliance must deny the Soviet Union freedom of action in the Eastern Mediterranean.

From a broader perspective, much of the importance ascribed to the Mediterranean, and especially the eastern sector, is its position linking Europe to the centres of turmoil and crisis in the Middle East and the Persian Gulf. This is one reason why, at NATO's insistence, naval arms control is specifically excluded from the CFE discussions in Vienna. The ability to project force into any of these regions in response to a crisis will be an ongoing NATO and US concern and a sustained focus of debate in defence planning circles.

An important factor influencing this debate will be the availability of secure bases in Greece and Turkey to sustain such operations. Money is usually the key to these leasing rights. Current trends suggest that even for restricted access the United States will continue to pay more and most likely get less in both the negotiations with Greece which began in 1987[5] and those which will begin in Turkey in 1990. In the case of Greece, the United States will be allowed continued access to most Greek facilities, but for a price. It is likely that if the price demanded by Greece is too high, the Americans will withdraw completely from these facilities, redirecting some of them to Turkey. In the case of Turkey, the United States will find the negotiations tough, with Ankara asking for increased security assistance, while at the same time perhaps restricting American (and possibly NATO) use of their facilities.

It is precisely the uncertainty of base availability over the long term that is the central problem in the South Eastern Flank. At the very least, it complicates planning. Moreover, ambiguity will not necessarily secure additional funding from the United States or NATO. Firmer parameters are needed to justify the maintenance of costly base access arrangements. If such parameters cannot be secured, the degree of uncertainty will be a factor in determining how much money the United States and NATO will pay. Reducing uncertainty, therefore, is a primary objective. Washington—and Brussels—must think more creatively about obtaining access to these bases and power projection alternatives in order to ensure that adequate assets will be available for various future contingencies.

No doubt the traditional patterns of security assistance from the United States and NATO members are now being eroded by the changes in the level of resources available. Domestic economic and political pressures and the arms control environment are already creating a situation where sharp reductions in defence spending are being contemplated by members of the Alliance. This will not change unless political reforms in the Soviet Union and Eastern Europe spin out of control, enough to result in hostile reactions from within. In fact, NATO's Secretary-General Woerner has rebuked NATO governments for beginning to spend less on defence, warning that the improvements in East–West relations should not signal 'cut-price security.'[6] Specifically for Greece and Turkey, this new climate will impact on the amount of security assistance that each will be provided. Inevitably, any aid provided to either Ankara or Athens will be bound up by their bilateral relations.

In this ever-changing international environment, Athens' defence and foreign policy will not always adhere to the West's views. The compliant Greece, so familiar during the period prior to 1974, has evaporated. Only one issue persists today that provides a broad political consensus: relations with Turkey. This issue alone will continue to affect most of Athens' security relations with NATO and the United States. As for Turkey, her leaders will continue to make compelling demands for additional military assistance, particularly in light of the terrorist activities that have taken place in South Eastern Turkey, Ankara's proximity to an unstable Middle East, and unreasonable southern neighbours. Furthermore, increased trade with the West and political integration with Europe, especially membership in the EEC, will be the basis for her future policy needs. If Turkey does not attain this latter goal, it is conceivable that Ankara will re-evaluate her policies with the West. The *raison d'être* of NATO membership—closer affiliation with the West—for both Ankara and Athens will become less relevant if their relations with the United States and other NATO members become disagreeable. The basis for both nations' defence policies is, therefore, not exclusively focused on NATO requirements nor on NATO threat perceptions. Defence policies for both nations are individual, precisely because they are regarded as national policies. As outside powers observe these machinations, an understanding of how such policies are achieved would be of mutual benefit.

The political leadership in Greece has strengthened democratic government. As the balance between civil-military influences has evolved, this leadership has sought to build consensus for the policies they now pursue. This will, at times, entail difficult relations with the United States and NATO, but this effort will be justified domestically by the fact that it has resulted in a firmer and more cohesive foundation of policy-making that is exclusively Greek; not a pliant state. By contrast, Turkey has been more 'loyal' to NATO and caused fewer problems within NATO councils and in relations with Washington. This has come about internally from a relatively cohesive, albeit passive, public opinion on national security issues. Unfortunately Ankara has not benefited from increased financial or military assistance as a result of this nor will it in the future. The relationship between the United States, NATO, Greece and Turkey will doubtless continue to be testy. National and NATO perspectives on stability and security of the South Eastern Flank will become more compatible if Ankara and Athens make an effort to cooperate with each other, and in turn justify the efforts of outside powers to engage themselves in its concerns. Unfortunately, the kind of leadership required to undertake such an effort is presently lacking in both capitals.

The new dynamism taking place in the Soviet Union and Eastern Europe, combined with the growing importance and increasingly perilous implications of local conflicts and crisis situations, requires qualitative improvements in Alliance cooperation between Ankara and Athens. Specific disagreements, lack of coordination and consultation may continue to offer the Soviet Union opportunities which Moscow's politically vigilant and dynamic new leadership may exploit. A more credible defence posture on the South Eastern Flank of NATO is a necessity. It cannot be pursued primarily by bilateral accords between the United States and Greece and Turkey nor with European countries. Relations can be strengthened by truly multi-lateral commitments linking Greece and Turkey more closely with Western Europe. This becomes a necessity with the potential today of out-of-area matters directly affecting Central Europe. Certainly, the solution does not lie in reducing or minimising mutual obligations.

Building long-term political stability and co-operation in Greece and Turkey will depend as much on diplomatic tact as on military prowess. The moulding of national interests into a coherent body of Alliance interest, while minimising and resolving the conflicting issues, is central to success on the South Eastern Flank of NATO. Can this and other major questions posed in this volume be sensibly addressed and answers found? The author personally believes that the solutions lie with the Alliance, but 'time will tell'.

Glossary of Acronyms

AAM	Air-to-Air Missile
ACE	Allied Commander Europe
AFSOUTH	Allied Forces Southern Europe
AIRSOUTH	Allied Air Forces Southern Europe
AMF	Allied Mobile Force
APC	Armoured Personnel Carrier
ASM	Air-to-Surface Missile
ATTU	Atlantic to the Urals
ASW	Anti-submarine Warfare
AWACS	Airborne Warning and Control System
CFE	Conventional Forces Europe Discussions
CINCSOUTH	Commander-in-Chief, Allied Forces Southern Europe
COMAIRSOUTH	Commander, Allied Air Forces Southern Europe (Naples)
C^{3}I	Command, Control, Communications and Intelligence
COMNAVSOUTH	Commander, Allied Naval Forces Southern Europe (Naples)
DECA	Defence and Economic Co-operation Agreement
DID	Defence Industry Directorate (Greece)
DIDA	Defence Development and Support Administration (Turkey)
DM	West German Mark
EEC	European Economic Community
ELINT	Electronic Intelligence
FIR	Flight Information Region
FMS	Foreign Military Sales
FIVEATAF	Fifth Allied Tactical Air Force
GDP	Gross Domestic Product
GNP	Gross National Product
ICAO	International Civil Aviation Organisation

INF	Intermediate-Range Nuclear Forces
JCS	Joint Chiefs of Staff
KKE	Communist Party of Greece
LANDSOUTH	Land Forces Southern Europe (Verona)
LANDSOUTHCENT	Land Forces South-Central Europe (Larisa)
LANDSOUTHEAST	Land Forces South-Eastern Europe (Izmir)
LOCs	Lines of Communication
MBT	Main Battle Tank
MLRS	Multiple-Launch Rocket System
NADGE	NATO Air Defence Ground Environment
NATO	North Atlantic Treaty Organisation
NAVOCFORMED	Naval On-Call Force Mediterranean
NAVSOUTH	Naval Forces Southern Europe
NOTAM	Note to Airmen
PASOK	Panhellenic Socialist Movement (Greece)
PKK	Kurdish Workers' Party
POL	Petroleum, Oil and Lubricants
SACEUR	Supreme Allied Commander Europe
SAM	Surface-to-Air Missiles
SEVENATAF	Seventh Allied Tactical Air Force
SIGNIT	Signal Intelligence
SIXATAF	Sixth Allied Tactical Air Force
SLOC	Sea Lines of Communication
SRA	Southern Region Amendment
SSMs	Surface-to-Surface Missiles
STRIKEFORSOUTH	Naval Striking and Support Forces Southern Europe
STVD	Southern Theatre of Strategic Operations
SWTVD	South-West Theatre of Strategic Operations
TVD	Soviet Theatre of Strategic Operations
TGS	Turkish General Staff
WEU	Western European Union
WTO	Warsaw Treaty Organisation

Chapter Notes

Chapter 1. A Legacy of Fragmentation

1. Turkey has approximately 600 kilometres of land frontier with the Soviet Union and borders Bulgaria. Greece verges on Albania, Bulgaria and Yugoslavia.
2. As quoted in 'NATO's Achilles Heel: Is the Southeastern Flank Beyond Repair?' by Monteagle Stearns, discussion paper for Workshop/Seminar on 28 May 1987, organised by the Foreign Service Institute, Washington, DC, p. 2.
3. Ibid., p. 4
4. Both Greece and Turkey sent contingents to the United Nations forces in Korea as part of their interest and support of this conflict.
     For details of this period see Bruce R. Kuniholm, *The Origins of the Cold War in the Near East*. (Princeton, New Jersey: Princeton University Press, 1980), pp. 350–78.
5. Stearns, 'NATO's Achilles Heel,' p. 5.
6. James Brown, 'The Politics of Transition in Turkey,' *Current History* (February, 1988): p. 71.
7. Stearns, 'NATO's Achilles Heel,' p. 7.
8. Henry Kissinger, *The Troubled Partnership* (New York: McGraw Hill, 1965), p. 35.
9. The population of Turkey is in excess of 52,000,000 with a total armed forces of 635,000 as compared to Greece's population of about 10,000,000 and standing forces of 214,000.
10. C. M. Woodhouse, *Something Ventured* (London: Granada Press, 1982), p. 133.
11. The British grant of independence was tied to a complex set of accords known as the Zurich-London Accords, 1959, and whose guarantors are Great Britain, Greece, and Turkey.
12. For details of President Lyndon Johnson's letter and President Inonu's reply see *Middle East Journal* (Summer, 1966): pp. 386–93.
13. When Brigadier Dimitrios Ioanides sought to eliminate Archbishop Makarios, he believed that he was doing Washington a service as well as ridding himself of an 'upstart' who attempted to undermine the authority of Athens. His attempt against Makarios' life triggered the Turkish invasion. Presently, there are some 26,000 Turkish troops stationed in Cyprus.
14. For details see *Congressional-Executive Relations and the Turkish Arms Embargo* (Washington: US Government Printing Service, 1980).
15. *Foreign Broadcast Information Service, Daily Report* (FBIS), VII, 13 May 1983: T–1.
16. Interview conducted in Ankara, Turkey, at the Ministry of Foreign Affairs on 28 May 1981.
17. For a complete discussion of the Aegean Sea issues, see Andrew Wilson, *The Aegean Sea*, Adelphi Paper, No. 155 (London: IISS, 1979–80).
18. Thanos Veremis, 'Greece and NATO: Continuity and Change,' in *NATO's Southern Allies; Internal and External Challenges*, ed. John Chipman (London, Routledge, 1988), p.274.
19. NATO military aircraft are exempt from filing flight plans with Athens, according to the 1944 ICAO agreement. Greece claims that this agreement permits enforcement of a nation's national rules and regulations.
20. The Berne Declaration, 1976, established a set of guidelines for future negotiations

over the continental shelf. See Andrew Wilson's 'The Aegean Sea,' Appendix I for the text of the Berne Declaration.

21. US House of Representatives, *Greek-Turkish Relations: Beginning of a New Era*, A Staff Report prepared for the Committee on Foreign Affairs, 100th Congress, 2nd Session (Washington, DC: December 1988), p. 22.

22. Turkey has not signed the Law of the Sea Treaty.

23. The islands that have been fortified are Chios, Samothraki, Kos, Lesbos, Rhodes, and Samos. It is estimated that some 27,000 Greek troops are stationed here. *Compendium of International Agreements and Other Legal Materials* (Naples, Italy: Allied Forces Southern Europe, 1985), pp. 4–6.

    The 1923 Lausanne Treaty demilitarised not only the Dardanelles and the Bosporus, but also the Greek and Turkish islands in the area. Subsequently, the 1936 Montreaux Convention authorised the remilitarisation of the Dardanelles and the Bosporus without mentioning the status of the adjacent islands. Holding that the latter treaty replaced the former in its entirety, the Greeks have assumed the right to remilitarise the islands in a treaty interpretation disputed by the Turks.

24. The Lemnos Island impasse also prevented the Alliance from producing an updated NATO-Warsaw Pact Comparison paper since Turkey refuses to accept Greek Defence Planning Questionnaire data that includes the forces on Lemnos. In May 1989, Prime Minister Ozal stated that Turkey would welcome Greek participation in NATO military exercises held in the Aegean Sea.

25. Greece did not participate in any NATO exercises from 1974–1978 and has participated selectively from 1978 to the present.

26. In 1985 Greece refused to refuel a British naval vessel when it called on a NATO depot in Souda Bay, Crete.

27. Sir Nicholas Henderson, *The Birth of NATO* (Boulder, Colo.: Westview Press, 1983), p. 72.

28. Ibid., p. 104.

29. Ibid.

30. In the period 1957–58 two NATO Secretaries General—Ismay and Spaak—acted as mediators in successive attempts to restore harmony to Anglo-Greek-Turkish relations.

Chapter 2. Politics of Continuity and Change

1. Constantine Tsoucalas, 'The Ideological Impact of the Civil War', *Greece in the 1940s: A Nation in Crisis*, ed. John Iatrides (London: University of New England, 1981), p. 328.

2. Thanos Veremis, 'Greece and NATO: Continuity and Change', *NATO's Southern Allies: Internal and External Challenges* (London: Routledge, 1988), p. 246.

3. Ibid.

4. Thanos Veremis, 'Greek Security: Issues and Politics', *Greece and Turkey*, ed. Jonathan Alford (London: Gower Publishing Co., 1984), p. 28.

5. The Centre Union party received 52.72 per cent or 2,424,477 votes out of 4,598,839. The Communists and the Socialists formed the United Democratic Left (EDA) which became the second parliamentary party in 1958, garnering 24 per cent of the vote. This party nurtured the discontent that existed against Karamanlis and the National Radical Union (ERE).

6. Two events set the stage for the 21 April coup: first, the discovery in May 1965 of a left-wing secret organisation known as the Shield (*Aspida*) and connected to Andreas Papandreou; second, the elections scheduled for May 1967, which George Papandreou and the Centre Union and the Left were certain to win. The latter event precipitated discussions within the general staff (including King Konstantine) for a possible *coup d'état*. Serious discussions began as early as February 1967. Several members of the General Staff were against a coup; thus, no decision was forthcoming. Colonel George Papadopoulos and his cohorts, who were members of a secret organisation known as the National Union of Young Officers (EENA) and were privy to the discussion of

the General Staff, realised that no action from this level would be forthcoming and instituted their own coup. The actual coup plan, given the name The Hawk (*Ierax*), was a General Staff contingency plan to implement a NATO war plan known as Prometheus II.

7. *The Times* (London), 15 July 1965.
8. Veremis, *NATO's Southern Allies*, p. 248.
9. Keith R. Legg, *Politics in Modern Greece* (Stanford: Stanford University Press, 1969). For a detailed discussion of 'Politics at the Extraparliamentary Level', see pp. 186–220.
10. Veremis, *NATO's Southern Allies*, p. 248.
11. Eight *coups d'état* have taken place in this century: coups led by Colonel N. Zorbas in 1909, Colonel George Plastiras in 1922, General J. Metaxas in 1933 and 1936, General G. Kondylas in 1926 and 1935, George Pangalos in 1925, and Colonel G. Papadopoulos 1967. Other attempted coups either failed or never got 'off the ground' (May 1951, March and early April 1967, February 1975, March 1982, February 1983 and November 1984).
12. Legg, *Politics in Modern Greece*, pp. 191–192.
13. James Brown, 'Military Intervention and the Politics of Greece', *Soldiers in Politics*, ed. Steffen W. Schmidt and Gerald A. Dorfman (Los Altos, Calif.: Geron-X, Inc., 1974), pp. 221–224.
14. Kosta Digkabe, *Oi Ekloges Sthn Ellada, 1844–1985* (*The Elections in Greece 1844–1985*), (Solonika, Greece: Malliares-Paidia Publishers, 1986), p. 87.
15. Ibid., pp. 51 and 89.
16. Veremis, *NATO's Southern Allies*, p. 252.
17. Beginning in February 1984 and subsequently in December 1984 and March 1985, a total of 6 Lieutenant Generals, 37 Major Generals and 79 Brigadier Generals were retired. Also, the Chief of the General Staff (General Nikolaos Kouris) is an Air Force officer, whereas historically this billet belonged to the Army. All the major slots of the armed forces were headed by Papandreou supporters or political neutrals. Professionalism is not a major criteria for selection to these posts.
18. The Navy was highly implicated in the King's counter-coup of December 1967. During the entire period of the Junta, the Navy was, for the most part, suspect.
19. Morris Janowitz, *The Military in the Political Development of New Nations* (Chicago: The University of Chicago Press, 1977), p. 134.
20. Legg, *Politics in Modern Greece*, p. 34.

   Clientage belongs to the corporate tradition of the Ottoman Empire. During the centuries of Turkish rule, it was customary for a local notable in Greece to intercede with the authorities on behalf of his fellow citizens. This role gave him prestige, power, and wealth; the villagers gained a sponsor and security. There was some reciprocity, since it was recognised that the notable had a call on the service or loyalty of those for whom he did favours. Conversely, the notable had an obligation to protect the interests of those who entered into this relationship; thus the client maintained a certain self respect. Clientage relationships continue to this day, especially in the rural areas, but also among some elements of the urban population.

21. Ibid., pp. 249–316.
22. Ibid., p. 307.
23. Cabinet ministers and their families tend to favour certain educational institutions (Protypon Gymnasium and Athens University). In addition, they travel and study extensively abroad. Furthermore, they belong to voluntary and élite organisations (the Athenian League, Society of Athenians, etc.). However, intra-élite conflicts and antagonisms exist between old aristocratic families (*tzakia*) and the newly mobilised strata of entrepreneurs (*neoplouti*). These élites are not homogeneous in outlook or philosophy, but they have interlocking relationships. The cabinet ministers tend to be all males, university educated and predominantly lawyers.
24. A. F. Freris. *The Greek Economy: In the Twentieth Century* (New York: St. Martin's Press, 1986), p. 148.
25. *International Herald Tribune*, 7 June 1988, p. 10.
26. Freris, *The Greek Economy*, p. 196.

27. *International Herald Tribune*, 7 June 1988, p. 10.
28. By threatening to veto the admittance of Spain and Portugal into the EEC, Papandreaou was able to apply leverage to his position in securing $1.5 billion European Currency Units ($1.25 billion) a year in various grants and aids.
29. In the first post-embargo year, 1978, both Greece and Turkey received about $175 million in military aid. The next year, the ratio of their aid ($148 million to Greece, $208 million to Turkey) was close to 7:10. This ratio has remained in effect informally by means of congressionally imposed cuts to Turkey's aid since 1980, although Turkey and subsequent administrations have opposed it. It should be highlighted that the 7:10 ratio applies to items being *offered and not what is taken*.
30. Prime Minister Karamanlis began the process in 1961 and Greece joined the EEC twenty years later.
31. S. Victor Papacosma, 'Greece and NATO', *NATO and the Mediterranean*, eds. Lawrence S. Kaplan *et al*. (Wilmington: Scholarly Resources, Inc., 1985), p. 209.
32. Ibid., p. 209. While Greece remained outside of the military command structure of NATO, Greece's military relations with the United States can be characterised, at best, as tentative.
33. Papacosma, *NATO and the Mediterranean*, pp. 210–211.
34. *New York Times*, 4 September 1986, p. 6.
35. Robert McDonald, 'Greece: The Search for a Balance', *The World Today* (Vol. 44, No. 6, June 1988), p. 101.
36. Likewise, the Prime Minister was to visit Turkey, but his visit was postponed because of domestic politics. Several high delegations from Greece have visited Ankara, including Foreign Minister K. Papoulis.
37. One scandal affects the Bank of Crete and a young wheeler dealer named George Koskotas, who has supposedly embezzled some $200 million. An even larger scandal is brewing involving the Hellenic Arms Industry (EVO) and the Munitions Cartridge Company (PYRKAL). Five of the top officials of these companies have been charged with financial improprieties. *New York Times*, 28 September 1989.
    If Parliament had been dissolved in an effort to break the political deadlock by holding elections, the Greek constitution forbids any further persecution of ministers and thus it would put an end to the 'catharsis' that was sought by New Democracy and Alliance partnership.
38. Mersin was the Mediterranean port that served the Turkish armed forces in their 1974 invasion of Cyprus, and continues to be the port from which operations and support of Turkish troops on the island are primarily conducted.
39. *World Military Expenditures and Arms Transfers 1987* (Washington: US Government Printing Office, 1988), p. 128.
40. Greece has bought arms and equipment from France (40 MIRAGE 2000, EXOCET missiles, AMX–30 tanks), Federal Republic of Germany (75 LEOPARD tanks, T–209 submarines, 24 F–104G STARFIGHTERS), Italy (armoured personnel carriers, Aspida surface-to-air missiles), Norway (surface-to-surface missiles), Netherlands (frigates), and Great Britain (HAMLET surface-to-air missiles). Other items include upgrade kits for the M48–A5 tank, STINGER and HARPOON missiles, and anti-submarine warfare helicopters.
41. SRA requires the recipient to pay transportation costs and the cost for any upgrading or repair of the equipment the country believes is necessary.
42. McDonald, 'Greece: The Search for a Balance', p. 101.
43. At the height of the Aegean Sea confrontation in March 1987, Papandreou dispatched Foreign Minister K. Papoulias not to Brussels but to Sofia, Bulgaria, to visit T. Zhivkov.
44. Greece is the only NATO member who does not recognise Israel *de jure*.
45. Veremis, *NATO's Southern Allies*, p. 263.
46. Foreign Broadcast Information Service (FBIS), (Washington: US Government Printing Office), 28 May 1986, S4–5.
47. *The Christian Science Monitor*, 29 September 1986. The Supreme Court of Greece, on 12 May 1989, upheld the US request for the extradition of Mohammed Rashid, a Palestinian, whom Washington has accused of planting a bomb on a Pan American

flight from Tokyo to Honolulu, in which one person was killed and 15 were wounded. The final decision is in the hands of the Minister of Justice, who has overruled extradition orders of two recent terrorism cases, not wanting to affect Greece's relations with the Palestinians. *Greece: The Week in Review*, 27 November 1989, p. 2–3.

48. Only five Libyans are officially accredited to the Greek Government, but more than 50 at the embassy had diplomatic immunity. Some 20 left Athens.

49. *The Christian Science Monitor*, 29 September 1986.

Chapter 3 Turkey. A Delicately Poised Ally

1. Kemal Ataturk was the first President of the Republic and the leader of the Republican People's Party. He was re-elected three times and died in office in 1938.

2. Ataturk had to fend off a conservative military faction which opposed his nation building and quelled three Kurdish insurrections (in 1925, 1930 and 1937). See Lincoln P. Bloomfield, Jr., 'Anarchy in Turkey,' *Conflict* (Vol. 2, No. 1, 1980), pp. 33-34.

3. By 1930, Robert College in Istanbul had become one of the most prestigious centres in Turkey for training its commercial and technical élite.

4. Dankwart A. Rustow, 'Turkey's Travails,' *Foreign Affairs* (Fall 1979), p. 84.

5. Ibid.

6. Another example was when Turkish approaches to Pakistan and Iraq (1954–55) satisfied Dulles' requests that the initiative for a common defence of the area must come from within the region.

7. The Electoral Law 1946 introduced direct universal suffrage and the secret ballot.

8. In December 1957, a plot by dissident officers to discredit the DP and the political system was unearthed. Officers continued to involve themselves in conspiratorial schemes until the May 1960 coup.

9. For a detailed discussion of the several extremist groups of this period, see Bloomfield. *Anarchy in Greece*, Vol. 2, pp. 40–2.

10. With the outbreak of civil war between the Turkish and Greek Cypriots, it was clear to Turkey that the outnumbered Turkish Cypriots were to be overrun. As a guarantor under the 1959 London-Zurich accords on Cyprus, the Turkish Air Force began to overfly the island and the armed forces mobilised for an invasion of Cyprus.

11. Other problems that plagued US-Turkish relations were port visits of the Sixth Fleet, differences and pace of modernising the Armed Forces, curtailment of poppy production and reduction of US economic assistance.

12. The Justice Party won 52.3 per cent of the popular vote.

13. Rustow, 'Turkey's Travails,' p. 88.

14. Law No. 1773 enacted in June 1973 outlined jurisdiction of civilian courts. Also, Articles 141, 142, and 163 were reversed. This allowed the state courts to arrest and detain any suspect leftist or right-wing Islamist, regardless of the presence or absence of a conventional crime.

15. The Republican People's Party received 185 seats; Justice Party 149; National Salvation Party 48; Democratic Party 45; Republican Reliance Party 13; the National Muslim Party 3; and Independents 6.

16. The discussion that follows is taken primarily from Rustow, 'Turkey's Travails,' pp. 90–94.

17. For example, when Fahri Koruturk resigned as President, the Grand National Assembly was unable to nominate a replacement because of the deadlock among the several political parties. Over 100 ballots were taken to no avail.

18. Rustow, 'Turkey's Travails,' p. 92.

19. James Brown, 'Military and Politics in Turkey,' *Armed Forces and Society* (Vol. 13, No. 2, Winter 1987), p. 241.
    It was reported that the National Security Council warned the politicians, both privately and publicly, at least six times during the first part of 1981.

20. For details of both Demeril's and Ecevit's responses, see *FBIS*, 3 January 1980, T1–2. Emphasis added by author.

21. The margin of victory to lift the bans on the politicians was quite close. For detailed

discussion, see *Middle East International* (London: Linco Printing, Inc.) 29 September 1987.

22. In November 1989, elections were held by the Grand National Assembly and Turgut Ozal was elected President of the Republic, replacing President K. Evren. The term of office is for six years.

23. The Constitutional Court, Turkey's court of last resort, declared on 9 October 1987, that Article 8 of the Election Law was unconstitutional. The Court's 6 to 5 decision concerned only the process of selecting candidates. This decision forced Prime Minister Ozal to reconvene Parliament to amend the election law and to change the election day from 1 November to 29 November 1987.

    In the results of the election, Ozal and the Motherland Party won 292 of 452 seats in Parliament, while the Social Democrats won 99 seats and the True Path Party of Suleyman Demirel took 59 seats. Bulent Ecevit failed to gain the 10 per cent needed for parliamentary representation and announced his withdrawal from active politics.

24. In March 1989, a deputy of the Motherland Party, Idris Arikan, wounded opposition True Path Party deputy A. Ceylan in the Grand National Assembly. Could this be a harking back to the pre-1980 era?

25. President Evren has suggested that perhaps the Communist Party should be re-established in Turkey. See *FBIS*, 14 December 1988, p. 29.

26. The Motherland Party of Prime Minister Ozal won only two mayoral positions out of 67 provinces, capturing overall 21.8 per cent of the vote, as opposed to the Social Democrats who won 39 mayoral positions and garnered 28.2 per cent, while the True Path Party won 16 seats and secured 25.6 per cent. The Moslem fundamentalist Prosperity Party won five positions and captured 9.7 per cent of the vote and the Democratic Left 9.7 and three seats.

27. These provinces are Bingol, Diyarbakir, Elazig, Hakkari, Mardin, Siirt, Tunceli and Van.

28. Turkey has had a long-standing agreement with Iraq that permits Ankara to pursue the PKK into Iraqi territory in order to attack Kurdish strongholds.

    In October 1989, two Syrian MIG–21s shot down a Turkish survey aircraft 13 miles inside Turkey, with the loss of five lives. Syria quickly apologised and launched an investigation. This incident added fuel to the Kurdish issue.

29. Upon the conclusion of the Iran-Iraq conflict, Iraq unilaterally attacked Kurdish villages, using chemical weapons against them. Some 70,000 fled to Turkey. It also appears that the PKK is now receiving support from Tehran. See *The Middle East* (London: I. C. Publications, Inc.) February 1989, No. 172, pp. 20–22.

30. An emphasis has been placed on the study of modern Turkish history and Kemalism. Cadets at the military high schools and military academies are required to take a minimum of one hour per week for all four years of their enrollment at each institution.

31. For specific details, see Brown, 'Military and Politics in Turkey,' pp. 245–247.

32. Only 10 per cent of the army cadets are from the eastern provinces, where the revolution took roots, whereas the percentage of the total population of Turkey is 14.6 per cent.

33. Brown, 'Military and Politics in Turkey,' p. 247.

34. Ibid.

35. Morris Janowitz, *The Military in the Political Development of New Nations*, p. 50.

36. The National Security Council consists of the Prime Minister, the Chief of the General Staff, the Ministers of Defence, Internal Affairs, and Foreign Affairs, the Commanders of the Army, Navy and Air Force and the Commander of the Gendarmerie, under the chairmanship of the President of the Republic.

    The Ministry of Defence is basically an adjunct to the Turkish General Staff. The defence minister's responsibilities include personnel, procurement, supplies, and implementation of the budget. All major decisions affecting the Turkish armed forces are made by the General Staff—the supreme body.

37. *FBIS*, 2 January 1980, T–1.

38. *Newspot*, 3 January 1986.

39. *Turkey: OECD Economic Survey, 1987* (Paris: Organisation for Economic Co-operation and Development, 1987), p.7.
40. *Country Report: Turkey* (London: Economic Intelligence Unit, 1988), pp. 1-5.
41. Ibid., 14.
42. Altogether the total amount of assistance was cut; Turkey will receive most of her monies in the form of grants rather than FMS credits.
43. Turkey has a number of important NATO installations. Among these is the AWACS air base at Konya, major intelligence gathering sites (Sinop, Pirinclik, Belbasi, etc.), Incirlik Air Base (for tactical fighters), several supply and munitions locations (conventional and nuclear) throughout Turkey, and 16 NADGE locations.

    The fundamental difficulty stems from US constitutional procedures which do not allow an administration to enter any commitments in advance. What the Reagan Administration was able to do was to sign a 'side letter' (a declaration of intent) promising to make every effort to get the maximum possible military aid for Turkey each year, in the face of possible congressional opposition.
44. *World Military Expenditures and Arms Transfer 1987*, p. 128.
45. Dankwart A. Rustow, *Turkey: America's Forgotten Ally* (New York: Council on Foreign Relations, 1987), p. 84.
46. Turkey joined the Baghdad pact in 1955 and the Central Treaty Organisation (CENTO) in 1959. These organisations did not involve Washington directly as a member; however, they sustained the United States' security strategy in the Middle East.
47. Tensions between Bulgaria and Turkey over the fate of the Turkish minority in Bulgaria have risen sharply since 1985. Bulgaria launched a violent campaign to compel all members of the minority, some one million, to change their Turkish names, rooted in Islam, to Bulgarian names, which are mainly of Orthodox Christian origin.
48. *ANKA Review* (Istanbul), 20 December 1988., p. 21
49. Another example of Ankara's sensitivity toward Moscow was her unwillingness to permit US intelligence experts to examine the MIG–29 that was flown by a defecting Soviet pilot to Trabzon. The MIG was released to the Soviets within 36 hours. *International Herald Tribune*, 5 May 1989, p. 2.
50. This resolution was passed by a small minority of the European Parliament; most members abstained.
51. 'What's Jamming the Door of Europe,' *The Middle East*, September 1987, No. 155, p. 40.
52. *ANKA Review*, 20 December 1988, p. 21.
53. Ibid.
54. The Constitutional Court ruled in March 1989 that it is illegal for female students to wear Islamic attire, particularly the head-scarf or 'turban', on university campuses. The verdict provoked Islamic demonstrations in Konya, Istanbul and elsewhere. More importantly, this issue has pitted Ozal and the 'Salvationist' elements of his party against President Evren and the Turkish Armed Forces. This is a very risky game for Ozal. First, he is creating doubts in the EEC about the genuineness of his commitment to the West, and in the Turkish General Staff, about the genuineness of his adherence to Kemalism. *Middle East International*, 17 March 1989, No. 346, p. 10.
55. For a detailed discussion, see 'Turkey's Middle East Gamble,' in *The Middle East*, No. 125 (March 1984), pp. 27–31.
56. Ibid.
57. In March 1986 Ankara agreed to accept a Syrian ambassador, the first since 1983.
58. *Turkish Daily News*, 10 August 1987, p. 1.

Chapter 4. Competition in the Mediterranean

1. Sergio A. Rossi, 'NATO's Southern Flank and Mediterranean Security,' *NATO's Maritime Flanks: Problems and Prospects*, eds. H. F. Zeiner-Gundersen et. al. (London: Pergamon-Brassey's, 1987), p. 48.

2. These events were the Islamic Revolution in Iran, the invasion of Afghanistan and the ten-year war between Iran and Iraq.

3. US House of Representatives, *US Military Installations in NATO's Southern Region*. Report prepared for the Subcommittee on Europe and the Middle East, 99th Congress, 2nd session (Washington, D.C.: October 7, 1986).

4. Michael MccGwire, 'Soviet Strategic Arms and Capabilities in the Mediterranean: Part I,' *Adelphi Papers, Part I, No. 229: Prospecs for Security in the Mediterranean* (London: The International Institute of Strategic Studies, Spring 1988), p. 14.

5. Ibid.

6. Thomas H. Etzold, 'The Soviet Union in the Mediterranean,' *NATO and the Mediterranea*, eds. Lawrence S. Kaplan, Robert W. Clawson, and Raimondo Luraghi (Wilmington, Del.: Scholarly Resources, Inc., 1984), p. 31.

7. Mark N. Katz, 'Soviet Policy in the Middle East,' *Current History* (Vol. 87, No. 526, February 1988), p. 58.

8. In June 1989 Iran's President, Ali Akbar Rafsanjani, visited Moscow and was able to consummate several substantial agreements amounting to $15 billion over the next fifteen years, providing economic, military and technical assistance in return for natural gas.

9. John Chipman, 'NATO and the Security Problems of the Southern Region: From the Azores to Ardahan,' *NATO's Southern Allies Internal and External Challenges*, ed. John Chipman (London: Routledge, 1988), p. 18.

10. Michael MccGwire, 'Soviet Strategic Arms Part 1,' p. 3.

11. For the text and a discussion of the Montreux Convention and its implications for Soviet naval planning, see Jesse W. Lewis, Jr, *The Strategic Balance in the Mediterranean* (Washington, D.C.: American Enterprise Institute, 1976), pp. 70–72, 155–169.

12. The USSR has successfully circumvented the Treaty's protocol on aircraft carriers thus far by declaring its four *Kiev*-class VTOL ships to be cruisers, on the basis of their cruiser-like bows. One of these vessels is attached to the Black Sea Fleet and comes and goes through the Straits at will. The Soviet Navy will once again have to grapple with the Protocols of the Convention with the completion of the first two large-deck carriers. The 65,000 ton *Tbilisi* is currently close to completion in the Black Sea. It is scheduled to become operational in 1992. Even if special dispensation is given to permit these carriers to exit the Turkish Straits *once* upon completion, the Treaty clearly prohibits regular transit, a fact which is likely to force the Soviet Union to decide upon an alternative basing site, limiting their value to the Fifth Escadra.

13. John Chipman, 'NATO and the Security Problems of the Southern Region,' p. 20.

14. See note 12 above for the effects of the Montreux Convention on these large-deck carriers.

   For a detailed discussion of this issue see Ted Greenwood 'Soviet Intimidation of the West: The Violation of the Montreux Convention,' *Global Affairs* (Fall 1988), pp. 50–69.

15. John Chipman, 'NATO and the Security Problems of the Southern Region,' p. 19.

16. This crisis was precipitated by the threats posed to King Hussein's regime by a variety of Palestinian groups and Syria.

17. Admiral Elmo Zumwalt, Jr., *On Watch* (New York: Quadrangle Books, 1976), p. 293.

18. Ibid., p. 297.

19. Ibid., pp. 297–298.

20. Michael MccGwire, 'Soviet Strategic Arms Part I,' p. 38.

21. James Cable, *Gunboat Diplomacy 1919–1979: Political Applications of Limited Naval Force*, 2nd ed. (London: Macmillan Press, 1981), pp. 264–266.

22. The Soviet Union has rebuilt the Syrian armed forces four times: Prior to 1967, after the 1967 war with Israel, again in 1973 and after Lebanon in 1982.

23. *The Military Balance, 1988–89*, (London: The International Institute for Strategic Studies, (Published Brassey's (UK) 1988), p. 42.

24. Other anchorages for the Fifth Escadra are located at Cape Passero, Italy, the Gulf of Hammamet off the coast of Tunisia and the Gulf of Sollum off the Libyan coast.

25. Prior to 1946, the Mediterranean was of little concern to the United States, despite

an occasional skirmish with Barbary pirates.

The ostensible purpose of the *Missouri's* visit was to deliver to Turkey the remains of the former Turkish ambassador Munier Ertegun, who had died in Washington in November 1944.

26. Jed C. Snyder, *Defending the Fringe: NATO, the Mediterranean and the Persian Gulf* (Washington, D.C.: The John Hopkins Foreign Policy Institute, 1987), p. 17.
27. Edward N. Luttwak and Robert G. Weinland, *Sea Power in the Mediterranean: Political Unity and Military Constraints* (Washington, D.C.: Center for Strategic and International Studies, 1979), p. 8.
28. James Cable, *Gunboat Diplomacy*, p. 78.
29. Jan S. Breemer, 'De-Committing the Sixth Fleet,' *Naval War College Review* (November-December 1982), pp. 27–28.
30. Jed C. Snyder, *Defending the Fringe*, p. 17.
31. These aircraft consist of TU–26s (Backfires), TU–225 (Blinders), with AS–4, AS–5, and AS–6 air-to-surface missiles.

Chapter 5. The Military Balance

1. The six geographical areas are Gibraltar Mediterranean (GIBMED), Western Mediterranean (MEDOC), Central Mediterranean (MEDCENT), North Eastern Mediterranean (MEDNOREAST), Eastern Mediterranean (MEDEAST), and South Eastern Mediterranean (MEDSOUEAST).
2. Because this volume focuses on Greece and Turkey, the discussion will only focus on the South Eastern region and not Northern Italy.
3. Lawrence L. Whetten, 'Turkey's Role in the Atlantic Alliance,' *Atlantic Quarterly* (Autumn 1984): p. 262.
4. The AMF's role is primarily a deterrent one, but if deterrence fails the AMF is intended to fight alongside host country troops to help contain an enemy advance. Such participation by a NATO force in a Flank country would help to multilateralise the conflict and show the enemy that NATO as a whole was concerned about the security of the attacked country. The AMF is not truly a fighting force: it is intended primarily 'to show the flag'. It should not be viewed as a force capable of providing reinforcements, but rather an immediate reaction unit which the Supreme Allied Commander Europe (SACEUR) would call upon for political reasons, to signal concern.

   The most important outside instrument of South-Eastern Flank security is to be found in the Rapid Reinforcement Plan adopted by NATO's Defence Planning Committee in December 1982. The plan envisages the involvement of over 2,000 US combat aircraft, up to 700 of which would probably be made available for a contingency in the Southern Region.
5. The land components of this force consist of infantry, armour, artillery, and helicopters from other NATO countries. Most of these units are based in their home countries. The air components are squadrons from the US, FRG, Italy and Canada.
6. During 1974–78, Greece began building military installations on these islands, which include bunkers and barbed wire, as well as emplacements for minefields and artillery pieces, anti-aircraft guns and light tanks.
7. 'A' Corps has its headquarters at Kozani, 'B' Corps at Veria, 'C' Corps at Thessaloniki, and 'D' Corps at Xanthi.
8. Syria is a fully-fledged Soviet client state which sports eight armoured and mechanised divisions, 4050 MBTs and about 450 combat aircraft.
9 This was the arrangement prior to 1975, at which time, because of Cyprus, 'D' Corps was created.
10. The first two MEKO-2000s were built at Golcuk in 1988, with at least two additional to be built in the very near future, along with the building of two corvettes. Also, some six 209 diesel submarines have been built.
11. 'West European and NATO Navies: Some Twenty Years,' *Proceedings* (March, 1989): p. 141.

12. Turkish naval assets are located at Golcuk, Istanbul, Izmir, Eregli, Kara Mursel, Foca and Akzac Karaagac Bay.
13. Two squadrons operate out of Golcuk and one out of the Black Sea port of Eregli.
14. The first ATAF is headquartered at Eskiseher and the second ATAF at Diyarbakir. Also, there is a transportation squadron, and eight squadrons of NIKE Hercules and two Rapier squadrons.
15. The air defence command shares responsibility for the operation and maintenance of NATO's 24 early warning radar network (NADGE—NATO Air Defence Ground Environment).
16. The first and most important is the Western TVD which encompasses all Central Europe, including the Iberian Peninsula, plus Sweden and Norway, This TVD is viewed by Soviet planners as the likely theatre for East-West confrontation. Operationally, victory in the Western TVD could come about by coordinating a breakthrough in the SWTVD, being the most unstable region of NATO.
17. The STVD begins in the Caucasus and Turkestan and extends to Eastern Turkey, Iran, Afghanistan, Syria, Pakistan and India.
18. East of a line running north and south of Giresun, Sivas to Hatay Province.
19. *NATO and the Warsaw Pact: Force Comparisons* (Brussels: NATO Information Service, 1984), pp. 21-23.
20. Libya's Ummaitiqah Air Base and Syria's Siyes base could be used to launch reconnaissance and fighter bomber operations.
21. Both Greece and Turkey have in the region of Thrace about 1,800 MBTs (M48–A5s, LEOPARDS and AMXs).
22. It is estimated that the Soviet Union's 7th Guard and 31st Army Corps have about 900 MBTs (T–54s and T–55s) against the Turkish Third Army's 650 M48A5s.

Chapter 6. The Strategic Geography: Land, Sea and Air Campaigns

1. In this chapter the author has not attempted to differentiate between a conventional and a nuclear conflict. In addition, adjacent portions of the WTVD are also part of the Warsaw Pact contingency planning.
2. The relations between Turkey and Bulgaria have deteriorated greatly since 1985. At that time authorities in Sofia launched a mass Bulgarisation programme desiring to obliterate any identity that ethnic Turks living in Bulgaria might have with their Turkish roots. Beginning in 1989, a mass migration of these persecuted peoples has taken place. As of this writing, an excess of 300,000 refugees have streamed into Turkey from Bulgaria.
3. The attack could also secure the right flank for a theatre operation in the STVD aimed at Iran and the Persian Gulf.
4. The land, sea and air campaigns as discussed in this chapter are from several sources. They are based primarily on the personal observations of the author who has travelled to many of these locations and has had detailed discussions with NATO officers. Also, see Hugh Faringdon, *Strategic Geography* (2nd ed.) (London: Routledge, 1989), and an excellent discussion by Phillip A Peterson, 'The Southwestern TVD in Soviet Military Planning'; paper presented at the Conference on New Technologies and International Armaments Co-operation, Istanbul, Turkey, 27–29, June 1989.

    The data on military force levels is from *The Military Balance, 1989–1990*. (London: The International Institute for Strategic Studies (Published Brassey's (UK) 1988).

    For detailed historical footnotes on how strategic geography in Greece and Turkey was used by invading armies, see Faringdon, pp. 196–224.
5. See Daniel N. Nelson, 'The Bulgarian People's Army,' in Jeffrey Simon (ed.) *NATO-Warsaw Pact Force Mobilisation* (Washington, DC: National Defense University Press, 1988), pp. 455–461.
6. If Yugoslavia and Albania actively co-operate with the Warsaw Pact, the ground threat to Greece, Turkey and Italy would increase considerably. Access to air bases in Southern Yugoslavia and Albania would permit the Warsaw Pact fighters to open a gap between Italy and Greece for use by Soviet bombers and perhaps naval vessels.

7. Faringdon, *Strategic Geography*, p. 223.
8. *The Voroshilov Lectures, Vol. I: Issues of Soviet Military Strategy*, Graham H Turbiville (ed.), (Washington, DC: National Defense University Press, 1989), p. 113.
9. Faringdon, *Strategic Geography*, p. 216.
10. The Black Sea Fleet's bases are located at Sevastopol and Balaklava in the Crimea, at Odessa in the west and at Poti close to Anatolia. It has impressive naval construction facilities up the River Bug at Nikolayev.
11. Faringdon, *Strategic Geography*, p. 218.
12. Ibid., pp. 215–216.
13. Joint airborne/amphibious combat operations resembling a Soviet assault landing were conducted in exercise SHIELD-82. Peterson, 'The Southwestern TVD in Soviet Military Planning,' p. 30.
14. Charles Pritchard, 'Warsaw Pact Amphibious Forces and the Turkish Straits,' *Dis Politika* [(Turkish Foreign Policy Institute), Vol. XIII, No. 1-2, 1986], p. 155.
15. Both the Greek and Turkish forces lack anti-tank weapons to be effective against Warsaw Pact MBTs. Furthermore, the rapid pace of the Soviet Union's deployment of reactive armour is further undermining NATO anti-tank capabilities.
16. As quoted in Peterson, 'The Southwestern TVD in Soviet Military Planning,' p. 31.
17. Ibid., pp. 31-32.
18. The Transcaucasus Military District has a unique Mountain Directorate which trains troops for combat in mountains. Faringdon, *Strategic Geography*, p. 210.
19. Ibid., pp. 210–211.
20. Ibid.
21. Ibid., p. 211.
22. Overall the Greek and Turkish forces have very little protective equipment and knowledge about chemical warfare.
23. The acquisition of a NATO multinational tanker fleet would provide fighters with considerably more loiter time and greater ability to intercept Soviet fighters and bombers.
24. S. G. Gorshkov, 'Navies in War and Peace,' *US Naval Institute Proceedings* (January-April, 1974), p. 36.
25. Ibid.
26. The Soviet Union would undertake mining activities by using either merchant vessels, submarines, or aircraft. For the latter, it would be demanding missions that would necessitate deep penetrations into the southeastern area.
27. These ports account for most of the dry-cargo reception capacity for ocean-going cargo ships. Ports that coastal vessels could use in Greece are Patras, Kalamata, Candia, and Irakleon.
28. To minimise this risk, NATO could keep these choke points under surveillance by maintaining maritime patrols on station.
29. Submarines pose a serious threat to these battle groups. It is conceivable to utilise decoy carrier battle groups. When this is done, it significantly reduces the threat but requires additional vessels.
30. Greece has AIM–7 (SPARROWS) and Turkey RAPIERS. It is anticipated that both will be securing Multiple-Launched Rocket Systems (MLRS) shortly.
31. Although both Greece and Turkey have acquired MIRAGE and F-16s recently, for the foreseeable future the south-eastern area will continue to rely heavily on older aircraft such as F–104s, F–4s, and F–5A/Bs.
32. Fighters from Bulgaria could operate against Greece and Western Turkey and the FENCERS and medium bombers from Vinnitsa and Smolensk Army Air could also come into play.
33. Success of these missions would depend on the shelter facilities available in Bulgaria and Romania.
34. Diego A. Ruiz Palmer and A. Grant Whitley, 'The Balance of Forces in Southern Europe: Between Uncertainty and Opportunity,' *The International Spectator* (Vol. XXIII, No. 1, January-March 1988), pp. 35–36.
35. Ibid., p. 39.

Chapter 7. Conflict Between Two Allies

1. As cited by Yahon Ramati in 'NATO's Southern Flank and Israel', a paper presented at the American Political Science Association annual meeting at Atlanta, Georgia, 31 August–3 September 1989, pp. 3–4.
2. This confrontation led the two Prime Ministers, Papandreou and Ozal, to meet in Davos and initiate a process toward institutionalising discussions between Greece and Turkey to improve their relations with a hope, but not a guarantee, of changing the substance of each other's policies.
3. This concept of the *Megali Idea* evolved in the early nineteenth century in Greece as the ideal of uniting all Greeks of the Ottoman Empire into one Greek nation with its capital in Constantinople.
4. There are some circles in Athens who believe that there exists a secret protocol between Greece and Bulgaria. The protocol is alleged to permit Greek forces to pass through Bulgaria in order to outflank Turkish units in Turkish Thrace..
5. *The Military Balance, 1988–1989* (London: The International Institute for Strategic Studies, (Published Brassey's (UK) 1988), pp. 69, 81, 87.
6. Ibid., pp. 87–88.
7. The Turks might be constrained in meeting this objective because of their inadequate engineering and transportation assets. Also, to defend against Greek air attacks they have only limited SAMs although they do possess RAPIERS and REDEYES. The NIKE-HERCULES units are primarily positioned in the Istanbul area.
8. The Greek and Turkish air forces are about equal and are affected by poor weather or night time capabilities. Whoever dominates the air would be in a position to press for interdiction attacks.
9. The two air forces have roughly similar aircrew readiness rates and annual flying hours. Informed observers of both suggest that Turkish tactical training is a bit more conservative and less aggressive than that of their Greek counterparts.
10. *The Military Balance, 1988–1989*, pp. 69, 80.

Chapter 8. Conventional Arms: Negotiations, Modernisation and Defence Industrial Development

1. These are the first arms reduction talks held by the two sides, unlike the Mutual Balanced Force Reduction Talks that included only eleven countries, because they focused narrowly on forces in Central Europe.
2. The existence of multiple capabilities will not be a criterion for modifying the scope of the negotiation:

    No conventional armaments or equipment will be excluded from the subject of the negotiation because they may have other capabilities in addition to conventional ones. Such armaments or equipment will not be singled out in a separate category.

    Nuclear weapons will not be a subject of this negotiation.

    Naval forces and chemical weapons will not be addressed.
3. In the East, the ATTU region includes all of Eastern Europe plus the Soviet military districts that lie west of the Urals, the Ural River, and the Caspian Sea. The relevant Soviet districts, along with their 'theatres of operation' (TVDs), are the Leningrad Military District (MD), which makes up the entire North-Western TVD; the Baltic, Byelorussian, and Carpathian MDS, which along with Poland, the German Democratic Republic (GDR), and Czechoslovakia make up the Western TVD; the Odessa and Kiev MDs, which together with Hungary, Romania, and Bulgaria make up the South–Western TVD; the Moscow, Volga, and Ural MDs, which make up the USSR's Central Reserve region; and the North Caucasus and Trans-Caucasus MDs, which make up the western half of the Southern TVD.
4. *To Strengthen Stability and Security* (Washington, DC: US Information Agency, 1987), p. 5.

    For the US and Canada only, forces stationed in Europe are counted in the CFE discussions. Those in home territory are excluded. For the US this means that only 30 per cent of ground forces and 10 per cent of the tactical air force are included, while for the Soviet Union this includes about 70 per cent of ground and air forces.

5. Ibid.
6. The CFE talks must serve to enhance the security of NATO and not to jeopardise it. The philosophy of the Harmel Report of some twenty years ago held twin concepts of deterrence and *détente* and this is discharged on the basis of adequately assumed security, not as an alternative to it.
7. This will permit the US to have a total of 225,000 personnel in Europe, because reinforcement of Europe from the US is more time-consuming than from the Soviet Union.
8. There are five categories for discussion in the CFE negotiations: MBTs, APCs, artillery, aircraft and personnel.
    Cutting Conventional Forces I (Brookline, Mass.: Institute for Defense and Disarmament Studies, 1989), XVI.
9. For example the Warsaw Treaty Organisation envisions that, in the first round, each alliance would reduce its alliance-wide holdings in various categories down by 15 per cent below current holdings of the Alliance with fewer. The second round would be deeper and reduce these categories further by 25 per cent.
10. Michael Moodie, 'Conventional Arms Control: An Analytical Survey of Recent Literature,' *The Washington Quarterly* (Winter 1989): p. 190.
11. Big cuts on the conventional side could bring phenomenal savings—on the order of in excess of $50 billion annually in the US, Soviet Union and in Europe.
12. *Cutting Conventional Forces* I, p. 390.
13. For example, NATO's proposed zones place the Kiev MD in the zone with Greece and Turkey. This was at the insistence of Turkey. This whole area behind the Urals may even be a threat to Turkey if reserve military districts are places of stockpiling of arms and equipment.
14. For specifics see *Cutting Conventional Forces* I, p. 390.
15. Ibid., p. 53.
16. See Air Vice-Marshal R. A. Mason, 'Airpower in Conventional Arms Control,' *Survival* (September/October 1989): pp. 397–413.
17. There is a point at issue here as to how training aircraft will be counted. NATO argues that such aircraft have potential combat capabilities. Rather than create specific criteria for defining trainers, NATO's plan demands that each side submits a list of proposals.
18. This includes the Second Army, XI Corps on Cyprus and elements of the Third Army.
19. *Defense News*, September 11, 1989: p. 58.
20. Since 1985 more than 2,000 people have been killed by terrorists in South-Eastern Turkey. Most of these incidents are by the PKK terrorist organisation.
21. On September 27, 1989 Turkey recognised the Jurisdiction of the European Court of Human Rights for a three-year period.
22. *Defense News*, March 27, 1989: p. 8.
23. *Cutting Conventional Forces* I, p. 65.
24. *Defense News*, March 27, 1989: p. 8.
25. Greece is considering the purchase of modernising kits for its F–4s and F–5s to extend their service life.
26. These two acquisitions will be completed by the middle of this year.
27. This includes installations on the islands of Lemnos, Mykonos, Skyros, and Rhodes.
28. This includes outdated SAMs and newly purchased West German twin 20 mm air defence guns and SKYGUARD firing Sparrow AAMs or 35 mm defence guns.
29. New taxiways and runways have been expanded and they have also built dispersed bases to provide operational facilities from the main bases.
30. Greece has expressed an interest in buying 12 new frigates in sets of four, that would be built in Greece.
31. Raytheon will sell to the Greek Navy four sonar systems for improved anti-submarine warfare. These will be hull-mounted and with variable depth sonar capability. These are valued at $30 million.

32. For the 1987–88 period, the Navy received only 18 per cent of the defence budget, while the Army and Air Force received 35 and 32 per cent respectively.
33. This aid is in addition to the normal assistance that is given to Turkey. This is worth about $350 million.
34. LTV will deliver 12 of these systems by 1990.
35. *The Military Balance, 1989–1990* (London: International Institute for Strategic Studies, 1989), p. 77.
36. Ibid.
37. *Defense News*, November 13, 1989, p. 42.
38. Ibid.
39. The US has identified two squadrons (40 aircraft) from Air Guard and Reserve Force for possible transfer to Turkey.
40. Turkey's early warning capabilities against the Warsaw Pact and other nations has markedly improved with the deployment of NATO AWACs at Konya.
41. For example, the $4.2 billion F–16 sale was accompanied by $150 million in direct offsets and $1.27 billion in indirect offsets.
42. *Defense News*, 21 August, 1989, reported improprieties and overcharges in the purchase of the Mirage 2000 and F–16 contracts.
43. HAI holds a major contract in the overhaul of GE J–79 engines used in the F–4s and F–5s stationed in Europe. In 1983, a 15-year contract with the French firm SNECMA to repair jet engines was also signed.
44. It has been reported that Libya purchased some $500 million of military equipment from EBO including the Artemis-30 twin anti-aircraft gun.
45. EBO also holds licences to produce light guns for Heckler and Koch (GA3 and GA4 assault rifles, machine guns, 20 mm cannons).
46. Hellenic Shipyard employs some 2,700 people. Labour unrest plagues this facility. The Elevsis Shipyard is currently building five tank landing ships for the Greek Navy.
47. Its name was changed in 1989 to the Undersecretariat for Defence Industries. This move is seen as an indication of the importance the government places on its role.
48. This is an agreement that relates directly to the transaction—for example, co-production or joint ventures.
49. *Defense News*, September 26, 1989: p. 28.
50. Ibid.
51. An executive committee consisting of the Prime Minister, Minister of Defence, Chief of the Turkish General Staff and the Undersecretary for DIDA makes all the final decisions.
52. It is anticipated that a contract will be signed in 1990.
53. The TUSAS plant is located some 20 kilometres from Ankara at Murted and employs some 1,000 people.
54. The offsets are allocated as follows: General Dynamics $800.5 million, General Electric $317.5 million and Westinghouse $152 million.

    As a consequence of the selection of the General Electric F110–GE–100 engine to power the Turkish F–16s, General Electric has joined together with Turkish partners to create TUSAS Engine Industries located at Eskisehir. At the present time, 232 Turks and 32 US employees are working here and when it goes into full production 420 relatively well-paid technicians will be employed, giving the economy of Eskisehir a needed boost.

    The choice of Eskisehir as the site of this new engine factory was primarily a political decision influenced by the proximity of the Eskisehir Air Force Base, which houses most of the aircraft engine maintenance facilities of the Turkish Air Force. Eskisehir is not a booming metropolis. It does not have a civilian airport and the road to Ankara is poor, at best. The city also has an unfavourable image among Turks. Hence it might also prove difficult to attract Turkish professionals.

    On the other hand, it is conceivable that Eskisehir, in the long term, will become the centre of the air defence industry in Turkey. It now claims two of the most important facilities in this sector—the Air Force base with its repair and overhaul facilities and the TUSAS engine factory.

55. Three TYPE 209s were built at Kiel and two of the MEKO 200s were built in Hamburg.

Chapter 9. Summary and Conclusion

1. *Congressional Quarterly: Weekly Report*, December 9, 1989, p. 3374.
2. A worst case scenario remains a political reversal of Gorbachev and a return back to hard-line Stalinist.
3. *Congressional Quarterly: Weekly Report*, December 9, 1989, p. 3380.
4. *The Wall Street Journal*, December 11 1989, p.14.
5. The clock was stopped on the Greek base negotiations because of the inability of Athens to secure a parliamentary majority during the elections in June and November 1989.
6. *Washington Times*, October 10 1989, p. 7.

Index

The Easte